T0076326

Developing on AWS with C#

A Comprehensive Guide on Using C# to Build
Solutions on the AWS Platform

Noah Gift and James Charlesworth

Beijing · Boston · Farnham · Sebastopol · Tokyo

Developing on AWS with C#

by Noah Gift and James Charlesworth

Copyright © 2023 O'Reilly Media, Inc. All rights reserved.

Published by O'Reilly Media, Inc., 1005 Gravenstein Highway North, Sebastopol, CA 95472.

O'Reilly books may be purchased for educational, business, or sales promotional use. Online editions are also available for most titles (*http://oreilly.com*). For more information, contact our corporate/institutional sales department: 800-998-9938 or *corporate@oreilly.com*.

Acquisitions Editor: Zan McQuade
Development Editor: Melissa Potter
Production Editor: Christopher Faucher
Copyeditor: Piper Editorial Consulting, LLC
Proofreader: Justin Billing

Indexer: WordCo Indexing Services, Inc.
Interior Designer: David Futato
Cover Designer: Karen Montgomery
Illustrator: Kate Dullea

October 2022:   First Edition

Revision History for the First Edition
2022-10-04:   First Release

See *http://oreilly.com/catalog/errata.csp?isbn=9781492095873* for release details.

978-1-492-09587-3

[LSI]

Table of Contents

Preface

If you had to pick two popular technologies to focus on that emerged over the last 20 years, it would be tough to pick two better choices than C# and AWS. Anders Hejlsberg designed C# for Microsoft in 2000, and a few years later, the .NET Framework and Visual Studio launched. Next, in 2004, Mono, a cross-platform compiler and runtime for C#, became widely available. This ecosystem has enabled unique platforms and technologies, including the cross-platform mobile framework Xamarin.

In an alternate universe in the early 2000s, Amazon switched to a service-oriented architecture that culminated in a 2002 release of public web services. As the services grew in popularity, Amazon released SQS in 2004 and Amazon S3 and EC2 in 2006. These storage, compute, and messaging services are still the core building blocks of Amazon Web Services (AWS). As of 2022, AWS has at least 27 geographic regions, 87 availability zones, millions of servers, and hundreds of services. These services include various offerings ranging from machine learning (SageMaker) to serverless (Lambda). This book shows what is possible with these two remarkable technology stacks. You'll learn the theory surrounding cloud computing and how to implement it using AWS. You will also build many solutions with AWS technology, from serverless to DevOps implemented with the power of the .NET ecosystem, culminating in many elegant solutions that use these two powerful technologies.

Who Should Read This Book

This book is for C# developers looking to explore the possibilities on AWS. The book could also be considered an introduction to AWS and cloud computing in general. We will introduce many cloud computing topics from a standing start, so if this is your first foray into cloud-based software development, then rest assured we will provide all the context you will need.

While C# is *technically* just a programming language and not a framework, we will be relating almost exclusively to .NET application developers building web applications. There will be passing references to Blazor and Xamarin but knowledge of these is absolutely not required. We also have content relevant to developers familiar with both the older .NET Framework, and to the newer .NET (previously *.NET Core*).

How This Book Is Organized

AWS offers over 200 services to build all kinds of cloud-based applications, and we have organised this book to cover the services we feel are most important to a C# developer. The chapters are structured as follows.

Chapter 1, "Getting Started with .NET on AWS", serves as an introduction to AWS and how to interact with and configure your services.

Chapter 2, "AWS Core Services", covers Storage and Compute in detail, two of the most widely used services that will also feel most familiar to a .NET application developer used to deploying to web servers.

Chapter 3, "Migrating a Legacy .NET Framework Application to AWS", serves as a brief overview of the many ways you can rapidly migrate an existing codebase to AWS, either from an existing physical or virtual machine, or another cloud provider.

Chapter 4, "Modernizing .NET Applications to Serverless", takes you one step further than migrating existing applications and looks at ways you can modernize the way your code is architected to follow a serverless model, with examples on AWS.

Chapter 5, "Containerization of .NET", is all about containers. If you are already using Docker containers for your .NET web application, this chapter will help you rapidly deploy these to a managed container service on AWS.

Chapter 6, "DevOps", did you know AWS has a fully managed continuous delivery service called CodePipeline? This chapter shows you how you can simplify your application's path to production using the tools provided on AWS.

Chapter 7, "Logging, Monitoring, and Instrumentation for .NET", Monitoring and Instrumentation for .NET continues on from DevOps to demonstrate some of the logging and monitoring functionality you can integrate into your applications. We will also look at manually pushing performance metrics directly from your C# code.

Chapter 8, "Developing with AWS C# SDK", is the final chapter of this book and offers a more in depth look at the SDK tools for C# that allow you to integrate AWS services into your code.

Finally, there are two appendixes that you might find helpful at the back of the book that didn't fit in cleanly in any chapter. Appendix A, "Benchmarking AWS", walks through how to benchmark AWS machines and Appendix B, "Getting Started with .NET", shows a brief C# and F# GitHub Codespaces tutorial.

Additionally, each chapter includes critical thinking questions and exercises. Critical thinking questions are a great starting point for team discussions, user groups, or preparation for a job interview or certification. The exercises help you learn by doing and applying the context of the chapter into a working code example. These examples could make excellent portfolio pieces.

Additional Resources

For those with access to the O'Reilly platform, an optional resource that may help you with your AWS journey is 52 Weeks of AWS-The Complete Series (*https://oreil.ly/kDf0Q*); it contains hours of walk-throughs on all significant certifications. This series is also available as a free podcast on all major podcast channels (*https://podcast.paiml.com*).

In addition to those resources, there are daily and weekly updates on AWS from Noah Gift at the following locations:

Noah Gift O'Reilly
On Noah Gift's O'Reilly profile (*https://www.oreilly.com/pub/au/3039*), there are hundreds of videos and courses covering a variety of technologies, including AWS, as well as frequent Live Trainings. Two other O'Reilly books covering AWS may also be helpful: *Python for DevOps* and *Practical MLOps*.

Noah Gift Linkedin
On Noah Gift's LinkedIn (*https://www.linkedin.com/in/noahgift*), he periodically streams training on AWS and in-progress notes on O'Reilly books.

Noah Gift Website
Noahgift.com is the best place to find the latest updates on new courses, articles, and talks.

Noah Gift GitHub
On Noah Gift's GitHub profile (*https://github.com/noahgift*), you can find hundreds of repositories and almost daily updates.

Noah Gift AWS Hero Profile
On Noah Gift's AWS Hero Profile (*https://oreil.ly/FyFvf*), you can find links to current resources involving work on the AWS platform.

Noah Gift Coursera Profile
On Noah Gift's Coursera profile (*https://www.coursera.org/instructor/noahgift*), you can find multiple specializations covering a wide range of topics in cloud computing with a heavy emphasis on AWS. These courses include:

- Cloud Computing Foundations (*https://oreil.ly/XcxeC*)

- Cloud Virtualization, Containers and APIs (*https://oreil.ly/mcacu*)

- Cloud Data Engineering (*https://oreil.ly/pVHGm*)

- Cloud Machine Learning Engineering and MLOps (*https://oreil.ly/724Sz*)
- Linux and Bash for Data Engineering (*https://oreil.ly/Ps1Mz*)
- Python and Pandas for Data Engineering (*https://oreil.ly/07ywX*)
- Scripting with Python and SQL for Data Engineering (*https://oreil.ly/rSBMG*)
- Web Applications and Command-Line Tools for Data Engineering (*https://oreil.ly/gDDHy*)
- Building Cloud Computing Solutions at Scale Specialization (*https://oreil.ly/VZo7x*)
- Python, Bash and SQL Essentials for Data Engineering Specialization (*https://oreil.ly/TpIUU*)

Pragmatic AI Labs Website

Many free resources related to AWS are available at the *Pragmatic AI Labs and Solutions website (https://paiml.com)*. These include several free books:

- *Cloud Computing for Data Analysis (https://oreil.ly/I4ADa)*
- *Minimal Python (https://oreil.ly/JD2Ha)*
- *Python Command Line Tools: Design Powerful Apps with Click (https://oreil.ly/7zxNa)*
- *Testing in Python (https://oreil.ly/uJ5cC)*

Conventions Used in This Book

The following typographical conventions are used in this book:

Italic

Indicates new terms, URLs, email addresses, filenames, and file extensions.

`Constant width`

Used for program listings, as well as within paragraphs to refer to program elements such as variable or function names, databases, data types, environment variables, statements, and keywords.

`Constant width bold`

Shows commands or other text that should be typed literally by the user.

`Constant width italic`

Shows text that should be replaced with user-supplied values or by values determined by context.

This element signifies a tip or suggestion.

 This element signifies a general note.

 This element indicates a warning or caution.

Using Code Examples

Supplemental material (code examples, exercises, etc.) is available for download at *https://oreil.ly/AWS-with-C-Sharp-examples*.

If you have a technical question or a problem using the code examples, please send email to *bookquestions@oreilly.com*.

This book is here to help you get your job done. In general, if example code is offered with this book, you may use it in your programs and documentation. You do not need to contact us for permission unless you're reproducing a significant portion of the code. For example, writing a program that uses several chunks of code from this book does not require permission. Selling or distributing examples from O'Reilly books does require permission. Answering a question by citing this book and quoting example code does not require permission. Incorporating a significant amount of example code from this book into your product's documentation does require permission.

We appreciate, but generally do not require, attribution. An attribution usually includes the title, author, publisher, and ISBN. For example: "*Developing on AWS with C#* by Noah Gift and James Charlesworth (O'Reilly). Copyright 2023 O'Reilly Media, Inc., 978-1-492-09587-3."

If you feel your use of code examples falls outside fair use or the permission given above, feel free to contact us at *permissions@oreilly.com*.

O'Reilly Online Learning

O'REILLY® For more than 40 years, *O'Reilly Media* has provided technology and business training, knowledge, and insight to help companies succeed.

Our unique network of experts and innovators share their knowledge and expertise through books, articles, and our online learning platform. O'Reilly's online learning platform gives you on-demand access to live training courses, in-depth learning paths, interactive coding environments, and a vast collection of text and video from O'Reilly and 200+ other publishers. For more information, visit *https://oreilly.com*.

How to Contact Us

Please address comments and questions concerning this book to the publisher:

O'Reilly Media, Inc.
1005 Gravenstein Highway North
Sebastopol, CA 95472
800-998-9938 (in the United States or Canada)
707-829-0515 (international or local)
707-829-0104 (fax)

We have a web page for this book, where we list errata, examples, and any additional information. You can access this page at *https://oreil.ly/AWS-with-C-sharp*.

Email *bookquestions@oreilly.com* to comment or ask technical questions about this book.

For news and information about our books and courses, visit *https://oreilly.com*.

Find us on LinkedIn: *https://linkedin.com/company/oreilly-media*.

Follow us on Twitter: *https://twitter.com/oreillymedia*.

Watch us on YouTube: *https://youtube.com/oreillymedia*.

Acknowledgments

Noah

It is always an honor to have the opportunity to work on an O'Reilly book. This book marks my fourth for O'Reilly, and I am working on the fifth book on Enterprise MLOps. Thank you to Rachel Roumeliotis (*https://oreil.ly/GbCM4*) for allowing me to work on this book and Zan McQuade (*https://oreil.ly/TyZX7*) for the excellent strategic direction.

Both my coauthor James Charlesworth (*https://oreil.ly/ReRkb*) and our development editor Melissa Potter (*https://oreil.ly/Sm2Nn*) are fantastic to work with, and I am lucky to work with two such talented people on a project this demanding. Thanks to Lior Kirshner-Shalom and from AWS, Nivas Durairaj (*https://oreil.ly/75Nab*), David Pallmann, and Bryan Hogan, who provided many insightful comments and corrections during technical reviews.

Thanks as well to many of my current and former students as well as faculty and staff at Duke MIDS (*https://oreil.ly/2SWqF*), Duke Artificial Intelligence Masters in Engineering (*https://oreil.ly/bTcbr*), UC Davis MSBA (*https://oreil.ly/ZB0SH*), UC Berkeley (*https://oreil.ly/cX4XH*), Northwestern MS in Data Science Program (*https://oreil.ly/i9AIB*) as well as UTK (*https://oreil.ly/u3rJi*) and UNC Charlotte (*https://oreil.ly/yCydZ*).

These people include in no particular order: Dickson Louie (*https://oreil.ly/gMxsP*), Andrew B. Hargadon (*https://oreil.ly/IEnYf*), Hemant Bhargava (*https://oreil.ly/Mgkru*), Amy Russell (*https://oreil.ly/ABcjv*), Ashwin Aravindakshan (*https://oreil.ly/fqVSg*), Ken Gilbert (*https://oreil.ly/8aoUi*), Michel Ballings (*https://oreil.ly/PouWU*), Jon Reifschneider (*https://oreil.ly/IsCsh*), Robert Calderbank (*https://oreil.ly/iQ0yY*), and Alfredo Deza (*https://oreil.ly/HvsSl*).

Finally, thank you to my family, Leah, Liam, and Theodore, who put up with me working on weekends and late at night to hit deadlines.

James

This is my first book with O'Reilly, and I have been overwhelmed by the support we have received from the team, especially Melissa Potter, without whom you would have suffered a lot more of my convoluted British spellings. I'd also echo Noah's thanks to the technical reviewers, specifically David Pallmann and Bryan Hogan at AWS.

The tech industry moves at such a rapid pace that you do not get anywhere without standing on the shoulders of giants. It is for this reason that I'd like to thank two of my former bosses, James Woodley (*https://oreil.ly/0ZmWS*) and Dave Rensin (*https://oreil.ly/dlL6x*), for all the advice, coaching, mentorship, and support over recent years.

Lastly, big shout out to my amazing wife, Kaja, who supports me through all my endeavors, I will always be your Richard Castle.

## CHAPTER 1

Getting Started with .NET on AWS

This chapter covers the basic scaffolding of essentials on your first day working with AWS and C#. These essentials include using cloud-based development environments such as AWS CloudShell and a traditional Visual Studio development environment that leverages the AWS SDK.

The material in this book sets you up for success by adding many code examples of doing .NET 6 development on AWS. You can view those code examples in the source code repository for the book (*https://oreil.ly/AWS-with-C-Sharp-examples*). Additionally, both traditional development methods like Visual Studio and new cloud native strategies like developing with AWS Cloud9 are covered. There is something for all types of .NET developers.

For scripting fans, there are also examples of using the AWS Command Line Interface and PowerShell for the AWS SDK. At the end of the chapter, there are discussion questions and exercises that you can use to build on the lessons covered. These exercises are an excellent tool for creating a comprehensive portfolio of work that gets you hired. Let's get started with a brief dive into cloud computing.

What Is Cloud Computing?

Cloud computing is the utility-type delivery of IT resources over the internet with utility-type pricing. Instead of purchasing and maintaining physical data centers and hardware, you can access IT services, such as computing, storage, and databases, on an as-needed basis from a cloud vendor.

Perhaps the best way to describe cloud computing is to take the view of the UC Berkeley Reliable Adaptive Distributed Systems Laboratory or RAD Lab. In their paper "Above the Clouds: A Berkeley View of Cloud Computing" (*https://oreil.ly/tsBGN*), they mention three new critical aspects of cloud computing: "the illusion of infinite computing resources," "the elimination of up-front commitment by cloud users," and "the ability to pay for the use of computing resources on a short-term basis as needed." Let's talk about these items in more detail.

Having taught thousands of students and working professionals cloud computing, I (Noah) have strong opinions on learning as quickly as possible. A key performance indicator, or KPI, is how many mistakes you can make per week. In practice, this means trying things out, getting frustrated, then working out the best way to solve what is frustrating you, and then doing that over and over again as quickly as possible.

One of the ways I encourage this in a classroom is by facilitating students to demo progress weekly on what they are working on and build a portfolio of work. Similarly, in this book, I recommend building out a series of GitHub projects that catalog your work and then building out demo videos explaining how your project works. This step accomplishes two things in learning cloud computing: teaching yourself better metacognition skills and building a portfolio of work that makes you more marketable.

The illusion of infinite computing resources

Machine learning is an excellent example of an ideal use case for "near infinite" computing resources. Deep learning requires access to large quantities of storage, disk I/O, and compute. Through elastic compute and storage, data lake capability via Amazon S3 opens up workflows that didn't exist previously. This new workflow allows users and systems to operate data where it resides versus moving it back and forth to workstations or specialized file servers. Notice in Figure 1-1 that the Amazon S3 storage system can seamlessly handle the scaling of computing, storage, and disk I/O with any number of workers that access the resource. Amazon S3 can do this not only because it contains near infinite elasticity but also due to redundant properties. This concept means that it not only scales but can virtually always be available because of the design around the idea that "things always fail" (*https://oreil.ly/X77BO*).

One definition of machine learning is a program that learns from historical data to create predictions. You can use AWS SageMaker Studio to train your own machine learning models without knowing anything about data science with a feature called Amazon SageMaker Autopilot. You can learn more about that service here (*https://oreil.ly/QsDeC*).

Resource Requirements of AI and ML

A data lake is often synonymous with a cloud-based object storage system like Amazon S3. It allows data processing "in place" without moving it around, and a data lake accomplishes this through near-infinite capacity and computing characteristics. A data lake is a centralized repository that allows you to store all your structured and unstructured data at any scale. When working in the film industry on movies like *Avatar* (*https://oreil.ly/ZgrZN*), the data was immense; it did need to be moved by an excessively complicated system. Now, with the cloud, this problem goes away.

Deep learning is a type of machine learning that uses neural networks to learn from large quantities of data to make predictions or find hidden patterns. Deep learning is suited to cloud computing via data lakes due to its requirement for large amounts of data and powerful GPUs. According to AWS, "Unlike traditional machine learning, deep learning attempts to simulate the way our brains learn and process information by creating artificial *neural networks* that can extract complicated concepts and relationships from data. Deep learning models improve through complex pattern recognition in pictures, text, sounds, and other data to produce more accurate insights and predictions." You can learn more about data lakes and deep learning in the O'Reilly book Noah wrote, *Practical MLOps*.

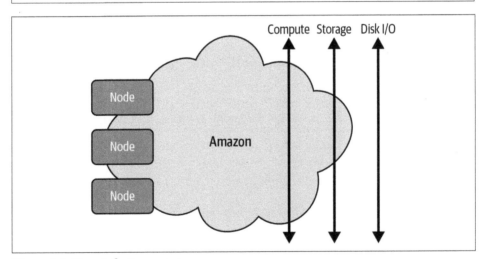

Figure 1-1. Near infinite compute

The elimination of up-front commitment by cloud users
    For many start-ups, spending hundreds of thousands of dollars on buying equipment to try out an idea is not feasible. The cloud enables an opportunistic way to develop software by eliminating high fixed costs before cloud computing. Not

only that, but you are not locked into a particular technology choice as you are in an on-premise data center.

The ability to pay for the use of computing resources on a short-term basis as needed

By switching to variable costs, companies only pay for what they need. The result is more efficient architectures that can respond to events and scale according to demand. As you can see, the critical cloud benefit is the ability to use elastic capabilities, namely, compute and storage. One such resource is an Elastic File System (EFS) on AWS. According to AWS, EFS (*https://aws.amazon.com/efs*) is a "simple, serverless, set-and-forget, elastic file system." It works well with the core elasticity capability of AWS in that it allows a developer to provision or tear down ephemeral resources like spot instances for a task yet interact with persistent storage available to all machines that use it. *Spot instances (https://aws.amazon.com/ec2/spot)* are compute instances you can bid on and obtain for up to 90% cost savings, making them ideal for workflows that can be run anytime or are transient.[1]

 AWS takes cost optimization very seriously and includes it as one of their AWS Well-Architected Framework (*https://oreil.ly/LzKgE*) pillars. According to AWS, "The AWS Well-Architected Framework helps you understand the pros and cons of decisions you make while building systems on AWS." Spot instances are a considerable part of the cost optimization story because they allow you to bid on unused capacity, achieving, as a result, up to 90% off regular on-demand pricing. For developers learning something, this resource is invaluable because you only "pay for what you need."

Fully managed networked file systems like EFS are helpful in that they provide a consistent network experience, like a persistent home directory or data share. "Amazon Elastic File System (Amazon EFS) automatically grows and shrinks as you add and remove files with no need for management or provisioning," according to official AWS documentation (*https://aws.amazon.com/efs*).

One of the most troublesome bottlenecks in dealing with large data is needing more compute, disk I/O (input/output), and storage to process a task, like counting the visits to a website for a company with terabytes of data. In particular, the ability to seamlessly use a file system mountable by a cluster of machines (i.e., EFS) and grow to meet the I/O demands of the cluster's aggregate work is a massive efficiency that did not exist until cloud computing.

---

[1] You can read more about EFS and spot instances in Chapter 6 in *Python for DevOps* (O'Reilly).

Another elastic resource is EC2 (*https://oreil.ly/dnQh1*) virtual computing environments, also known as instances. EC2 instances are a basic level of scalable computing capacity provided by AWS. They have many features, including using Amazon Machine Images (AMIs) that package a complete server install. They are handy for scaling web services, trying out prototypes, or bidding on spare capacity, as with AWS Spot Instances. Spot Instances open up entirely new ways of working because virtual machines can be disposable, i.e., discarded when not needed, and used when the costs are low enough to justify their use.

Types of Cloud Computing

One consideration to be aware of is the types of cloud computing: IaaS (Infrastructure as a Service), PaaS (Platform as a Service), FaaS (Function as a Service), and SaaS (Software as a Service). Let's discuss each in detail.

IaaS

This option offers the basic building blocks of cloud computing, including networking, storage, and computing. It provides the closest abstraction to traditional IT resources and the most flexibility.

PaaS

This option is a hosted service that takes care of all IT management and allows a developer to focus only on building the business logic. An excellent example of an AWS PaaS is AWS App Runner (*https://aws.amazon.com/apprunner*), which allows for continuous delivery of .NET applications with minimal effort. This type of offering removes the need to manage IT infrastructure. It allows an organization to focus on the deployment and management of applications.

FaaS

FaaS is fascinating as a development paradigm because it allows a developer to work at the speed of thought. AWS Lambda is the canonical example of this model due to its automatic management of the compute resources.[2] For a .NET developer, it is perhaps the most efficient way to deploy logic to the cloud since the code only runs when responding to an event.

SaaS

This option provides a complete product available to purchase, freeing up an organization from needing to either host or develop this offering. An excellent example of this type of product is a logging and monitoring analysis service.

---

2 The AWS whitepaper "Developing and Deploying .NET Applications on AWS" (*https://oreil.ly/Y2dEQ*) explains AWS Lambda's mechanisms.

Other ("as a service")

There are newer "as a service" offerings made available by cloud computing. These services are discussed in more detail a little later in the book.

The general intuition is that IaaS means you pay less but have to do more, SaaS means you pay more but do less, and PaaS lies in the middle.[3] This concept is similar to walking into a big warehouse store and either buying flour to make pizza, buying a frozen pizza, or buying a cooked slice of pizza at the counter on your way out. Whether we're talking about pizza or software, you pay less but do more in situations where you have expertise and time to do things yourself. Alternatively, the convenience of higher level service, i.e., a hot slice of pizza, is worth leveraging the experts.

While the raw cost of IaaS may be less, it is also closer to the traditional way of doing things in physical data, which may not always mean it is cheaper. IaaS may not always be more affordable because the total ROI (return on investment) may be higher since you need to pay for highly trained staff to develop and manage applications on top of IaaS. Additionally, some traditional paradigms like running a web service in a virtual machine may cost more money than an event-driven AWS Lambda function that only runs when invoked.

Another way to describe an efficient event-driven service like AWS Lambda is to call it a *cloud native service*. Cloud native services are new offerings created due to efficiencies made possible by cloud computing and offer paradigms not available in traditional IT infrastructure, such as responding to web events versus running a web server 24/7. In concrete terms, an AWS Lambda function could run for just a few seconds of combined compute time per day. Meanwhile, a traditional web service would run 24/7 regardless of whether it's receiving thousands of requests per second or just a dozen requests in a day. This concept is similar to the lights in a parking garage: you could waste electricity lighting an empty garage or you could use sensor lights that only turn on when motion triggers them. In this case, IaaS may be a more expensive solution when the ROI of the resources required to build it and the application's run-time inefficiencies are fully considered in the cost.

Another way to refer to services that require little to no management on your part is *managed services*. An excellent example of a managed service is Amazon Cloud-Search. The managed service in the AWS Cloud makes it simple and cost-effective to set up, manage, and scale a search solution for your website or application. Managed services are the opposite of IaaS, which require experts to set up, run, and maintain them.

---

3 You can read more detail about how AWS sees cloud computing in their "Overview of Amazon Web Services" whitepaper (*https://oreil.ly/aPuLH*).

AWS uses the term *managed services* to refer to PaaS, SaaS, and FaaS services. You'll likely only see the term *managed services* used in AWS documentation.

Next, let's dive into how to get started with AWS.

Getting Started with AWS

An ideal place to get started with AWS is to sign up for a free tier account (*https://aws.amazon.com/free*). When you initially create the account note, you need to set both an account name and the email address for the root user as shown in Figure 1-2.

Sign up for AWS

Root user email address
Used for account recovery and some administrative functions

AWS account name
Choose a name for your account. You can change this name in your account settings after you sign up.

Verify email address

OR

Sign in to an existing AWS account

Figure 1-2. Sign up for AWS

Once you create an account, the first thing to do is to lock away your AWS account root user access keys.[4] on how to lock your AWS account root user access keys.] You don't want to use the root user for everyday tasks but instead create an IAM admin user.[5]

This is because if you expose the account credentials, it is possible to lose control of your AWS account. A fundamental security principle is the principle of least privilege (PLP), which states that you should "start with a minimum set of permissions and grant additional permissions as necessary." Additionally, the root user account should

---

4 The AWS Identity and Access Management guide has a detailed list of *https://oreil.ly/x90WL*

5 To create an admin IAM user, follow the official AWS guide (*https://oreil.ly/ogmRn*).

enable AWS multifactor authentication (MFA) on the AWS root user account to review the step-by-step instructions on how to secure your account with MFA.[6]

It is worth noting that a standard stumbling block in getting up to speed quickly with cloud computing is the terminology. Fortunately, AWS has a detailed and updated glossary of terms (*https://oreil.ly/5s83K*) worth bookmarking.

A straightforward way to use AWS is via the AWS web console. Let's tackle this next.

Using the AWS Management Console

The AWS Management Console, as shown in Figure 1-3, is the central location to control AWS from a web browser.[7] The Services tab shows a hierarchical view of every service on the platform. Adjacent to this tab is a search box that allows you to search for a service. We find ourselves using the search box frequently, as it is often the quickest way to navigate to a service. Adjacent to the search box is the AWS CloudShell icon, which appears as a black and white terminal icon. This service (*https://aws.amazon.com/cloudshell*) is a great way to quickly try out commands on the AWS platform, like listing S3 buckets (*https://oreil.ly/SvdPd*)—containers for object storage—in your account or running a command against a managed natural language processing API like AWS Comprehend (*https://aws.amazon.com/compre hend*).

Conceptually, an S3 bucket is similar to consumer cloud storage like Dropbox, Box, or Google Drive.

The circled N. Virginia tab shows the AWS region currently used. It is common to toggle to different regions to launch virtual machines or try services in another region. Often, but not always, new services first appear in the N. Virginia region, so depending on what region your organization is using, they may need to toggle to N. Virginia to try out a new service and then back again. Likewise, suppose a new service appears in a different region like US West (Oregon). You may find yourself trying that new service out in that region and then needing to toggle back to your primary region.

---

6 See the AWS multifactor authentication guide (*https://oreil.ly/6a24r*).

7 You can read more about the AWS Management Console in the in the official documentation (*https://oreil.ly/UT4d1*).

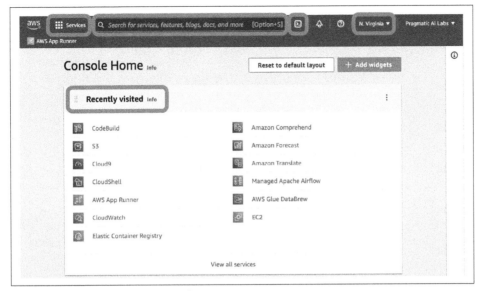

Figure 1-3. Using the AWS Console

The cost of services (*https://oreil.ly/QU1ur*) and transferring data out of AWS may vary between regions.

Finally, the Recently visited tab shows services recently used. After prolonged use of AWS, it is common to have most of the daily services appear in this section, providing a helpful shortcut menu to use AWS. Another thing to note is that you can "star" (*https://oreil.ly/Q14E7*) an item in the console to add it to the Favorites tab, as shown in Figure 1-4. This process can be a convenient way to access services you use often.

Figure 1-4. Favorites in the AWS Management Console

Next, let's look at utilizing the AWS communities and documentation resources.

Utilizing the AWS Communities and Documentation

A tremendous variety of documentation is available for learning about the AWS platform in various forms and depth. Let's discuss these resources next.

The .NET on AWS website

The .NET on AWS website (*https://oreil.ly/cS5eZ*) is the central location for information about using .NET with AWS. From here, readers can find service and SDK documentation, AWS toolkits and migration tools, getting started tutorials, developer community links, and other content.

It is wise for a .NET developer to bookmark this website since it has a curated view of helpful resources. One of my favorite sections is the .NET Community tab (*https://oreil.ly/de3mt*). This section has a link to many popular developer communities, as shown in Figure 1-5 including Twitter, re:Post, Stack Overflow, Slack, GitHub, and Global AWS User Groups.[8]

Figure 1-5. Developer communities for .NET

One of the more valuable sections of the community portal is the links to YouTube channels and developer blogs. Finally, there are links to open source .NET projects that AWS invests in, including .NET on AWS (*https://github.com/aws/dotnet*) and AWS SDK for .NET (*https://github.com/aws/aws-sdk-net*).

Next, let's look at the AWS SDK for .NET documentation.

---

8 Additionally, there are links to famous .NET developers like Norm Johanson (*https://oreil.ly/P9DOO*), François Bouteruche (*https://oreil.ly/AcSmE*), and Steve Roberts (*https://oreil.ly/rV9m7*).

AWS SDK for .NET documentation

You can learn to develop and deploy applications with the AWS SDK for .NET at the official website (*https://aws.amazon.com/sdk-for-net*). This website includes several essential guides, including the Developer Guide (*https://oreil.ly/4xmTZ*), the API Reference Guide (*https://oreil.ly/EHPkN*), and the SDK Code Examples Guide (*https://oreil.ly/Y0f0G*).

Another essential resource is the necessary development .NET tools on AWS, shown in Figure 1-6. These include AWS Toolkit for Rider, AWS Toolkit for Visual Studio, AWS Toolkit for Visual Studio Code, and AWS Tools for Azure DevOps.

Figure 1-6. Explore .NET tools on AWS

We'll dig into the AWS SDK later in the chapter. Next, let's take a look at the AWS service documentation.

AWS service documentation

AWS has so many services that it can be overwhelming at first to understand which service is appropriate for the task at hand. Fortunately, there is a centralized web page, the AWS documentation website (*https://docs.aws.amazon.com*), containing guides and API references, tutorials and projects, SDKs and toolkits, as well general resources like FAQs and links to case studies.

One item to call out is that AWS has many SDKs and toolkits, as shown in Figure 1-7, including the AWS CLI. It can be helpful for a .NET developer to see examples in many languages to get ideas for solutions you can build .NET. The AWS Command Line Interface (*https://aws.amazon.com/cli*) is often the most efficient documentation for a service since it abstracts the concepts at a level that makes it easy to understand what is going on. An excellent example of this concept is the following command to copy a folder recursively into AWS S3 object storage:

```
aws s3 cp myfolder s3://mybucket/myfolder --recursive
```

Each whitespace separates the command's actions, i.e., aws then s3 for the service, the action s3, and the rest of the command. There is no quicker way to learn a service on AWS than to invoke it from the command line in many cases.

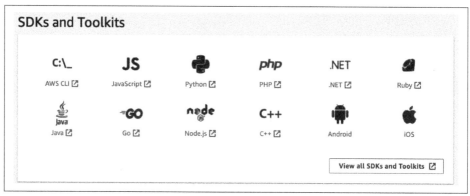

Figure 1-7. Explore AWS SDK and toolkits

Next, let's talk about installing the AWS Command Line.

Using the AWS Command Line Interface

According to the official AWS documentation (*https://aws.amazon.com/cli*), "The AWS Command Line Interface (CLI) is a unified tool to manage your AWS services. With just one tool to download and configure, you can control multiple AWS services from the command line and automate them through scripts."

There are four essential methods to interact with the AWS Command Line Interface.[9] Let's discuss each briefly.

AWS CloudShell
> AWS CloudShell (*https://aws.amazon.com/cloudshell*) is a cloud native browser-based shell, meaning that it takes advantage of the unique properties of the cloud by preinstalling the AWS CLI for you. You can choose between the Bash shell, PowerShell, or Z shell (*https://oreil.ly/3prep*).

AWS Cloud9
> AWS Cloud9 (*https://aws.amazon.com/cloud9*) is a cloud native interactive development environment (IDE) that has deep hooks into AWS with unique development tools suited to developing not just for the cloud but inside the cloud itself.

Linux shells
> By using the Amazon Linux 2 AMI (*https://oreil.ly/rWRSi*), you automatically get access to the command-line tools for AWS integration. Alternatively, you can install the AWS CLI on any Linux system (*https://oreil.ly/xVxX1*).

---

9 There is a detailed user guide (*https://oreil.ly/XmZuZ*) to interacting with the AWS Command Line Interface.

Windows command line

Managed AWS Windows AMIs (*https://oreil.ly/iX5tt*) come with AWS CLI. Alternatively, you can download and run the 64-bit Windows installer (*https://oreil.ly/0qrv9*).

Next, let's discuss the installation notes about each of these methods.

You can watch a more detailed walk-through of using the AWS CloudShell, including interacting with Bash, ZSH, PowerShell, S3, Lambda, Python, IPython, Pip, Boto3, DynamoDB, and Cloud9 on YouTube (*https://oreil.ly/F9y5o*) or O'Reilly (*https://oreil.ly/4J4Me*).

How to install AWS CloudShell and AWS Cloud9

There is no installation process necessary for AWS CloudShell and AWS Cloud9 because they are already included in the AWS Console experience, as shown in Figure 1-8. Notice that searching for both tools brings them both up in search results, allowing you to "star" (i.e., add them as favorites) or click on them. Finally, the terminal icon can also launch AWS CloudShell. One key advantage of these cloud native terminals is they are fully managed and up-to-date and automatically manage your credentials.

Figure 1-8. Selecting AWS Cloud9 and AWS CloudShell

How to install the AWS CLI

The AWS CLI installation comes with AWS Cloud9 or AWS CloudShell. If you need to install the AWS CLI locally on Windows, a detailed guide (*https://oreil.ly/JDsuk*) is on the AWS website.

How to install AWSPowerShell.NETCore for AWS

If you need to run PowerShell for AWS locally on Windows, Linux, or macOS, you can refer to the PowerShell Gallery (*https://oreil.ly/omRZp*) to find the latest version of AWSPowerShell.NETCore and installation instructions for Windows, Linux, and macOS. AWSPowerShell.NETCore is the recommended version of PowerShell for working with AWS because it has comprehensive cross-platform support. Generally, though, you can install the following PowerShell command: `Install-Module -Name AWSPowerShell.NetCore`.

An alternative to installing PowerShell on a local operating system is using AWS CloudShell since it comes preinstalled. Next, let's talk about how this process works.

Using PowerShell with AWS CloudShell

An excellent guide for using AWS Tools for PowerShell lives on the AWS website (*https://oreil.ly/zOG86*). Let's look at a simple example to supplement the official documentation. In the following example, as shown in Figure 1-9, we create an AWS bucket by invoking the `New-S3Bucket` cmdlet to create a new Amazon S3 bucket.

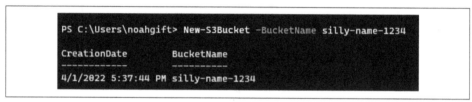

```
PS C:\Users\noahgift> New-S3Bucket -BucketName silly-name-1234

CreationDate          BucketName
------------          ----------
4/1/2022 5:37:44 PM   silly-name-1234
```

Figure 1-9. Create AWS bucket in AWS PowerShell

Next, we can go to the AWS Console, select S3, and verify it appears, as shown in Figure 1-10.

Name	AWS Region	Access	Creation date
○ silly-name-1234	US East (N. Virginia) us-east-1	Objects can be public	April 1, 2022, 13:37:45 (UTC-04:00)

Figure 1-10. Show AWS bucket in AWS S3 Console

It is worth mentioning that PowerShell for AWS offers a sophisticated and high-level interface to control and interact with services on AWS, including EC2, S3, Lambda, and more. You can further explore those in the AWS documentation (*https://oreil.ly/2V072*).

The AWS CloudShell supports three shells: PowerShell, Bash, and Z shell. To use PowerShell, you type **pwsh**. You can explore all AWS CloudShell features using the official documentation (*https://oreil.ly/z1CC4*). The AWS CloudShell comes with 1 GB of persistent storage in */home/cloudshell-user*. The action menu, as shown in Figure 1-11, allows you to perform many practical actions, including downloading and uploading files, restarting the terminal, deleting the data in the home directory, and configuring the tabs layout of the terminal.

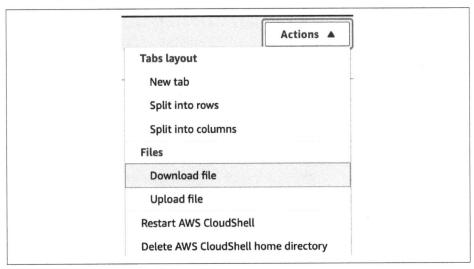

Figure 1-11. AWS CloudShell action menu

Fortunately, the AWS CloudShell PowerShell is straightforward, similar to local PowerShell. First, to use AWSPowerShell.NetCore, import it as shown in the following sequence, echo content into a file, and write it to the bucket created earlier. Finally, run Get-S3object to verify the file's creation in S3, which you can see in Figure 1-12.

```
Import-Module AWSPowerShell.NetCore
echo "This is data" > data.txt
Write-S3object -BucketName silly-name-1234 -File data.txt
Get-S3object
```

```
PS /home/cloudshell-user> Import-Module AWSPowerShell.NetCore
PS /home/cloudshell-user> echo "This is data" > data.txt
PS /home/cloudshell-user> Write-S3object -BucketName silly-name-1234 -File data.txt
PS /home/cloudshell-user> Get-S3object

cmdlet Get-S3object at command pipeline position 1
Supply values for the following parameters:
BucketName: silly-name-1234

ChecksumAlgorithm : {}
ETag              : "bd7090333ff9eabec6a4c1f9461aaaff"
BucketName        : silly-name-1234
Key               : data.txt
LastModified      : 4/1/2022 6:51:54 PM
Owner             : Amazon.S3.Model.Owner
Size              : 13
StorageClass      : STANDARD
```

Figure 1-12. AWS CloudShell create file S3

Another feature of the CloudShell and PowerShell environment is invoking C# code. To get started using PowerShell with C#, you can create a C# snippit and embed it in a script called *./hello-ps-c-sharp.ps1*. The C# code comes after the $code = @" block and then terminates at "@. The general idea is that if you are using PowerShell inside of AWS CloudShell, you can use existing snippets of helpful C# to enhance a PowerShell script without needing a full-fledged editor:

```
$code = @"
using System;
namespace HelloWorld
{
        public class Program
        {
                public static void Main(){
                        Console.WriteLine("Hello AWS Cloudshell!");
                }
        }
}
"@

Add-Type -TypeDefinition $code -Language CSharp
iex "[HelloWorld.Program]::Main()"

Install-Module -Name AWS.Tools.Installer -Force
```

Next, run it in your PowerShell prompt:

```
PS /home/cloudshell-user> ./hello-ps-c-sharp.ps1
Hello AWS Cloudshell!
PS /home/cloudshell-user>
```

Consider using Bash and PowerShell, depending on which one makes more sense in a given context. If you are doing something with pure .NET capabilities, then PowerShell is an easy win. On the other hand, you may find some documentation for scripting a solution with Bash on the AWS website. Instead of rewriting the example, simply use it and extend in Bash, saving you time.

In the following example, we use a Bash hash to store a list of Cloud9 IDs and then get information about them:

```
#!/usr/bin/env bash
# Loop through a list of Cloud9 Environments to find out more information

declare -A cloud9Env=([env1]="18acd120518340df8a73ccaab641851e"\
    [env2]="2c9eb66bf53b4083b9ab6345bae70dad"\
    [env3]="f104b0141c284a41af0c75fea7890770" )

## now loop through the above hash to get more information
for env in "${!cloud9Env[@]}"; do
  echo "Information for $env: "
```

```
      aws cloud9 describe-environments --environment-id "${cloud9Env[$env]}"
      done
```

We don't have to use Bash in this particular situation because there is excellent documentation on how to solve the problem in PowerShell for AWS. PowerShell can do the same thing as Bash and has deep C# integration. Notice the following example shows the PowerShell method of looping through several IDs stored in a hash:

```
# PowerShell script that loops through Cloud9 to get environment information

$cloud9Env = @{ env1 = "18acd120518340df8a73ccaab641851e";
                env2 = "2c9eb66bf53b4083b9ab6345bae70dad";
                env3 = "f104b0141c284a41af0c75fea7890770" }

foreach ($env in $cloud9Env.GetEnumerator()) {
        Write-Host "Information for $($env.Key):";
        Get-C9EnvironmentData $($env.Value)
}
```

To summarize, the AWS CloudShell is a great companion for the C# developer, and it is worth having in your toolkit. Now let's use Visual Studio for AWS, a preferred environment for experienced .NET developers who use AWS.

Using Visual Studio with AWS and AWS Toolkit for Visual Studio

Getting set up with Visual Studio with AWS is a straightforward process. The required components are an AWS account, a machine running a supported version of Windows, Visual Studio Community Edition or higher, and AWS Toolkit for Visual Studio (*https://aws.amazon.com/visualstudio*). Please refer to this official AWS documentation for further details on setting up Visual Studio for AWS if this is your first time configuring it.

If you want to use the latest .NET 6 features, you need to use Visual Studio 2022. In practice, your best experience for Visual Studio with deep AWS integration is a Windows environment running the latest version of Visual Studio. For example, a Mac version of Visual Studio exists, but the AWS Toolkit does not work on Mac.

The AWS SDK for .NET has deep integration with the Visual Studio environment, as shown in Figure 1-13. It includes interacting with AWS Core Services, including Amazon S3 and Amazon EC2, through the AWS Explorer integration installed as part of AWS Toolkit for Visual Studio.

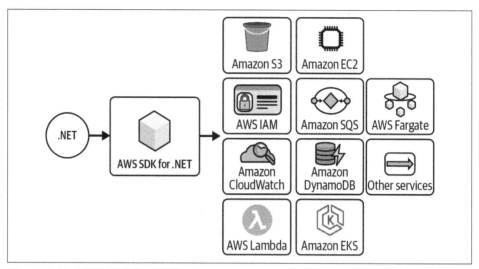

Figure 1-13. AWS SDK for .NET

According to the official AWS documentation, the AWS Toolkit for Visual Studio is an extension for Microsoft Visual Studio running on Microsoft Windows that makes it "easier for developers to develop, debug, and deploy .NET applications using Amazon Web Services." This integration includes multiple ways to deploy applications and manage services. A component of this integration manifests itself in the Server Explorer Toolbox, or AWS Explorer, as shown in Figure 1-14. The AWS Explorer lets you manage and interact with AWS resources like Amazon S3 or EC2 instances within a Microsoft Windows Visual Studio environment.

Notice how straightforward it is to dive into many popular AWS services with a mouse click.

Visual Studio is a popular development for .NET for two reasons: it is both a fantastic editor and a rich ecosystem for .NET developers. The AWS Toolkit for Visual Studio taps into this ecosystem as an extension for Microsoft Visual Studio on Windows, making it easier for developers to develop, debug, and deploy .NET applications using Amazon Web Services. You can see a complete list of the features available by reviewing the installer's official documentation (*https://oreil.ly/v2Xne*).

Note that Visual Studio Code (*https://oreil.ly/yWme7*) and JetBrains Rider (*https://oreil.ly/vVrq5*) both have AWS Toolkits.

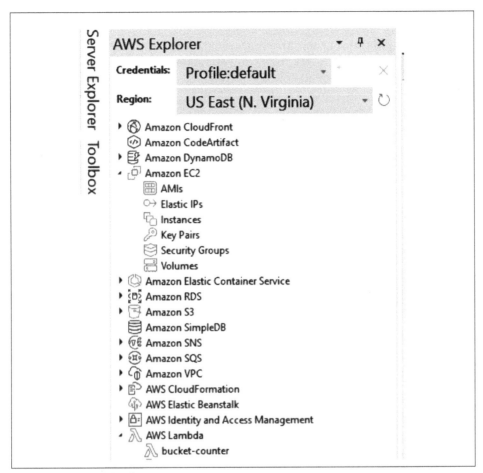

Figure 1-14. AWS Explorer

The AWS Explorer installation does require three key steps:[10]

1. Install the AWS Toolkit for Visual Studio

   Download the *AWS Toolkit for Visual Studio 2022* (*https://oreil.ly/v2Xne*) and install the package on your Windows machine that has a local installation of Visual Studio.

---

10 There is a detailed set-up guide (*https://oreil.ly/9ikNn*) available for AWS Toolkit for Visual Studio.

2. Create an IAM user and download credentials

   Create an IAM user in the AWS Console and apply the *principle of least privilege*.[11] Ensure that you select the access key option, as shown in Figure 1-15, and then download the credentials in CSV format when prompted.

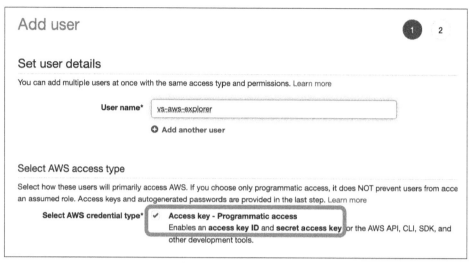

Figure 1-15. Create an IAM user for Visual Studio

3. Add credentials to Visual Studio

   Finally, add the credentials you downloaded in CSV form to AWS Explorer, as shown in Figure 1-16.

 Extra special consideration is needed in downloading keys from AWS to use on any local development machine because if they are compromised, the privileges of those keys are available to whoever owns them. Using the PLP, a developer should select IAM privileges that correspond only with the functions that are strictly necessary to develop the solutions you create on AWS.

---

11 There is a detailed guide (*https://oreil.ly/4kG24*) about the concept of principle of least privilege (PLP) in the AWS documentation. The core idea of PLP is only to give out permissions when needed.

Figure 1-16. Add credentials

Once AWS Toolkit for Visual Studio installs, it is also good to be vigilant about updating the tool shown in Figure 1-17 since it is actively under development with new features from AWS. You will see new updates to the AWS Toolkit for Visual Studio as notifications in Visual Studio.

Figure 1-17. Upgrading AWS Toolkit for Visual Studio

Next, let's look at getting started with the AWS SDK.

Getting Started with the AWS SDK

The best method to learn a new technology is to build something. Let's get started with the AWS SDK by making a Console App that targets .NET 6 using the AWSSDK.S3 package from NuGet. The steps are as follows:

1. Create a new Console App targeting .NET 6.

   Inside Visual Studio, create a new Console Application that serves as the vessel for the AWS S3 tool developed.

2. Install AWSSDK.S3 via NuGet.

   With the newly created Console App loaded, choose Tools, then NuGet Package Manager, then Manage NuGet Packages for Solution. Search for AWSSDK.S3 and install it into your Console Project.

3. Create the code.

   Build the following Console App by replacing the *Program.cs* file with the content shown in the following example.

 Another way to install NuGet Packages is to right-click on the project and select Manage NuGet Packages.

```csharp
using System;
using System.Threading.Tasks;

// To interact with Amazon S3.
using Amazon.S3;
using Amazon.S3.Model;

// Create an S3 client object.
var s3Client = new AmazonS3Client();

// Display Prompt
Console.WriteLine("AWS Bucket Lister" + Environment.NewLine);

// Process API Calls Async List AWS Buckets
var listResponse = await s3Client.ListBucketsAsync();
Console.WriteLine($"Number of buckets: {listResponse.Buckets.Count}");

// Loop through the AWS buckets
foreach (S3Bucket b in listResponse.Buckets)
{
```

```
    Console.WriteLine(b.BucketName);
}
```

 For fans of the command line, it is worth noting that you can also use the dotnet command-line tool to create a Console Application as in the following snippet: dotnet new console --framework net6.0.[12]

The Console App result then details a list of S3 buckets that the AWS user who has run the .NET application had, as shown in Figure 1-18.

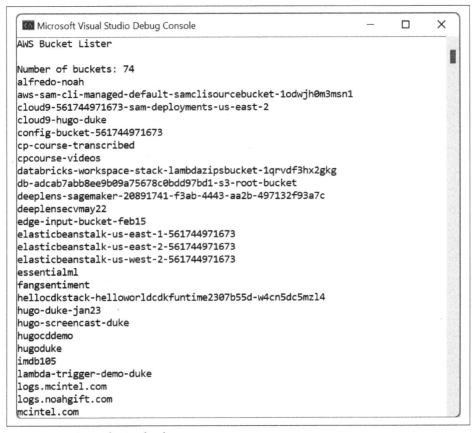

Figure 1-18. Async listing buckets

You can also watch a walk-through of building this S3 Console Application from scratch on O'Reilly (*https://oreil.ly/itGcO*) or You-Tube (*https://youtu.be/DGI_Vd04DpM*).

A follow-up step to this Console Application would be to extend the functionality to create buckets and not just list them, as shown in this AWS tutorial (*https://oreil.ly/jKBKl*) for the AWS SDK for .NET.

Next, let's wrap up everything covered in this chapter.

Conclusion

Cloud computing is a crucial driver of innovation in technology because it opens up more efficient ways to work.[13] By leveraging near-infinite resources and cloud native managed services, developers can enhance their productivity by focusing on the problem at hand versus issues unrelated to building a solution, like systems administration. This chapter covered how to start working with Amazon Cloud Services, first using a CloudShell, then moving to a full-fledged Visual Studio code environment.

The Visual Studio environment benefits from the AWS Toolkit, which has advanced features for interacting with the AWS Cloud. The AWS SDK is available directly inside Visual Studio via the NuGet package manager. The AWS SDK allows for straightforward integration into Visual Studio solutions like Console Applications. We used the AWS SDK to build out Console Applications with low-level services like AWS S3 and high-level AI APIs like AWS Comprehend.

A recommended next step for readers is to view the critical thinking discussion questions to reflect on how you could leverage the full power of AWS. You can take these questions and discuss them with your team or a coworker learning AWS. Additionally, several challenge exercise suggestions below serve as good practice for building AWS services that target .NET 6. Some of these services are not covered in detail yet, so you are welcome to skip them until they are covered in later chapters.

Next up, in Chapter 2, we cover AWS Core Services. These include AWS Storage, EC2 Compute, and services like DynamoDB. These services are the foundation for building cloud native applications that leverage the power of the .NET ecosystem.

---

13 In part, Amazon is the leader in cloud computing due to its culture, which describes itself in its leadership principles. These principles include frugality, customer obsession, and invent and simplify, among a few. You can read more about Amazon's leadership principles (*https://www.amazon.jobs/en/principles*).

Critical Thinking Discussion Questions

- What are the key differences between using Bash versus PowerShell in the AWS Cloudshell?
- When would it be advantageous to use PowerShell versus Bash and vice versa?
- How could mastering the command-line dotnet tools improve productivity?
- Could the AWS Toolkit for Visual Studio benefit even nondevelopers in your organization, e.g., the operations team? Why or why not?
- What are the advantages of prototyping C# web services by deploying right from Visual Studio?

Challenge Exercises

- Build a C# or an F# Console App and deploy to AWS CloudShell. Consider how the unique properties of a cloud-based development environment could help you automate workflows on the AWS Cloud, considering they don't require API keys and are available without needing to deploy to AWS compute services to run.
- Refer to the AWS CDK (*https://oreil.ly/EKZqZ*)[14] in C# documentation and create an S3 bucket via CDK.
- Build and deploy an Elastic Beanstalk application using Visual Studio and the AWS Toolkit for Visual Studio Code (*https://oreil.ly/yWme7*).
- Install one of the 600+ packages available for AWS with NuGet inside of Visual Studio (*https://oreil.ly/82yRo*).
- Create a hello world AWS Lambda function using the AWS Console in any supported language, then invoke it via VS Code and the AWS Toolkit for Visual Studio Code.

---

14 AWS CDK is a library that automates the deployment of resources in AWS.

## CHAPTER 2

AWS Core Services

The most popular raw materials to build a house include steel, brick, stone, and wood. These raw materials each have unique properties that enable a home builder to construct a house. Similarly, AWS Core Services are the foundational materials necessary to build complex systems. From a high level, these services include computing and storage.

When home builders construct a home, they follow comprehensive building codes, typically pulled from an international standard known as the I-Codes (*https://oreil.ly/MLp72*). According to the International Code Council, these modern safety codes aim to help ensure the engineering of "safe, sustainable, affordable and resilient structures." Similarly, the AWS Well-Architected Framework (*https://oreil.ly/Nxhnd*) provides "guidance to help customers apply best practices in design, delivery, and maintenance of AWS environments," according to AWS.

These general design principles (*https://oreil.ly/IVCQk*) are critical in understanding how to use AWS Core Services effectively. Let's briefly discuss them:

Stop guessing your capacity needs
> In a nutshell, it is a poor strategy to guess capacity. Instead, a system should incorporate the ability to add or remove resources dynamically.

Test systems at production scale
> The cloud allows for fully automated provisioning of resources; this allows a developer to test an application in an identical environment to production. The ability to replicate a production environment solves the "it works on my machine" problem endemic to the software engineering industry.

Automate to make architectural experimentation easier
> Automation results in less work over the long term, allowing the developer to audit, track changes, and revert them if needed.

Allow for evolutionary architectures
> The core idea is to design a system you expect to change. When designing software, we should consider dynamic natural systems such as trees and rivers versus static systems such as bridges or roads.

Drive architectures using data
> Data science is a popular discipline, but it doesn't confine itself only to business problems. Software systems need to use data science to identify the changes necessary to keep the system performing as designed.

Improve through game days
> An adequately architected system needs to have a complete simulation run regularly; it may be impossible to test all scenarios thoroughly without this.

Keep these principles in mind as we move through the chapter. Next, let's discuss AWS storage in more detail.

AWS Storage

Storage is an excellent example of a topic that, on the surface, is simple but can quickly explode into complexity. At the core of storage for AWS is Amazon Simple Storage Service, also known as AWS S3 (*https://docs.aws.amazon.com/s3/index.html*). It launched in 2006 as one of the first services available to the public from AWS. As of 2021, there are 100 trillion objects stored in S3.[1] If you want an example of "big data," this is as good as it gets.

While S3 is the first storage solution launched by AWS, there are many other options. Using a .NET developer-centric view, one way to begin is to divide storage into two broad categories: core storage and database.

Let's break down both briefly.

Core storage
> Core storage refers to the low-level storage components used by all services on AWS, and examples include both object-storage Amazon S3 and Amazon Elastic Block Store (EBS). AWS core storage options include object-storage Amazon S3, Amazon Elastic Block Store (EBS) (*https://aws.amazon.com/ebs*), fully managed network file storage such as Amazon File System (EFS) (*https://aws.amazon.com/efs*), and Amazon FSx for Windows File Server (*https://aws.amazon.com/fsx/windows*) (an example of one type of FSx option) and finally, utility storage services which include AWS Backup and Storage Gateway (*https://oreil.ly/3Zz6U*).

---

1 AWS S3 also regularly gets "peaks of tens of millions of requests per second" (*https://oreil.ly/x1fhi*).

Database

At a high level, a database is an organized collection of data accessed from a computer system. Database storage options include relational databases, including Amazon RDS (*https://aws.amazon.com/rds*), key-value databases, Amazon DynamoDB (*https://aws.amazon.com/dynamodb*), and special-purpose databases like Amazon Neptune (*https://oreil.ly/XdkCw*) (to query graph-based data).

With this breakdown out of the way, let's dive deeper into developing with S3 storage. S3 storage is critical to master since it offers various cost-effective tiers for dealing with object data.

Developing with S3 Storage

One way to look at S3 is as a high-level service that stores and retrieves objects at scale. For a developer, this perspective allows you to focus on developing the business logic for an application versus managing a high-performance object storage system. Let's first identify the key benefits of Amazon S3:

Durability

Durability refers to the concept of ensuring data is not lost. S3 Standard storage tier provides 99.999999999% (or eleven 9s) of durability (*https://aws.ama zon.com/s3/faqs*).

Availability

Availability refers to the concept of accessing your data when you need it. The S3 Standard storage tier has 99.99% (or four 9s) of availability.

Scalability

Scalability is the ability to increase capacity to meet demand. S3 offers near-infinite capacity in disk I/O and storage as a managed service. It can store single objects of 5 TB or less.

Security

S3 has both fine-grained access control and encryption in transit and rest.

Performance

The performance of the S3 filesystem supports many different access patterns, including streaming, large files, machine learning, and big data.

There are a few different ways to interact with S3 as a developer. The first option is through the .NET SDK. The example in Chapter 1 that lists the buckets in S3 is an excellent example of that process. You can also interact with S3 indirectly by using managed services that use S3. Examples of these managed services that use S3 include

AWS Athena[2] and AWS SageMaker. With Athena (*https://aws.amazon.com/athena*), you can query all of S3 via serverless SQL queries but don't need to worry about the logistics of dealing with servers. Likewise, Amazon SageMaker,[3] a fully managed machine learning service, heavily uses S3 to train machine learning models and store the model artifacts. A key reason for that is that S3 is serverless and scales without needing management by the user.

Another way to use S3 is by tapping into the S3 Lifecycle configuration (*https://oreil.ly/g0lpM*). The Lifecycle configuration allows sophisticated automated workflows to migrate data to different storage tiers and archive data. Let's look at these storage classes.

S3 Standard
Ideal for frequently accessed data and helpful for various use cases, including cloud native applications, content, gaming, and big data.

S3 Standard IA (infrequent access)
This storage class has the same benefits as S3 Standard but offers a different cost model, making it ideal for items like older log files since retrieval is a higher cost.

S3 One Zone-IA
The One-Zone (storing data in a single availability zone (*https://oreil.ly/suFRM*)) option is helpful for scenarios where the lowest cost possible is the goal. An example use case is a secondary backup because it is cost-effective as a secondary copy of data to protect against permanent loss due to the malfunction of the primary backup system.

Amazon S3 Glacier Deep Archive
Glacier is a secure, durable, and low-cost option ideal for data archival. It works well with S3 Lifecycles as the end delivery point.

In Figure 2-1, you can see how Amazon S3 plays a unique role as the hub of data activity beyond just storing media assets or HTML files. A challenging constraint in building global scale platforms or machine learning systems is storage capacity and disk I/O. AWS provides a core service, S3, that eliminates those constraints. As a result, the elastic nature of S3 with the near-infinite storage and disk I/O creates a new type of workflow where AWS-managed services build on top of this core service, for example, AWS SageMaker (*https://oreil.ly/x5n5M*) or AWS Glue (*https://oreil.ly/XYwNg*).

---

2 AWS Athena is an "interactive query service" that allows for easy analysis of data in S3 via SQL. You can read more about it in the getting started guide (*https://oreil.ly/N5lV8*).

3 You can read more about the managed service SageMaker in the official docs (*https://oreil.ly/FwqXr*).

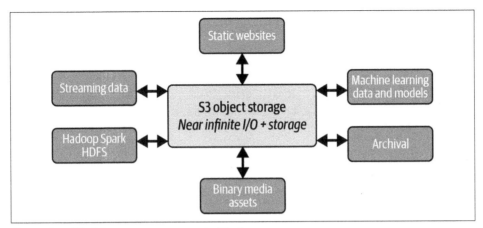

Figure 2-1. S3 object storage as a central hub

One of Noah's favorite use cases for Amazon S3 is to host static websites. In the O'Reilly book *Python for DevOps*, he covers a complete walk-through of how to build a Hugo (*https://gohugo.io*) website that uses AWS CodePipeline (*https://aws.amazon.com/code pipeline*), Amazon S3, and Amazon CloudFront CDN (*https:// aws.amazon.com/cloudfront*). You can also view a walk-through of the steps necessary to deploy a Hugo S3 site on AWS on YouTube (*https://oreil.ly/3pLIJ*) and O'Reilly (*https://oreil.ly/qRzVl*).

Another standout example of AWS building on top of S3 is the use of S3 for log files queried by Athena (*https://oreil.ly/3R0zl*).

Now that you understand the different storage classes for S3 object storage, let's discuss Elastic Block Store (EBS) storage.

Developing with EBS Storage

EBS is high-performance, network-attached storage. EBS storage (*https://aws.ama zon.com/ebs*) works by mounting block storage to an individual EC2 instance. EBS volumes act like raw, unformatted block devices (*https://oreil.ly/DiuJq*) (physical hard drives) but are virtualized and available as a service. Finally, EBS is block-level storage attached to an EC2 instance as opposed to S3, which stands on its own, holds data as objects, and is accessible from many instances.

Let's discuss the key benefits and use cases of EBS.

Benefits
EBS storage for data needs to be quickly accessed yet has long-term persistence. This storage type provides a dedicated high-performance network connection and the ability to provision dedicated disk I/O. Other key features include creat-

ing a snapshot for both backups to S3 or creating custom Amazon Machine Images (AMIs).

Use cases

EBS storage is ideal for web applications and database storage. High-performance dedicated disk I/O also comes in handy for building high-performance file servers that share data via Server Message Block (SMB) or Network File System (NFS) protocol.

One notable use of EBS is that through io2 Block Express (*https://oreil.ly/K7hok*) high-performance provisioned input/output operations per second (IOPs) allows for the creation of a "SAN in the Cloud" as shown in Figure 2-2. Notice how EBS storage provisioned in this manner creates a high-performance Microsoft SQL server instance that serves as the focal point of a business intelligence (BI) system.

This BI web service could feature an ASP .NET web service provisioned through Elastic Beanstalk, thus allowing for rapid autoscaling as data-intensive queries peak during heavy usage. Other use cases of the "SAN in the cloud" concept include deploying high-performance NoSQL servers or specialized analytics platforms like SAP HANA or SAS Analytics.

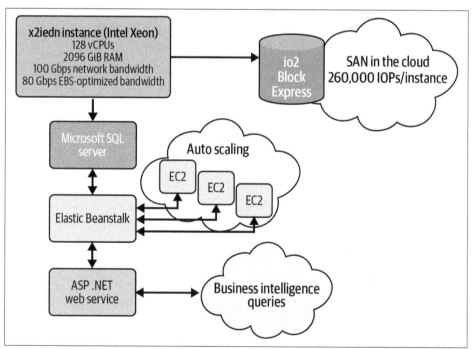

Figure 2-2. EBS SAN in the cloud with SQL server

Another type of storage is instance storage (*https://oreil.ly/tHqaY*). This storage type is temporary block storage for instances and is ideal for buffers, caches, or scratch partitions. A key difference with instance storage is that you cannot detach an instance store volume from one instance and attach it to a different instance. Unlike EBS storage, instance storage terminates when the instance stops, hibernates, terminates, or fails the underlying disk drive.

There's one use case that EBS does not address: if you have multiple instances that need to use the same storage, you need a new solution. In this case, you could use both Amazon EFS and Amazon FSx for Windows File Server. Let's discuss this topic next.

Using Network Storage: EFS and FSx

In the early internet era of the late 1990s and early 2000s, network storage was a large part of how large-scale Unix computer networks worked at universities and commercial organizations. NFS, or the Network File System, is a protocol developed by Sun Microsystems in 1984 and became ubiquitous in that early internet era.

One key issue NFS storage solved early on is the ability to create a portable home directory. This capability meant that users could create a terminal-based connection from any workstation and their shell configuration files and data were available. The downside of NFS storage-based systems is that the NFS file server is the central hub; as a result, it often causes a bottleneck in workflows as the system is overwhelmed with requests.

When the cloud era arrived in the early 2000s, many organizations moved to the cloud and built systems that didn't utilize centralized network storage anymore. Instead, they moved to block storage mounted on one machine or object stored mounted via a distributed filesystem like Hadoop. With the availability of EFS (*https://aws.amazon.com/efs*) (managed NFS) and FSx (*https://aws.amazon.com/fsx/windows*) (managed Windows network storage), the advantages of a centralized network mount point are back without the drawback of bottlenecks from the poor performance of centralized file servers.

A great example of NFSOps is shown in Figure 2-3. NFSOps describes using a network file system as a method of deploying software and configuration. Changes to the source code in GitHub trigger a build process through a Jenkins (*https://www.jenkins.io*) deployment server. This deployment server has an EFS mount point associated with it. As a result, the build server can use Rsync to deploy the script changes to the network mount point in a few milliseconds.

With the deployment process solved, this diagram shows a real-world solution used in a computer vision system. Because this particular workload uses access to centralized storage, this workflow mounts EFS as the "source of truth," allowing thousands of spot instances to use, read, and write data simultaneously. Further, the source code that performs the read and writes operations is stored on the EFS volume, dramatically simplifying configuration and deployment.

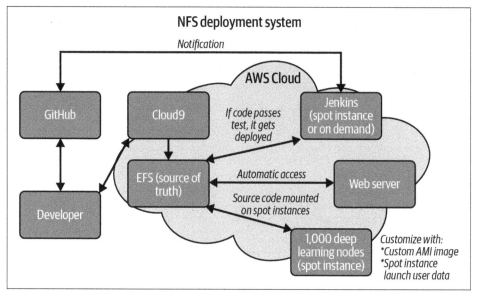

Figure 2-3. NFSOPs: using NFS storage to enhance operations

For .NET developers, there are also many exciting new workflows opened up by FSx for Windows. An excellent example in Figure 2-4 shows an FSx mount point that communicates with multiple instances of an Elastic Beanstalk–hosted .NET web service.

Another standard workflow for FSx is to develop feature films by mounting the storage endpoint for each editing workstation. In this AWS blog post (*https://oreil.ly/ 9pwQk*), you can read about how a film company used the editing software package DaVinci Resolve on AWS to create a feature film from home editing suites. Using FSx as a central file system in an animated film pipeline for major motion pictures is becoming a popular option for media companies. Because the web service can mount the file system, it can track the location of the assets as part of an asset management workflow. When an animator needs to render the entire file sequence, they send the work to ECS for batch processing. Since ECS also has access to the same file system (*https://oreil.ly/Kf1q4*), it allows for fast and seamless integration to the workflow for animators.

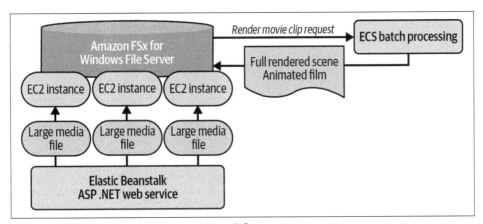

Figure 2-4. FSx for Windows in media workflow

The media industry has a long history of high-performance file servers coupled with high-performance computing (HPC) clusters. An excellent example of a modern cloud-based version is this blog post on virtual production (*https://oreil.ly/si1VM*) with Epic Games using FSx.

Using either EFS or FSx for Windows opens up new cloud-native architectures and is worth investigating further using the example tutorial on the AWS documentation website (*https://oreil.ly/NZMNd*). Next, let's discuss compute options available on AWS.

Using AWS Compute Core Services

Amazon EC2 provides resizable compute capacity with several essential details, including the ability to provision servers in minutes, automatically scale instances up or down, and only pay for the capacity you need. A necessary aspect of this service is that elasticity is built into the foundation of both the service and the integration with other AWS services.

Use cases for EC2 instances include servers ranging from web to database, where a developer wants more fine-grained control of the deployment process. While managed services like AWS App Runner offer a huge convenience over managing servers yourself, there are scenarios where a developer needs lower-level access to the EC2 instances. This service also allows complete control of the computing resources, meaning you can spin up a Linux and a Microsoft Windows instance. Further, you can optimize costs by using different pricing plans.

Next, let's explore these different compute options in finer-grained detail.

Comparison of AWS Compute Core Services

Another way to think about AWS EC2 is to look at how the official documentation compares AWS compute resources (*https://aws.amazon.com/products/compute*) in a more granular manner than discussed earlier in the chapter. In their official "Overview of Amazon Web Services" whitepaper (*https://oreil.ly/3HihF*), AWS breaks down computing into several categories:

Instances (virtual machines)
> Secure, resizable compute capacity in the cloud. EC2 instances and AWS Batch (fully managed batch processing at any scale) are two examples.

Containers
> Containers provide a standard way to package your application into a single image. According to the AWS documentation, running containers on AWS "provides developers and admins a highly reliable, low-cost way to build, ship, and run distributed applications at any scale." Examples include AWS App Runner[4] and Amazon Elastic Container Service (ECS).

Serverless
> This computing service allows running code without provisioning or managing infrastructure and responding to events at any scale. AWS Lambda is an example of serverless technology.

Edge and hybrid
> Edge services process data close to where the data resides versus processing in a data center. This service delivers a consistent AWS experience wherever you need it by providing the ability to use the cloud, on-premise, or at the edge. AWS Snow Family is an example.[5]

Cost and capacity management
> AWS helps you determine cost and capacity management by providing services and tools. It is up to the customer to test workloads against the recommended instance types to fine-tune price performance. Elastic Beanstalk is an example of one of the services in this category.[6]

---

4 AWS App Runner lets you package a container into a microservice that continuously deploys. You will see an example of this service in the container chapter.

5 The Snow Family (*https://aws.amazon.com/snow*) is a set of "Highly-secure, portable devices to collect and process data at the edge, and migrate data into and out of AWS."

6 According to AWS, AWS Elastic Beanstalk (*https://aws.amazon.com/elasticbeanstalk*) "is an easy-to-use service for deploying and scaling web applications and services."

Another way to reason about these choices is represented in Figure 2-5. Note that there is an inverse relationship between higher infrastructure control and faster application deployment. Fully managed services that also include additional production features like AWS Lambda and Fargate are at the far extreme, allowing for the quickest application development and deployment. This relationship is not a perfect rule in all situations, and exceptions exist, perhaps in a condition where developing an AWS Lambda microservice is harder to build and deploy than an AWS App Runner microservice for a particular domain.

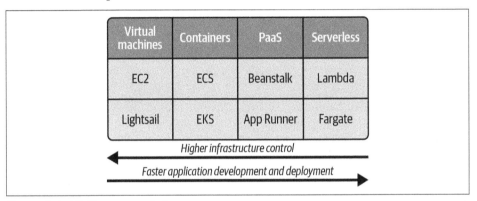

Figure 2-5. AWS compute choices

With our knowledge of EC2 core services, let's talk about getting started with EC2.

Using EC2

At the surface level, EC2 "just works" by allowing you to launch a compute instance and use it for tasks. At a deeper level, EC2 has a vast collection of features (*https:// oreil.ly/AiRbJ*). From a developer's perspective, let's dive into key parts of EC2 worth noting:

Amazon Machine Images (AMIs)
AMIs are preconfigured templates that conveniently install the software necessary for a server instance. There are AWS-recommended AMIs for Linux, Windows (*https://oreil.ly/7ymoo*), and even macOS. Notice in Figure 2-6 that the AMI Catalog is accessible by navigating inside the AWS console to the EC2 dashboard and selecting images. The quickstart AMIs are the commonly used AMIs, including Amazon Linux 2 and Windows. The "My AMIs" section is where custom AMIs appear. Finally, there is both a marketplace and a community of AMIs available.

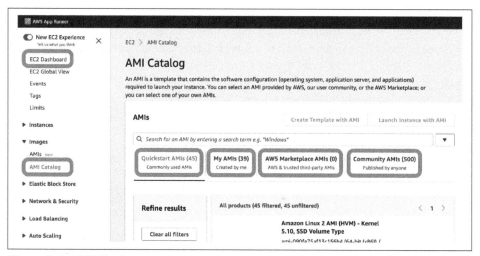

Figure 2-6. AMI Catalog

Instance types

In total, hundreds of instance types (*https://aws.amazon.com/ec2/instance-types*), arranged by category, including Compute Optimized, Memory Optimized, Accelerated Computing (hardware accelerators), and Storage Optimized. A best practice is to assess the needs of your application and perform load testing to ensure it meets the cost and performance requirements you expect.

Firewall

EC2 has a firewall called security groups (*https://oreil.ly/05rcL*) that enables granular configuration of protocols, ports, and IP ranges for inbound and outbound access to instances.

Metadata

You can create and use tags to enable resource tracking and automation of EC2 instances.

Elastic IP addresses

Static IPv4 addresses can be dynamically assigned to EC2 instances, thus enhancing elasticity and automation.

Virtual Private Clouds (VPC)

While VPC is a separate service, it has deep integration (*https://oreil.ly/7rcng*) with EC2. Virtual networks create an isolated environment with precise controls for connecting to other resources in AWS.

With the basics out of the way, let's look at what is involved in provisioning an EC2 instance in Figure 2-7. Notice how the instance launch can also use "User data" to assign custom commands at launch or select between EBS or instance storage. Other critical decisions include setting up a security group that opens up ports necessary for networking between services. Other configurable options include selecting the appropriate IAM role and giving the EC2 instance the ability to communicate with Amazon S3.

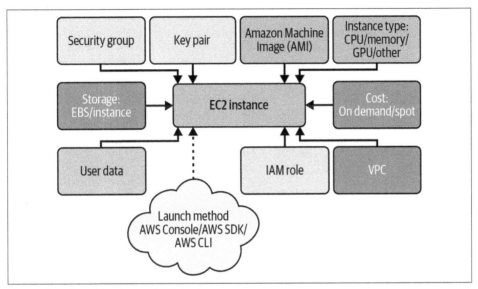

Figure 2-7. Provisioning an EC2 instance

 You can view an entire walk-through of how to provision EC2 instances from AWS CloudShell or the AWS Console in the follow‐ ing YouTube Video (*https://oreil.ly/4FvEP*) or on O'Reilly (*https:// oreil.ly/rltV3*).

It is essential to mention that a regular Bash terminal works well for automating EC2. Notice the following commands that launch an instance, describe it, then terminate it:

```
aws ec2 run-instances --image-id ami-033594f8862b03bb2
aws ec2 describe-instances --filters "Name=instance-type,Values=t2.micro"
aws ec2 terminate-instances --instance-ids i-00cbf30e33063f1a4
```

 A recommended resource for doing a deep dive on EC2 instance types is the AWS Knowledge Center document "How do I choose the appropriate EC2 instance type for my workload?" (*https:// oreil.ly/Lop74*)

Now that you know how to use EC2 in more detail, let's discuss networking with EC2.

Networking

AWS networking consists of a global infrastructure that enables EC2 instances to work globally and is reliable and distributed. Notice in Figure 2-8 that each region is distinct geographically and has multiple availability zones.

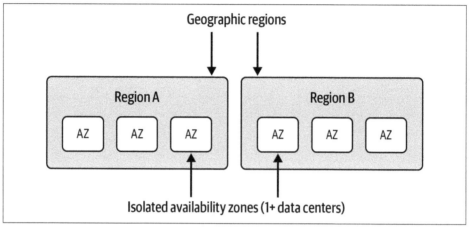

Figure 2-8. AWS regions and zones

There are more than 25 regions globally and more than 85 availability zones. This data means each region has at least 3 availability zones on average. Fortunately, it is easy to use AWS CloudShell and PowerShell to get your region's exact number of availability zones. Launch an instance of AWS CloudShell as a user with privileges to query EC2 via an IAM role. Next, import `AWSPowerShell.NetCore` and then query the available zones available in your AWS CloudShell's region:

```
Import-Module AWSPowerShell.NetCore
Get-EC2AvailabilityZone
```

 Under the region level, the AZs interconnect with high-bandwidth, low-latency networking, which is also encrypted. The network performance is sufficient to accomplish synchronous replication between AZs. The AZs are physically separated to achieve a real disaster recovery solution.

You can get more fine-grained control by assigning the output to a PowerShell variable `$zones` and then using `$zones.count` to count the exact number of availability zones in your region in the status "available":

```
$zones = Get-EC2AvailabilityZone -Filter @{ Name="state";Values="available" }
$zones.count
```

The output shows that with only a couple of lines of code, it is straightforward to script EC2 from PowerShell using the convenient AWS CloudShell as the development environment:

```
PS /home/cloudshell-user> Import-Module AWSPowerShell.NetCore
PS /home/cloudshell-user> $zones = Get-EC2AvailabilityZone -Filter `
  @{ Name="state";Values="available" }
PS /home/cloudshell-user> $zones.count
6
```

 You can check out the PowerShell documentation (*https://oreil.ly/ LNsQJ*) to see all of the flags available. There is also a demo walk-through of this process on YouTube (*https://youtu.be/ MeeZ3fnJsqM*) and O'Reilly (*https://oreil.ly/e75S2*).

Now that you understand EC2 networking in more detail, let's talk about EC2 pricing options.

Using EC2 Pricing Options

While purchasing options may not be top of mind to many developers, it is an important consideration. One of the five pillars of the AWS Well-Architected Framework is cost optimization (*https://oreil.ly/C170R*). In particular, this framework recommends that you "adopt a consumption model," i.e., pay only for the computing resources you require. Let's break down the different pricing options available for EC2:

On-demand instances
These instances are ideal for spiky workloads or prototyping. You pay for computing in increments as granular as a second, and there is no long-term commitment.

Reserved instances
These instances are noteworthy for committed, steady-state workloads. For example, once a company has a good idea of the configuration and load of its architecture in the cloud, it will know how many instances to reserve. There are options for both one-year or three-year commitments, leading to a significant discount from on-demand instances.

Savings plans
This plan is suited to Amazon EC2 and AWS Fargate, as well as AWS Lambda workloads because it lets you reserve an hourly spend commitment. The discounts are the same as reserved instances with the added flexibility in exchange for a dedicated hourly spend commitment.

Spot instances

These are ideal for fault-tolerant workloads that can be both flexible and stateless. A good example would be doing a batch job that can run during the day, say, transcoding video. These instances are available at up to 90% off on-demand pricing.

Dedicated hosts

Another option for workloads requiring single tenancy or software licenses is to use a dedicated physical server.

It is helpful to understand the options for pricing on AWS because they can make or break the effectiveness of moving to the cloud. With that information covered, let's move on to security best practices for AWS.

Security Best Practices for AWS

Security isn't optional for software engineering; it is a core requirement for any project. What may be surprising to newcomers to cloud computing is that moving to the cloud increases the security profile of projects. One way to explain this concept is through the unique AWS concept called the "shared responsibility model" (*https://oreil.ly/6q23h*) shown in Figure 2-9.

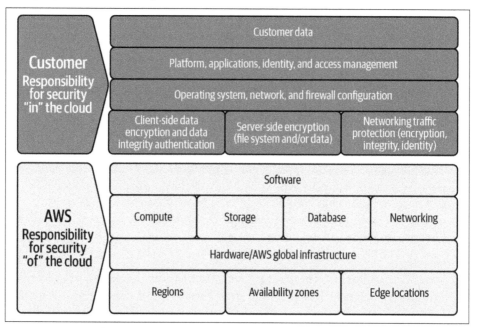

Figure 2-9. AWS shared responsibility model

Notice that AWS is responsible for the entire global infrastructure, including the physical security requirements. The customer then builds on top of that secure foundation and is responsible for items like customer data or firewall configuration.[7]

A great place to start designing a secure system on AWS is by following the guidelines available from the AWS Well-Architected Framework website (*https://oreil.ly/uaGGU*). There are seven design principles. Let's take a look:

Implement a strong identity foundation
Use the principle of least privilege (PLP) to assign just enough access to resources for a user to accomplish their assigned tasks. Use the identity and access management (IAM) system to control users, groups, and access policies while eliminating static credentials.

Enable traceability
It is critical to enable real-time monitoring, alerting, and auditing of changes to a production environment. This capability works through a comprehensive logging and metric collection system that allows actionability.

Apply security at all layers
The best defense is a layered approach where every component of cloud computing, from computing to storage to networking, adds security hardening.

Automate security best practices
Automating security best practices as code allows for an efficient and idempotent way to minimize organizational risk.

Protect data in transit and at rest
Data needs protecting both in its location and when it moves. This best practice happens through combined encryption, tokenization, and access controls.

Keep people away from data
Manual data processing is an antipattern to avoid as it introduces humans into the loop, which can inflict intentional and unintentional security holes.

Prepare for security events
A consistent theme at Amazon is "design for failure." Similarly, it is essential to have a plan for dealing with security incidents and processes that aligns with organizational needs with security.

---

7 Further, you can find detailed information about security by visiting the Security Pillar (*https://oreil.ly/BJtas*) section of the AWS Well-Architected Framework site.

One of the big takeaways for AWS security is how critical automation is to implementing security. DevOps is at the heart of cloud-native automation, which is the focus of Chapter 6. With the foundational best practices of security out of the way, let's discuss the AWS best-practice encryption.

Encryption at Rest and Transit

Encryption is a method of transforming data that makes it unreadable without access to a secret encryption key.[8] At the center of the encryption strategy in transit and rest is that data becomes exposed in an unencrypted form at no point.

"Transit" refers to sending data from one location to another, such as from a user's mobile phone to a banking website. *Rest* refers to the storage of the data; for example, data that resides in a database is at rest.

A good analogy would be to consider the concept of sealing perishable foods by vacuum packing the product. Vacuum packing removes oxygen, thus extending the product's shelf life and preserving it. As soon as the seal breaks, the food item instantly degrades. Similarly, data exposed in an unencrypted form exposes itself to instant risk and breaks down best practices in storing and managing data. AWS solves this problem by providing services that allow you to encrypt your data comprehensively throughout the lifecycle of data operations on the platform.

One essential item to consider is that for encryption to work, there is an encryption key (*https://oreil.ly/QJzoP*). Privileged users can access data only if they have that key.

Now that we have covered encryption, let's continue to drill down into security concepts on AWS by next covering the principle of least privilege.

---

8 You can read more about this topic via the AWS whitepaper "Logical Separation on AWS" (*https://oreil.ly/9wDGf*).

PLP (Principle of Least Privilege)

The mail delivery person does not have a key to your house because of the principle of least privilege (PLP). It is a security best practice for non-IT people and IT people alike that says to never give more access to resources than necessary. You can see this principle in action in Figure 2-10. The mail delivery person has access to the mailbox but not the house. Similarly, the family has access to the house, but only the parents can access the safe. This concept means with AWS, you give users the least amount of access and responsibility necessary to complete their tasks.

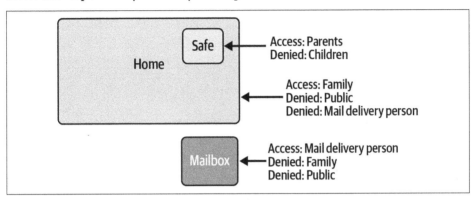

Figure 2-10. Principle of least privilege example

PLP protects both the resource as well as the recipient of the privilege. Consider the case of the safe-in-the-house scenario. There may be something in the safe that is dangerous to the children, and it protects both the safe and the child from not having access. With AWS, this design principle is in effect: only assign IAM policies with the least privileges to get the task completed.

This approach works in a real-world microservice architecture like the one shown in Figure 2-11. Notice how an AWS Lambda microservice is listening to AWS S3. When a user uploads a new profile picture, the AWS Lambda function uses an "S3 Read Only" policy since this service only needs to accept the event payload from S3, which includes the name of the image uploaded and the S3 URI, which contains the full path to the image. The AWS Lambda microservice then writes that metadata to the DynamoDB table using a role that includes the ability to access that particular table and update it.

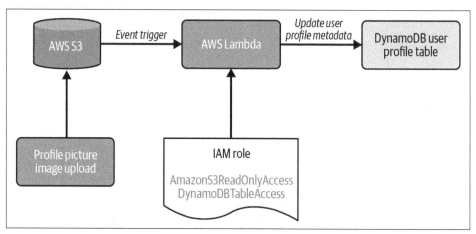

Figure 2-11. Serverless profile picture profile updater microservice

This PLP workflow prevents both security holes as well as developer errors. Limiting the scope of what a microservice does strictly by what it needs to perform its task diminishes organizational risk. This risk may not be apparent to systems developed without PLP, but it doesn't mean the risk doesn't exist.

With a deeper understanding of implementing security, let's discuss a central component in any securely designed system on AWS, AWS Identity and Access Management.

Using AWS Identity and Access Management (IAM)

At the center of securely controlling access to AWS services is IAM (*https://oreil.ly/ xaPQq*). With AWS IAM, you can specify who or what can access services and resources in AWS, centrally manage fine-grained permissions, and analyze access to refine permissions across AWS, as you can see in Figure 2-12.

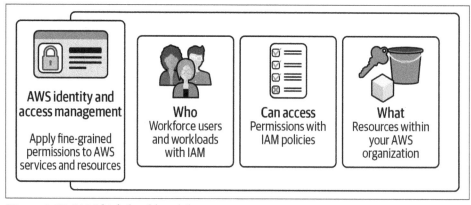

Figure 2-12. IAM high-level breakdown

To understand how IAM works in more detail, Figure 2-13 shows how a principal is a person or application that can request an AWS resource by authenticating. Next, a user (Account ID 0123*) must be authorized to create a request, where policies determine whether to allow or deny the request. These rules are identity-based policies, other policies, and resource-based policies that control authorization.

After the request approval, the actions available come from the service itself, i.e., `CreateDatabase`, `CreateUser`, or whatever the service supports. Finally, after the approval of the operations in the request for the service, they are performed on the resource. An example of a resource is an EC2 instance or an Amazon S3 bucket.

You can read a very detailed overview of this process by reading the Understanding How IAM Works User Guide (*https://oreil.ly/GkiUm*). The IAM service has five critical components: IAM users, IAM groups, IAM roles, and IAM permissions and policies (bundled together for brevity). Let's discuss each one:

IAM users
    A user is an entity you create in AWS to represent either a person or an application. A user (*https://oreil.ly/etisJ*) in AWS can have programmatic access via an access key, AWS Management Console access via a password, or both. An access key enables access to the SDK, CLI commands, and API.

IAM groups
    An IAM user group (*https://oreil.ly/hawd3*) is a collection of IAM users. Using groups allows you to specify permissions for multiple users.

IAM roles
    An IAM role (*https://oreil.ly/hQyBG*) is an IAM identity with specific permissions. A typical scenario is for a service like EC2 to have a role assigned with special permissions to call the AWS API, say, download data from S3 without needing to keep API keys on the EC2 instance.

IAM permissions and policies
    You manage access (*https://oreil.ly/oi6u2*) to AWS by creating or using default policies and attaching them to IAM identities like users, groups, and roles. The permissions in these policies then set what is allowed or denied.

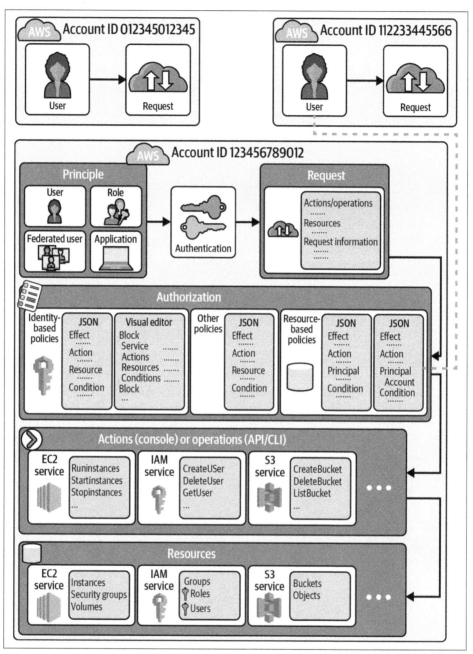

Figure 2-13. How IAM works

With a deeper understanding of identity and access management on AWS out of the way, let's switch topics to building NoSQL solutions on AWS with DynamoDB.

Developing NoSQL Solutions with DynamoDB

The CTO of Amazon, Werner Vogel, points out (*https://oreil.ly/qSNzq*) that a "one size database doesn't fit anyone." This problem is illustrated in Figure 2-14, which shows that each type of database has a specific purpose. Picking the correct storage solutions, including which databases to use, is crucial for a .NET architect to ensure that a system works optimally. An excellent resource for comparing AWS Cloud databases is found on the AWS products page (*https://oreil.ly/qK0no*).

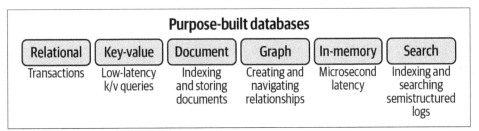

Figure 2-14. Each type of database has a purpose

Maintenance is a consideration in designing a fully automated and efficient system. Suppose a particular technology choice is being abused, such as using a relational database for a highly available messaging queue. In that case, maintenance costs could explode, creating more automation work. So another component to consider is how much automation work it takes to maintain a solution.

At the core of DynamoDB (*https://aws.amazon.com/dynamodb*) is the concept of a distributed database that is eventually consistent.[9] In practice, the database can automatically scale up from zero to millions of requests per second (*https://oreil.ly/ZRZvt*) while maintaining low latency.

Let's break down the critical DynamoDB concepts via characteristics, use cases, and key features:

Characteristics
> DynamoDB is a fully managed nonrelational key-value and document database that performs at any scale. It is also serverless and ideal for event-driven programming. Enterprise features of DynamoDB include encryption and backups.

---

[9] A foundational theorem in theoretical computer science is the CAP theorem (*https://oreil.ly/aM06S*), which states that there is a trade-off between consistency, availability, and partition tolerance. In practice, this means that many NoSQL databases, including DynamoDB, are "eventually consistent," meaning they eventually converge the new writes to different nodes to create a consistent view of the data.

Use cases

This service works well for simple high-volume data that must scale quickly and doesn't require complex joins. It also is ideal for solutions that require high throughput and low latency.

Key features

Some key features include NoSQL tables and the ability to have items with different attributes. DynamoDB also supports caching and peaks of 20M+ requests per second.

We have covered the basics of DynamoDB; next, let's build a simple application using DynamoDB.

Build a Sample C# DynamoDB Console App

Let's build a simple DynamoDB application in C# that reads data from a table. There are many ways to create a table manually, including Figure 2-15, in which you first navigate to the DynamoDB interface and then select "Create table."

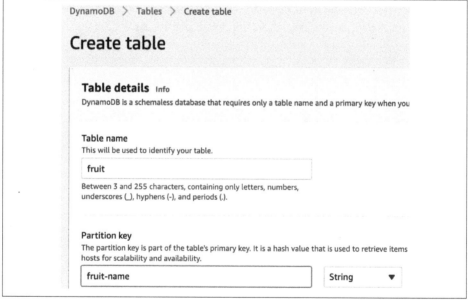

Figure 2-15. Create a DynamoDB table in Amazon Console

Another way to create a table and populate it with values is by using Visual Studio AWS Explorer, as shown in Figure 2-16.

Figure 2-16. Create a DynamoDB table in Visual Studio Explorer

Yet again, we populate the table with fruit. We can do it via the .NET SDK or the console if we want to query it, as shown in Figure 2-17.

Figure 2-17. Query table

To create an application to query DynamoDB, open up Visual Studio and create a new Console Application, then install the DynamoDB NuGet package (*https://oreil.ly/BChf7*) as shown in Figure 2-18.

Figure 2-18. Install DynamoDB

With the installation out of the way, the process to query the table, print out the entire table, and pick a random fruit is addressed in the following C# code example:

```csharp
using System;
using System.Collections.Generic;

// To interact with AWS DynamoDB
using Amazon.DynamoDBv2;
using Amazon.DynamoDBv2.DocumentModel;

// Create client ❶
var client = new AmazonDynamoDBClient();
var fruitTable = Table.LoadTable(client, "fruit");

// Display Prompt
Console.WriteLine("Table Scan " + Environment.NewLine);

// Scan ❷
ScanFilter scanFilter = new ScanFilter();
Search search = fruitTable.Scan(scanFilter);

//All Fruit ❸
var fruitList = new List<string> ();

//print ❹
do
{
    var documentList = await search.GetNextSetAsync();

    foreach (Document document in documentList)
    {
        var fruit = document.First().Value;
        Console.WriteLine($"Fruit: {fruit}");
        fruitList.Add(fruit);    //Add scanned fruit to list
    }
} while (!search.IsDone);
```

```
//Now pick a random fruit
var random = new Random();
int index = random.Next(fruitList.Count);
Console.WriteLine($"Random Fruit: {fruitList[index]}");
```

❶ First, create a client.

❷ Next, scan the table.

❸ Then, make a list to hold the results.

❹ Finally, loop through the table results, put them in the list, and randomly pick a fruit to print.

The results of the Console Application in Figure 2-19 show a successful table scan and selection of random fruit.

```
Microsoft Visual Studio Debug Console                                    —   □   ×
Table Scan

Fruit: strawberry
Fruit: pear
Fruit: apple
Random Fruit: strawberry

C:\Users\noahgift\source\repos\noahgift\ScanDynamoDB\ScanDynamoDB\bin\Debug\net6.0\ScanDynamoDB.exe (process 10444) exit
ed with code 0.
To automatically close the console when debugging stops, enable Tools->Options->Debugging->Automatically close the conso
le when debugging stops.
Press any key to close this window . . .
```

Figure 2-19. Table scan Console App

Check out the AWS docs GitHub repo (*https://oreil.ly/gol15*) for more ideas on building applications. It is an excellent resource for ideas on building solutions with DynamoDB.

A CRUD application creates, reads, updates, and deletes items from a database. This CRUD example (*https://oreil.ly/1SdtM*) for DynamoDB is a great resource to refer to when building this style of application on DynamoDB.

Now that you know how to build solutions with DynamoDB let's discuss a complementary service: the Amazon Relational Database Service (RDS).

Amazon Relational Database Service

RDS is a service that lets you point and click to set up an enterprise database in the cloud. The times before RDS were dark days for developers who have experienced running their own SQL database. The list of tasks necessary to properly administer a database is quite staggering. As a result, many positions called DBAs or database administrators filled the role of helping keep SQL systems alive like Microsoft SQL Server, MySQL, and Postgres. Now many of those tasks are features in RDS.

The features synthesize into a uniform solution that creates agility for .NET projects. The critical win of RDS is that it allows a developer to focus on building business logic, not fighting the database. This win occurs because RDS alleviates the pain of managing the database and will enable developers to focus on building the application. Let's look at a select list of the core features that highlight the power of RDS:

Core features
> RDS is easy to use. It also has automatic software patching, which reduces security risks. Best practice recommendations are baked into the product and include access to SSD storage, dramatically increasing the service's scalability.

Reliability
> The service includes the ability to create automated backups and build database snapshots. Finally, a best practice of multi-AZ deployments allows for a robust recovery option in an availability zone outage.

Security and operations
> RDS includes significant encryption capabilities, including using this in both rest and transit. Further network isolation allows for increased operational security and fine-grained resource-level permissions. Also, there is extensive monitoring via CloudWatch, which increases the cost-effectiveness of the service.

With the core features of RDS out of the way, let's discuss a fully managed serverless solution next.

Fully Managed Databases with Amazon Aurora Serverless v2

The cloud native world of serverless is addictive to develop solutions with because of the straight line between your thoughts and their implementation as business logic. With the addition of Amazon Aurora Serverless v2 (*https://oreil.ly/E5QJZ*), the ability to execute quickly on business logic as code is enhanced further.

Here is a subset of the benefits of the Amazon Aurora Serverless v2:

Highly scalable
Instances can scale to hundreds of thousands of transactions in a fraction of a second.

Simple
Aurora removes the complexity of provisioning and managing database capacity.

Durable
Aurora storage is self-healing via six-way replication.

The critical use cases include the following:

Variable workloads
Running an infrequently used application that peaks 30 minutes a few times a day is a sweet spot for this service.

Unpredictable workloads
A content-heavy site that experiences heavy traffic can count on the database automatically scaling capacity and then scaling back down.

Enterprise database fleet management
Enterprises with thousands of databases can automatically scale database capacity by each application demand without managing the fleet individually.

Software as a service (SaaS) applications
SaaS vendors that operate thousands of Aurora databases can provision Aurora database clusters for each customer without needing to provision capacity. It automatically shuts down the database when not in use to reduce costs.

Scaled-out databases split across multiple servers
It is common to break high write or read requirements to numerous databases. Aurora Serverless v2's capacity is met instantly and managed automatically, simplifying the deployment.

Putting all this together, a SaaS company could build an architecture as shown in Figure 2-20 where each client has one dedicated serverless pipeline of AWS Step Functions that orchestrate via AWS Lamba payload that proceed to Aurora Serverless v2.

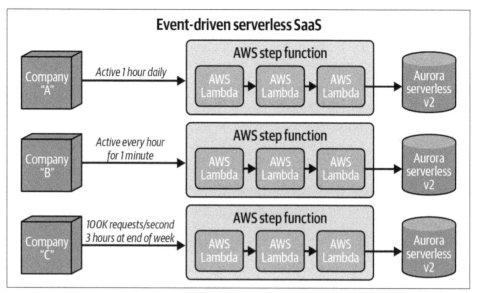

Figure 2-20. SaaS company architecture with Aurora Serverless

The benefit of this architecture is that it is easy to debug the pipeline for each paying customer. Additionally, the complexity of managing server load for each client is alleviated since the entire pipeline uses autoscale serverless components.

 One notable example of developing a .NET Web API using Aurora Serverless is at this blog post by AWS (*https://oreil.ly/WUmb9*).

This chapter covered a wide variety of essential topics for mastering AWS. Let's wrap up the highlights.

Conclusion

AWS Core Services are the foundation that allows a developer to build sophisticated solutions. In this chapter, we covered the core services of computing and storage. This coverage included recommendations on using service options for services like EC2 and S3 and managed services.

It is important to note that for both EC2 and S3, there is an extensive selection of pricing options. The appropriate pricing option for a given architecture is critical in building a well-architected AWS system. Fortunately, AWS provides detailed monitoring and instrumentation on pricing and valuable tools in the AWS Cost Management Console (*https://oreil.ly/8EZtn*).

The chapter covered both traditional and NoSQL databases, including an example of using DynamoDB to build a simple Console Application. Take a look at the critical thinking questions and exercises to challenge yourself to apply this material to your scenarios. The next chapter covers migrating a legacy .NET application to AWS.

Critical Thinking Discussion Questions

- What are new workflows for architecting software made available by network filesystems like Amazon EFS and Amazon FSx?
- What are the advantages of prototyping solutions with AWS EC2 spot instances?
- What compute and database services should a small startup of one to three developers gravitate toward for building SaaS APIs?
- What compute services should a company with a large data center moving to the cloud consider?
- How could your organization translate the spirit of the blog post "A One Size Fits All Database Doesn't Fit Anyone" (*https://oreil.ly/W4H4a*) into a plan for how to use the correct types of databases for the problems it faces?

Exercises

- Build a CRUD (create, read, update, delete) C# Console App for AWS S3.
- Build a CRUD (create, read, update, delete) C# Console App for AWS DynamoDB.
- Build a CRUD (create, read, update, delete) C# Console App for AWS RDS for Aurora Serverless v2.
- Change the DynamoDB example to select a fruit without needing to scan the table randomly.
- Launch a Windows EC2 instance, install a custom tool or library on it, convert it to an AMI (*https://oreil.ly/fgPD9*), and launch an EC2 instance with your custom AMI (*https://oreil.ly/zkG9o*).

## CHAPTER 3

Migrating a Legacy .NET Framework Application to AWS

In the previous chapters, we have seen some of the exciting tools and services that AWS gives us as developers. We are next going to take a look at what we can do with some of our legacy .NET applications and explore what is made possible by moving them to the cloud.

Software development is not, as we're sure you are uncomfortably aware, a pursuit solely of greenfield projects, clean repos, tidy backlogs, and the latest toolsets. Organizations of all sizes can have legacy code, some of which may still be running on premises, internal tools, APIs, workflows, and applications that are actively used but not actively maintained. Migrating these to the cloud can provide your organization with cost savings, increased performance, and a drastically improved ability to scale.

In this chapter, you will learn how to choose, plan, and execute the migration of a web application running on IIS and built on either .NET Framework or .NET Core/6+.

 With the release of .NET 5 in November 2020, Microsoft has renamed .NET Core to simply ".NET". In these next chapters, we will refer to .NET Core and all future versions as .NET and the previous, legacy version of the framework as .NET Framework.

Choosing a Migration Path

Every .NET application will have a different path to the cloud and, while we cannot create a one-size-fits-all framework for migrating a legacy .NET application, we *can* learn from the migrations of those that came before us. In 2011, the technology research company Gartner identified five migration strategies for migrating on-premises software to the cloud (*https://oreil.ly/KFvfw*). These were known as "The 5 Rs" and over the years have been refined, adapted, and expanded as new experiences emerged, growing to encompass all the challenges you might face migrating and modernizing a legacy web application.

For migrating some of your code to AWS we now have 6 Rs, any of which could be applied to a legacy .NET web application running on IIS and built in either .NET Framework or the more recent incarnation .NET:

- Rehosting
- Replatforming
- Repurchasing
- Rearchitecting
- Rebuilding
- Retaining

The first five of these strategies have increasing levels of effort and complexity; this, however, is rewarded with increasing value and ability to iterate going forward. We will delve deeper into some of these approaches later in this chapter.

Rehosting

Rehosting is the process of moving an application from one host to another. It could be moving an application from running in a server room on a company's premises to a virtual machine in the cloud, or it could be moving from one cloud provider to another. As a strategy for migration, rehosting does not change (or even require access to) the source code. It is a process of moving assets in their final built or compiled state. In the .NET world, this means *.dll* files, *.config* files, *.cshtml* views, static assets, and anything else required to serve your application. It is for this reason that rehosting is sometimes called the "lift and shift" approach to migration. Your entire application is lifted out as-is and shifted to a new host.

The advantages of rehosting your application include being able to take advantage of the cost savings and performance improvements possible on a cloud-hosted virtual machine. It can also make it easier to manage your infrastructure if you can rehost your lesser maintained or legacy applications alongside your more actively developed code on AWS.

For an overview of some of the tools and resources available, should you choose to follow this migration path, see "Rehosting on AWS" on page 66.

Replatforming

The replatforming approach goes one step further than simply rehosting and changes not just *where* but also *how* your application is hosted. Unlike rehosting, replatforming *could* involve changes to your code, although these changes should be kept to a minimum to keep the strategy viable.

There are many definitions of what constitutes a "platform," but one platform we as .NET developers are all aware of is Internet Information Services (IIS) running on Windows Server. Replatforming would be the process of migrating your application *away* from IIS and onto a more cloud native hosting environment such as Kubernetes. Later in this chapter, we will explore one type of replatforming in more detail: "Replatforming via Containerization" on page 71.

Repurchasing

This strategy is relevant when your application depends on a licensed third-party service or application that cannot run on a cloud infrastructure. Perhaps you use a self-hosted product for customer relationship management (CRM) or content management system (CMS) functionality in your application that cannot be migrated to the cloud. Repurchasing is a migration strategy for applications that rely on these products and involves ending your existing, self-hosted license, and purchasing a new license for a cloud-based replacement. This can either be a cloud-based version of a similar product (for example, Umbraco CMS to Umbraco Cloud), or a replacement product on the AWS Marketplace.

Rearchitecting

As the name implies, rearchitecting deals with the overall architecture of your application and asks you to think about how you can make changes to facilitate its move to the cloud.[1] For a legacy .NET Framework application, this will almost certainly mean moving to .NET. Microsoft in 2019 announced that version 4.8 will be the last major release of .NET Framework and, while it will continue to be supported and distributed with future releases of Windows, it will not be actively developed by Microsoft.[2]

History has sculpted out a fairly linear journey for rearchitecting a monolithic web application, as shown in Figure 3-1.

---

1 This migration strategy is sometimes called "refactoring"; however, this can be a chameleon of a term, so I'll be sticking to "rearchitecting" for this book.

2 You can find the .NET Framework support policy here (*https://oreil.ly/FJImk*).

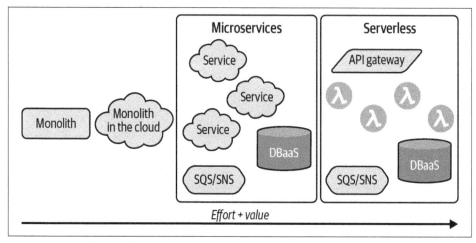

Figure 3-1. Evolution of monolith web applications

We will take a deeper dive into porting .NET Framework to .NET in the section "Rearchitecting: Moving to .NET (Core)" on page 75.

Rebuilding

Sometimes your legacy codebase fails to pass the effort versus value benchmark for migration and you have no choice but to rebuild from scratch. You are not, of course, starting entirely from scratch. You will be able to migrate some of your business logic; all those solved problems your legacy codebase has taken years to navigate through can be re-created on a new codebase. However, the code itself—the architecture, the libraries, databases, API schemas, and documentation[3]—will not be coming with you.

Retaining

The final migration strategy on this list is really just *none of the above*. Perhaps your legacy application has some special requirements, cannot be connected to the internet, will have to go through a prohibitively lengthy recertification process. There are many unique and often unforeseen reasons why some legacy codebases cannot be migrated to the cloud, or cannot be migrated at the present moment in time. You should only migrate applications for which a viable business case can be made, and if that is not possible, then selecting *none of the above* is sometimes your best option.

---

[3] I will admit to looking up from my screen and taking a long sip of coffee before adding "documentation" to this list. My cat gave me the same knowing stare that you are.

Choosing a Strategy

The migration strategy you choose will depend upon the current architecture of your application, where you want to get to, and how much you are willing to change in order to get there. The chart in Figure 3-2 summarizes the decisions you can make in order to choose the migration path most appropriate for your individual use case.

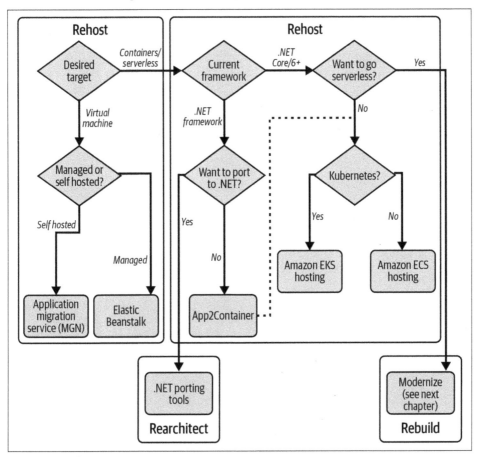

Figure 3-2. Choosing a strategy

AWS Migration Hub Strategy Recommendations

For further assistance in choosing a migration strategy, AWS offers a tool called AWS Migration Hub Strategy Recommendations (*https://oreil.ly/56iyO*). This service gathers data from your existing servers, augments it with analysis of your source code and SQL schemas, then recommends a migration strategy from those we have covered previously.

Strategy Recommendations is part of the AWS Migration Hub: a set of tools for analyzing an infrastructure planning for and then tracking a migration to AWS. The Migration Hub is available at no additional charge; you only pay the cost of any tools you use and any AWS resources consumed in the process

To get started with Strategy Recommendations, we first need to give it as much data about our existing infrastructure as possible. We can do this with the AWS Application Discovery Service (*https://aws.amazon.com/application-discovery*), another service accessible from the AWS Migration Hub. To start application discovery, navigate to discovery tools in the AWS Management Console (*https://oreil.ly/Vkp65*) for your home region[4] and choose from one of three methods to collect the data shown in Figure 3-3.

Figure 3-3. Application Discovery Service collection methods

Let's walk through a quick setup using the discovery agent. Before we start, ensure you have the AWS CLI installed and you have an IAM user access key (and secret). You can use the following commands to save these values in your AWS configuration files. These settings will then be used by all the tools in this chapter.

```
$ aws configure set aws_access_key_id <your-key-id>
$ aws configure set aws_secret_access_key <your-key-secret>
$ aws configure set default.region <home-region>
```

Next, open up a PowerShell terminal on one of the Windows servers you want to begin collecting data for, then download the agent installer:

```
PS C:\> mkdir ADSAgent
PS C:\> cd .\ADSAgent\
PS C:\ADSAgent> Invoke-WebRequest
https://s3.us-west-2.amazonaws.com/aws-discovery-agent.us-west-2/windows/latest/
ADSAgentInstaller.exe -OutFile ADSAgentInstaller.exe
```

---

4 Your home region in the AWS Migration Hub is the region in which migration data is stored for discovery, planning, and migration tracking. You can set a home region from the Migration Hub Settings page.

Next set your home region for the AWS Migration Hub, your access key ID, and secret.

And run the discovery agent installer on this server:

```
PS C:\ADSAgent> .\ADSAgentInstaller.exe REGION=$AWS_REGION KEY_ID=$KEY_ID
KEY_SECRET=$KEY_SECRET INSTALLLOCATION="C:\ADSAgent" /quiet
```

This will install the agent into the new folder you created, *C:\ADSAgent*. Back in the Migration Hub section of the AWS Management Console, you can navigate to Discover → Data Collectors → Agents and, if all has gone well, the agent you installed should appear in the list. Select the agent and click Start Data Collection to allow ADS to begin collecting data about your server.

 If your agent does not show up, ensure your server is allowing the agent process to send data over TCP port 443 to *https://arsenal-discovery.<your-home-region>.amazonaws.com:443*.

The discovery agent will poll its host server approximately every 15 minutes and report data including CPU usage, free RAM, operating system properties, and process IDs of running processes that were discovered. You will be able to see your servers in the Migration Hub by navigating to Discover → Servers on the dashboard. Once you have all your servers added to ADS, you are ready to begin collating the data necessary for strategy recommendations.

The Strategy Recommendations service has an automated, agentless data collector you can use to analyze your .NET applications running on the servers you now have in ADS. To get started navigate to Strategy → Get Started in the Migration Hub console and follow the wizard to download the data collector as an Open Virtual Appliance (OVA). This can then be deployed to your VMware vCenter Server. Full instructions for setting up the data collector can be found in the AWS documentation (*https://oreil.ly/LRIeN*).

Once your data collector is set up, you can move to the next page of the wizard and select your priorities for migration. Figure 3-4 shows the priorities selection screen in Strategy Recommendations. This will allow AWS to recommend a migration strategy that best fits your business needs and plans for the future. Select the options that most align with your reasons for migrating.

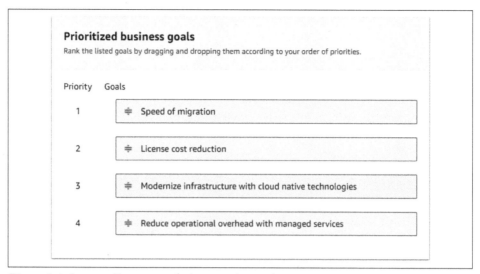

Prioritized business goals

Rank the listed goals by dragging and dropping them according to your order of priorities.

Priority	Goals
1	≑ Speed of migration
2	≑ License cost reduction
3	≑ Modernize infrastructure with cloud native technologies
4	≑ Reduce operational overhead with managed services

Figure 3-4. Strategy Recommendations service goals

After running data analysis on your servers, the service will give you recommendations for each application, including a link to any relevant AWS tools to assist you with that type of migration. In Figure 3-5, you can see the tool is recommending we use rehosting as a migration strategy onto EC2 using the Application Migration Service, which we will look at next.

Strategy options (1) Info

Data last analyzed 1 day ago. You can reassess your portfolio to see updated recommendations.

Filter strategy options by property or value

Strategy	Destination	Application components	Tool	Status
Rehost	Amazon Elastic Cloud Compute (EC2)	5	Application Migration Service	Recommended
Replatform	-	0	-	Not recommended
Relocate	-	0	-	Not recommended
Refactor	-	0	-	Not recommended

Figure 3-5. AWS recommending the rehost strategy

Rehosting on AWS

The approach for rehosting your legacy .NET application onto AWS will vary depending on how your application is currently hosted. For web apps deployed to a single server running IIS, you can easily replicate this environment on an Amazon EC2 instance on AWS. If your .NET application is currently deployed to a managed environment (an "app service" as other cloud providers might call it), then the equivalent on AWS is Elastic Beanstalk, and you should find the experience of working

---

with Elastic Beanstalk familiar. We will cover migrating managed hosting to Elastic Beanstalk later on in the section "Elastic Beanstalk" on page 70, but first, let's take a look at the case of rehosting a virtual machine running IIS over to EC2.

Application Migration Service (MGN)

The latest AWS offering for performing a lift-and-shift migration to EC2 is called the *Application Migration Service*, or MGN.[5] This service evolved from a product called CloudEndure that AWS acquired in 2018. CloudEndure is a disaster recovery solution that works by creating and maintaining replicas of your production servers on AWS EC2 and Elastic Block Store (EBS). This replication concept can be repurposed for the sake of performing a lift-and-shift rehosting. You simply set up replication to AWS then, when you are ready, switch over to running your application exclusively from your AWS replicas, allowing you to decommission the original server. An overview of how the Application Migration Service replicates your servers is shown in Figure 3-6.

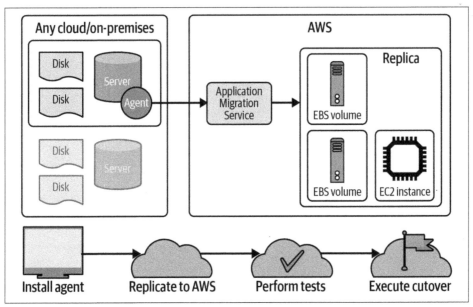

Figure 3-6. Overview of the Application Migration Service

---

5 Interestingly, the three letter abbreviation *MGN* for Application Migration Service is a contraction and not an initialism. Perhaps *AMS* was too similar to *AWS*.

The Application Migration Service is accessed via the AWS Management Console; type "MGN" into the search or find it in the menu of the Migration Hub as in Figure 3-7.

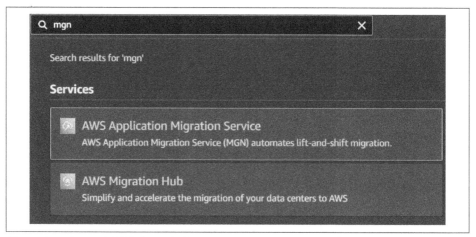

Figure 3-7. Access MGN through the AWS Management Console

Set up of the Application Migration Service begins by installing the replication agent onto your servers, similar to how we installed the discovery agent for the Application Discovery Service. First log onto your Windows server and open up a PowerShell window as Administrator to download the agent installer for Windows. Replace <region> with the AWS region you would like to migrate your servers into:

```
PS C:\> mkdir MGNAgent
PS C:\> cd .\MGNAgent\
PS C:\MGNAgent> Invoke-WebRequest
https://aws-application-migration-service-<region>.s3.<region>.amazonaws.com
/latest/windows/AwsReplicationWindowsInstaller.exe
  -OutFile C:\MGNAgent\AwsReplicationWindowsInstaller.exe
```

Next put your region, access key ID, and secret into variables if you haven't already and execute the installer:

```
PS C:\ADSAgent> $AWS_REGION="<region>"
PS C:\MGNAgent> $KEY_ID="<your-key-id>"
PS C:\MGNAgent> $KEY_SECRET="<your-key-secret>"

PS C:\MGNAgent> .\AwsReplicationWindowsInstaller.exe --region $AWS_REGION
  --aws-access-key-id $KEY_ID --aws-secret-access-key $KEY_SECRET
```

The agent installer will ask you which disks on this server you want to replicate and then will get to work syncing your disks to AWS. You can see the status of the agent installer operations in the console window as shown in Figure 3-8.

Figure 3-8. MGN replication agent console window

If you head back over to the MGN Management Console, you will be able to see your server under Source Servers in the menu. Click on your server name and you can see the status of the replication for this server as shown in Figure 3-9. It can take a while to get through all the stages, but once complete, the status in the console will change to "Ready For Testing." One nice feature of the Application Migration Service is the ability to spin up an instance of a server from a replica and test that everything is as you expect it to be, without interrupting or otherwise interfering with the replication itself.

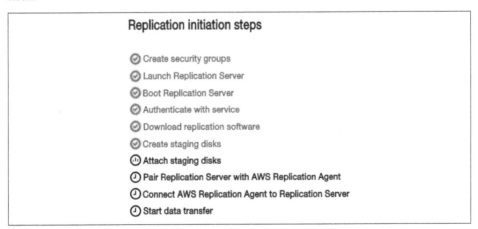

Figure 3-9. MGN replication status in the Management Console

To test a server, select "Launch test instances" from the "Test and Cutover" action menu of your source server. This will launch a new EC2 instance that should mirror the original Windows server you replicated, with transfer of licenses handled automatically by the Application Migration Service. You can connect to the EC2 instance with Remote Desktop (RDP) by selecting it in the list of EC2 instances from the Management Console once it becomes ready. When you are happy that the test instance is working the way you expect it to, you can execute the final stage of the migration: cutover.

If you refer back to the stages of application migration via replication in Figure 3-6, you can see the final stage being Execute Cutover. This is where we create the resources for all our source servers (that is: spin up a new EC2 instance for each server), stop replication of our old servers, and allow us to decommission the original servers we installed the replication agents onto.

So now we have all our servers running like-for-like on EC2 and we have performed the lift-and-shift rehosting, what's next? Staying inside the realm of *rehosting*, we can go one step further and take advantage of AWS's managed environment for running a web application: Elastic Beanstalk.

Elastic Beanstalk

Elastic Beanstalk is a *managed* hosting environment for your web application. It supports a variety of backend stacks such as Java, Ruby, or PHP, but it is the .NET Framework support that we are most interested in here. The difference between hosting our app on a Windows server on EC2, as we did in the previous section, and using Elastic Beanstalk can be distilled down to one key discrepancy.

With an unmanaged server, you upload your compiled and packaged website files to a server and then tweak the settings on that server in order to handle web traffic. With a managed service, you upload your package to the cloud, and the service will take care of the rest for you, setting up load balancers and dynamically scaling virtual machines horizontally. Managed services are the real draw for deploying your applications to the cloud and the more you lean into having AWS manage your infrastructure for you, the more you can concentrate on just writing code and solving problems for your business. Later in this book, we will cover serverless programming and how you can architect your .NET applications to be more serverless, a concept rooted in managed services as much as possible. You can think of Elastic Beanstalk as an equivalent to "App Service," which you may be familiar with from a slightly *bluer* cloud provider.

So let's get started with our first managed service on Elastic Beanstalk. The simplest way to deploy code is by using the AWS Toolkit for Visual Studio. With the AWS Toolkit installed, deploying to Elastic Beanstalk really is as simple as right-clicking your solution and selecting "Publish to Elastic Beanstalk." Figure 3-10 shows the toolkit in use in the Solution Explorer of Visual Studio.

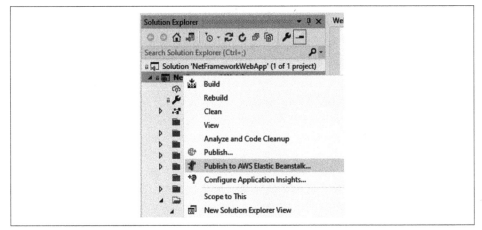

Figure 3-10. Publishing to Elastic Beanstalk directly from Visual Studio

There is of course also a CLI tool you can use in your CI pipeline. To get started with the Elastic Beanstalk CLI, see the EB CLI Installer (*https://oreil.ly/8aKRX*) on GitHub. The CLI tool allows you to publish your code directly to Elastic Beanstalk from AWS CodeBuild or GitHub.

Lastly, there is one final tool worth mentioning if you are thinking of trying out Elastic Beanstalk, and that is the Windows Web App Migration Assistant (WWMA) (*https://oreil.ly/8e4Q2*). This is a PowerShell script that you can run on any Windows Server with an IIS hosted web application to automatically migrate the application onto Elastic Beanstalk. This is useful if you have a legacy .NET application that is no longer maintained and you want to take advantage of the benefits of Elastic Beanstalk but you no longer perform releases for this app. It is a true *rehosting* tool that simply moves the compiled website assets from your *C:\inetpub* folder on the server into EC2 instance(s) managed and scaled by Elastic Beanstalk.

Replatforming via Containerization

As a migration strategy, replatforming is concerned with looking at the *platform* on which our .NET application is running and exploring moving somewhere else. In the case of a .NET Framework web application, that *platform* will be some version of Windows Server running IIS. While previously we looked at Elastic Beanstalk as a way of getting more out of this infrastructure, Elastic Beanstalk still hosts your application on IIS on Windows Server, albeit in a much more scalable and efficient way. If we want to really push the envelope for scalability and performance, while still keeping away from the original source code (these are "legacy" applications, after all), then we need to move away from IIS and onto something else. This is where containerization comes in.

We're going to skip over exactly what containerization is and why it matters as we have Chapter 5 later in this book dedicated to containerization of .NET. Suffice to say moving your legacy .NET application from Windows Server web hosting to containers unlocks both performance and cost benefits to your organization, all without having to touch any of that legacy code.

App2Container is a command-line tool from AWS that runs against your .NET application running on IIS on a Windows Server. It analyzes your application and dependencies, then creates Docker container images that can be deployed to an orchestration service in the cloud such as Elastic Container Service (ECS) or Amazon Elastic Kubernetes Services (EKS). Because App2Container runs on an application that is already deployed to a server, it doesn't need access to your source code and sits right at the end of a deployment pipeline. For this reason, App2Container is perfect for quickly replatforming an old application that is not being actively developed and you don't want to be rebuilding; simply skip right to the last two steps of the pipeline shown in Figure 3-11 and containerize the production files.

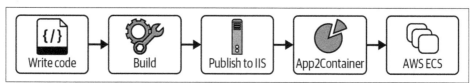

Figure 3-11. Deployment pipeline of .NET Framework application using App2Container

To containerize a .NET application, you first need to download and install App2Container onto the server running your application. You can find the installation package on AWS's website (*https://oreil.ly/UIZzD*). Download, unzip, and run .*install.ps1* from an administrator PowerShell terminal on the application server. This will install the `app2container` command-line utility. If you haven't already, make sure your application server has the AWS Tools for Windows PowerShell installed and you have a default profile configured that allows you access to manage AWS resources from your application server. If your server is running on an EC2 instance (for example, if you rehosted it using the Application Migration Service, see "Rehosting on AWS" on page 66), then these tools will already be installed as they are included on the Windows-based machine images used in EC2. Once you have confirmed you have an AWS profile with IAM permissions to manage AWS resources, you can initialize App2Container by running:

```
PS C:\> app2container init
```

The tool will ask about collecting usage metrics and ask you for an S3 bucket to upload artifacts, but this is entirely optional and you can skip through these options. Once initialized, you are ready to begin analyzing your application server for running .NET applications that can be containerized. Run the `app2container` `inventory` command to get a list of running applications in JSON format, and then pass in the JSON key as the `--applcation-id` of the app you want to containerize, as shown in Figure 3-12:

```
PS C:\> app2container inventory
PS C:\> app2container analyze --application-id iis-example-d87652a0
```

```
Administrator: Windows PowerShell                                   —  □  ✕

PS C:\> app2container inventory
{
    "iis-example-d87652a0": {
        "siteName": "ExampleSite",
        "bindings": "http/*:8080:",
        "applicationType": "iis",
        "discoveredWebApps": []
    }
}
PS C:\> app2container analyze --application-id iis-example-d87652a0
✓ Created artifacts folder c:\a2c\iis-example-d87652a0
✓ Generated analysis data in c:\a2c\iis-example-d87652a0\analysis.json
Analysis successful for application iis-example-d87652a0

Next steps:
1. View the application analysis file at c:\a2c\iis-example-d87652a0\analysis.json
2. Edit the application analysis file as needed.
3. Start the containerization process using this command: app2container containerize --application-id
iis-example-d87652a0
```

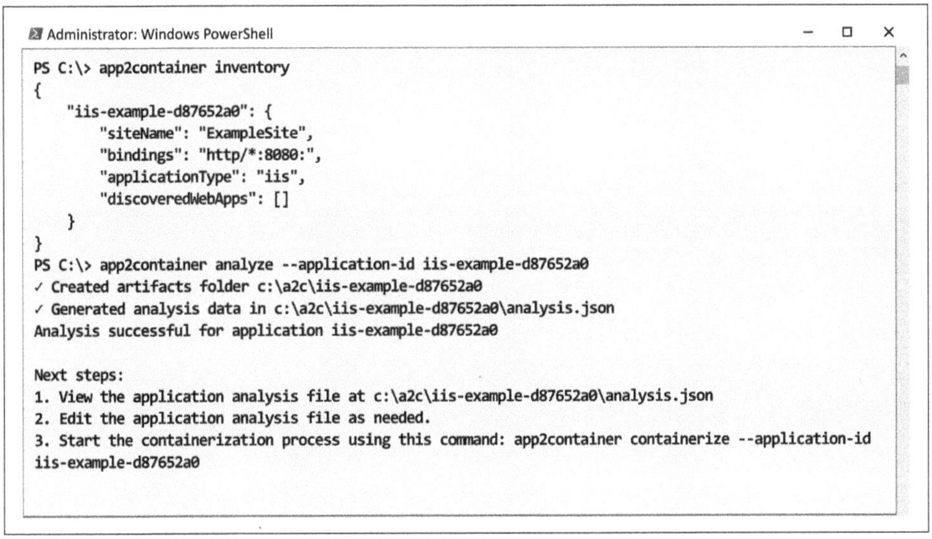

Figure 3-12. Listing the IIS sites capable of being containerized

We are encouraged to take a look at the *analysis.json* file that is generated for us, and we echo that sentiment. A full list of the fields that appear in *analysis.json* can be found in the App2Container User Guide (*https://oreil.ly/HCIa6*), but it is worth spending the time exploring the analysis output as these settings will be used to configure our container. You can edit the `containerParameters` section of *analysis.json* before containerizing if required. It is also worth opening up *report.txt* in the same folder as this is where any connection strings will be added by the analyze command. When you are ready, run the `containerize` and `generate` commands to build a docker image then generate all the artifacts you need to deploy it to either ECS or EKS:[6]

```
# Create a Dockerfile
PS> app2container containerize --application-id iis-example-d87652a0

# Generate a deployment
PS> app2container generate app-deployment --application-id iis-example-d87652a0
```

---

6 We will revisit these two container orchestration services later in this book, but in a nutshell ECS is a simpler and more "managed" service for running containers without the added complexity of dealing with Kubernetes.

The second command here (`generate app-deployment`) will upload your containers to Elastic Container Registry (ECR) and create a CloudFormation template you can use to deploy your app to (in this case) ECS. The tool will show you the output destination of this CloudFormation template (see Figure 3-13) and give you the command you need to deploy it to AWS.

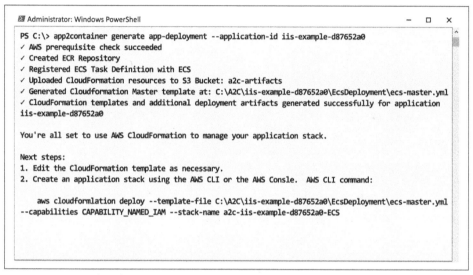

```
PS C:\> app2container generate app-deployment --application-id iis-example-d87652a0
✓ AWS prerequisite check succeeded
✓ Created ECR Repository
✓ Registered ECS Task Definition with ECS
✓ Uploaded CloudFormation resources to S3 Bucket: a2c-artifacts
✓ Generated Cloudformation Master template at: C:\A2C\iis-example-d87652a0\EcsDeployment\ecs-master.yml
✓ CloudFormation templates and additional deployment artifacts generated successfully for application
iis-example-d87652a0

You're all set to use AWS CloudFormation to manage your application stack.

Next steps:
1. Edit the CloudFormation template as necessary.
2. Create an application stack using the AWS CLI or the AWS Consle.  AWS CLI command:

    aws cloudformlation deploy --template-file C:\A2C\iis-example-d87652a0\EcsDeployment\ecs-master.yml
--capabilities CAPABILITY_NAMED_IAM --stack-name a2c-iis-example-d87652a0-ECS
```

Figure 3-13. Results of App2Container deployment generation

This has been a brief overview of App2Container from AWS, but much more is possible with this tool than we have covered here. Instead of performing the containerization on the application server itself, App2Container also lets you deploy a worker machine either to EC2 or your local virtualization environment. This would be useful if you wanted to protect the application server, which could be serving a web application in production, from having to spend resources executing a containerization process. Since App2Container is a CLI tool, it would also be simple to integrate into a full deployment pipeline for code you are still actively working on and releasing changes to. If you refer back to Figure 3-11, you can see how App2Container can be used to *extend* an existing .NET deployment pipeline into containerization without touching anything further upstream, including your code.

One final note on App2Container is framework version support, which has been expanding with new releases of the tool. You can use App2Container on both .NET Framework and .NET 6+ applications running on both Windows and, more recently, Linux. For .NET Framework, the minimum supported version is .NET 3.5 running in IIS 7.5. Java applications can also be containerized with App2Container, in a similar way to that we have explored here, so it's not just us C# developers who can benefit.

Rearchitecting: Moving to .NET (Core)

So far we have looked at migration approaches for our .NET applications that do not involve making changes to the code, but what can we do if changing the code is acceptable? In the next chapter we will be looking at modernizing .NET applications; however, if your application is still built on .NET Framework, the first step down every modernization path will almost certainly be a migration to .NET 6+. The road ahead for .NET Framework applications is not a long one and, aside from the rehosting and replatforming approaches we have covered in this book, you will eventually be approaching the topic of migrating framework versions. .NET is, after all, a complete rewrite of Microsoft's framework, and feature parity was not an aim. APIs have changed, namespaces like `System.Web.Services` are no longer present, and some third-party libraries that you rely on may not have been migrated, forcing you to replace them with an alternative. For these reasons, it is vital to do as much investigation as possible in order to assess the lift required in migrating your legacy .NET Framework application to modern .NET.

While there is no such thing as a tool that will automatically refactor your entire solution and convert your .NET Framework monolith to .NET 6+, what does exist are a handful of extremely useful tools to analyze your project, perform small refactoring tasks, and give you an insight into where you will find compatibility problems. I'm going to give you a brief insight into two of these tools: the .NET Upgrade Assistant from Microsoft, and the Porting Assistant from AWS.

Before you start, however, it is worth becoming familiar with which .NET Framework technologies are unavailable on .NET 6+ (*https://oreil.ly/1JaqV*). These include almost everything that used the Component Object Model (COM, COM+, DCOM) such as .NET Remoting and Windows Workflow Foundation. For applications that rely heavily on these Windows-only frameworks, one of the migration strategies we discussed earlier in this chapter may be more appropriate. Applications that use Windows Communication Foundation (WCF) can take advantage of the CoreWCF project (*https://github.com/CoreWCF/CoreWCF*) in order to continue using WCF features on modern .NET.

Microsoft .NET Upgrade Assistant

With the releases of .NET 5 and 6, Microsoft cemented its vision for a unified single framework going forward, with .NET 6 being the long-term support (LTS) release of the platform. In order to assist migration of .NET Framework applications to this new, unified version of the framework, Microsoft has been developing a command-line tool called the *.NET Upgrade Assistant*. The Upgrade Assistant is intended to be a single entry point to guide you through the migration journey and wraps within it the more longstanding .NET Framework conversion tool try-convert. It is a good idea to use try-convert from within the context of the Upgrade Assistant as you will get more analysis and guidance toward the strategies most applicable to your project.

The types of .NET Framework applications that this tool can be used with at time of writing are:

- .NET class libraries
- Console Apps
- Windows forms
- Windows Presentation Foundation (WPF)
- ASP.NET MVC web applications

The .NET Upgrade Assistant has an extensible architecture that encourages the community to contribute extensions and analyzers/code fixers. You can even write your own analyzers to perform automatic code refactoring based on rules you define. The Upgrade Assistant comes with a set of default analyzers that look for common incompatibilities with your code and offer a solution. For example, the HttpContext CurrentAnalyzer looks for calls to the static System.Web.HttpContext.Current, a pattern often employed in controller actions of .NET Framework applications that will need to be refactored since HttpContext.Current was removed in .NET Core. In Figure 3-14, you can see an example of the message this analyzer emits when HttpContext.Current is found in your code.

So let's get going with an upgrade. For this example, we have created a very simple ASP.NET MVC web application in Visual Studio 2019 using .NET Framework version 4.7.2. There is a controller action that takes the query string from the web request, adds it to the ViewBag, then displays it on the *Index.cshtml* Razor view. The output of this website can be seen in Figure 3-14.

Figure 3-14. Example ASP.NET MVC website running in a browser

We have purposefully added a couple of things to this example that we *know* are not compatible with .NET Core and later versions of the framework. First, as introduced earlier, we have a call to `HttpContext.Current` on line 9 of *HomeController.cs* (Example 3-1). This will need to be replaced with a call to an equivalent HTTP context property in .NET 6. We also have a Razor helper in *Index.cshtml*, the `@helper` syntax for which is not present in later versions of .NET (Example 3-2). We have this code checked into a Git repository with a clean working tree; this will help view the changes to the code that the .NET Upgrade Assistant will make by using a Git diff tool.

Example 3-1. HomeController.cs

```
using System.Web.Mvc;

namespace NetFrameworkMvcWebsite.Controllers
{
    public class HomeController : Controller
    {
        public ActionResult Index()
        {
            ViewBag.QueryString =
                System.Web.HttpContext.Current.Request.QueryString;

            return View();
        }

    }
}
```

Example 3-2. Index.cshtml

```
@{
    ViewBag.Title = "Home Page";
}

<div class="jumbotron">
    <p class="lead">This is a simple MVC application using .NET Framework</p>

    <h2>The query string is <strong>@ViewBag.QueryString</strong></h2>
</div>

<hr />

@WriteIndexFooter("Footer written using a Razor helper")

@helper WriteIndexFooter(string content)
{
    <footer>
        <p>@content</p>
    </footer>
}
```

To get started with the .NET Upgrade Assistant, first install it as a .NET CLI tool:

```
dotnet tool install -g upgrade-assistant
```

Next, in the directory that contains your solution file, run the upgrade assistant and follow the instructions to select the project to use as your entry point:

```
upgrade-assistant upgrade NetFrameworkMvcWebsite.sln
```

Depending on the type of .NET Framework project you have (WebForms, WPF etc.), the upgrade assistant will give you a different set of steps. We have an ASP.NET MVC Web Application, so we are offered a ten-step process for the upgrade, as follows:

```
Upgrade Steps

Entrypoint: D:\Code\CSharpBookExamples\NetFrameworkMvcWebsite\
NetFrameworkMvcWebsite.csproj
Current Project: D:\Code\CSharpBookExamples\NetFrameworkMvcWebsite\
NetFrameworkMvcWebsite.csproj

1. [Complete] Back up project
2. [Complete] Convert project file to SDK style
3. [Complete] Clean up NuGet package references
4. [Complete] Update TFM
5. [Complete] Update NuGet Packages
6. [Complete] Add template files
7. [Complete] Upgrade app config files
    a. [Complete] Convert Application Settings
    b. [Complete] Convert Connection Strings
    c. [Complete] Disable unsupported configuration sections
```

```
       d. [Complete] Convert system.web.webPages.razor/pages/namespaces
  8. [Complete] Update Razor files
       a. [Complete] Apply code fixes to Razor documents
       b. [Complete] Replace @helper syntax in Razor files
  9. [Complete] Update source code
       a. [Complete] Apply fix for UA0001: ASP.NET Core projects should not
       reference ASP.NET namespaces
       b. [Complete] Apply fix for UA0002: Types should be upgraded
       c. [Complete] Apply fix for UA0005: Do not use HttpContext.Current
       d. [Complete] Apply fix for UA0006: HttpContext.DebuggerEnabled should be
       replaced with System.Diagnostics.Debugger.IsAttached
       e. [Complete] Apply fix for UA0007: HtmlHelper should be replaced with
       IHtmlHelper
       f. [Complete] Apply fix for UA0008: UrlHelper should be replaced with
       IUrlHelper
       g. [Complete] Apply fix for UA0010: Attributes should be upgraded
       h. [Complete] Apply fix for UA0012: 'UnsafeDeserialize()' does not exist
 10. [Next step] Move to next project

Choose a command:
    1. Apply next step (Move to next project)
    2. Skip next step (Move to next project)
    3. See more step details
    4. Configure logging
    5. Exit

 >
```

Most of the steps are self explanatory; step 2 in my example is "Convert project to SDK style". This means reformatting the *.csproj* file to the newer .NET format that starts with <Project Sdk="Microsoft.NET.Sdk">. As you go through these steps, use a source control diff tool (e.g., KDiff, VS Code, or the Git Changes window in Visual Studio) to see the changes being made to your code and project files.

The logs from the upgrade assistant are stored in Compact Log Event Format (CLEF) inside the directory in which you ran the tool. It will also create a backup of your project; however, this is not particularly useful if you have everything checked into source control (you *do* have everything checked into source control, right?).

You can see from the preceding list that step 9c was Do not use HttpContext.Current. This is coming from the HttpContextCurrentAnalyzer we introduced earlier, and the fix from this analyzer will change all usage of HttpContext.Current in your code to HttpContextHelper.Current. We do still get a warning about HttpContextHelper.Current being obsolete and to use dependency injection instead; however, this doesn't prevent my upgraded code from compiling. The upgrade assistant also refactored my @helper syntax in the Razor view (step 8b) and replaced it with a .NET 6 compatible helper method. The code after running the upgrade assistant looks like this (Examples 3-3 and 3-4):

Example 3-3. HomeController.cs

```
namespace NetFrameworkMvcWebsite.Controllers
{
    public class HomeController : Microsoft.AspNetCore.Mvc.Controller
    {
        public Microsoft.AspNetCore.Mvc.ActionResult Index()
        {
            ViewBag.QueryString = HttpContextHelper.Current.Request.QueryString;

            return View();
        }

    }
}
```

Example 3-4. Index.cshtml

```
@using Microsoft.AspNetCore.Mvc.Razor
@{
    ViewBag.Title = "Home Page";
}

<div class="jumbotron">
    <p class="lead">This is a simple MVC application using .NET Framework</p>

    <h2>The query string is <strong>@ViewBag.QueryString</strong></h2>
</div>

<hr />

@WriteIndexFooter("Footer written using a Razor helper")

@{ HelperResult WriteIndexFooter(string content)
        {
            <footer>
                <p>@content</p>
            </footer>
                return new HelperResult(w => Task.CompletedTask);
    }
}
```

AWS Porting Assistant

Another tool you can use to aid your migration from .NET Framework is the porting assistant provided by AWS themselves. This is a Windows application that you download to the machine on which you have your .NET Framework solution. Although the porting assistant runs locally on your code, it will need to connect to AWS in order to retrieve NuGet package upgrade information from an S3 bucket; it is for this reason that you need to set it up with a local AWS profile as shown in Figure 3-15.

No resources will be created on your AWS profile. The porting assistant can be downloaded from the AWS Porting Assistant page (*https://oreil.ly/31UMk*).

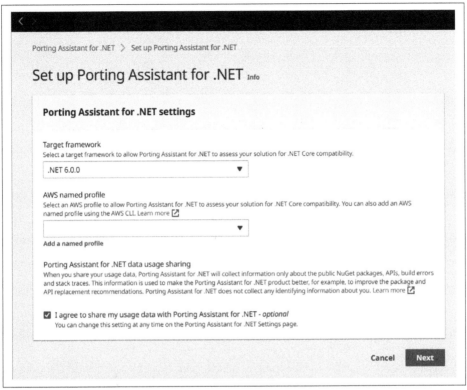

Figure 3-15. Running the .NET Porting Assistant from AWS

If we step through the wizard and use the same ASP.NET MVC web application we used for the Microsoft Upgrade Assistant, we can see that it has correctly identified the solution is targeting .NET Framework 4.7.5, and we have 7 incompatible NuGet packages and 15 incompatible APIs. This is the *15 of 17* values highlighted in Figure 3-16. You can see more information about these in the relevant tabs of the porting assistant including links to the code that has been identified as incompatible.

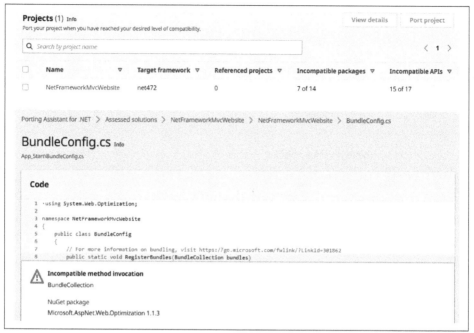

Figure 3-16. AWS Porting Assistant analysis results

When you are ready, click Port Solution to begin making the changes to your project files. The application will ask you where you would like to save the ported solution to; having your code in source control means you can choose "Modify source in place". Unlike Microsoft's tool, the AWS Porting does actually let you fine-tune which versions you would like to upgrade your NuGet packages to in the UI. For this example, we have simply left the defaults in place for all packages and stepped through the assistant. You can see now from Figure 3-17 that the project files have been upgraded and the project is now showing in the porting assistant as .NET 6.

Projects (1) Info
Port your project when you have reached your desired level of compatibility.

Q Search by project name

Name ▽	Target framework ▽
NetFrameworkMvcWebsite	net6.0

Figure 3-17. AWS Porting Assistant complete

If you click the link to open in Visual Studio, you will see the solution loads and your NuGet packages will have been upgraded to versions compatible with .NET Core/6+. Where the porting assistant's help ends, however, is by refactoring all the unsupported code. When we try to build this, we will still get errors that `System.Web.HttpContext` does not exist and "the helper directive is not supported," so it may be worth trying out all tools available and comparing your results. Overall, the .NET Porting Assistant from AWS does provide a very quick and accessible UI for visualizing and assessing the effort involved in refactoring your .NET Framework code to work with modern .NET.

Conclusion

The strategies and tools we have covered in this chapter will help you move an existing application running on IIS to AWS. From the basic "Rehosting on AWS" on page 66 of an application without touching the original source, to "Rearchitecting: Moving to .NET (Core)" on page 75 and making inroads into modernization of your codebase. Whichever strategy you choose, you will benefit from at least some of the advantages of running .NET in the AWS cloud; however, it is worth considering the next steps for your application. Some of the approaches we have covered here will leave your code in the exact same state as it was before you migrated. If you were not actively developing your codebase before the migration, then you will not be in a much better position to do so after choosing one of these paths. For a codebase you intend to continue to develop, to iterate on, and to add functionality to, you should to modernize your legacy application. Modernization will involve not just moving to .NET 6+ (although that will be a prerequisite); it will also involve replacing third-party dependencies, replacing external services, and refactoring the architecture of your application to use patterns that better exploit the cloud environment you are now running in. All these will be covered in the next chapter, in which we will cover the term *serverless* and how it can apply to you as a .NET developer.

Critical Thinking Discussion Questions

- Which is the easiest for a small start-up of the six Rs in a migration strategy?
- Which is the easiest for a large enterprise of the six Rs in a migration strategy?
- What are strategies to programmatically convert thousands of Windows services to containers using App2Container?
- What is a robust enterprise use case for the Porting Assistant for .NET?
- What are the advantages of Elastic Beanstalk applications in migration from on-premise to the AWS Cloud in an enterprise setting?

Exercises

- Build a hello world Blazor app on a Windows Server, then use App2Container to convert it to a Docker container image.

- Deploy the Strategy Recommendations collector on an Amazon EC2 instance.

- Run the AWS Migration Hub Orchestrator (*https://oreil.ly/bRnkz*).

- Build a hello world Blazor app on a Windows Server, then use App2Container to convert it to a Docker container image and deploy it to AWS App Runner.

- Build a hello world Blazor app on a Windows Server, then use App2Container to convert it to a Docker container image and deploy it to Fargate using AWS Copilot (*https://oreil.ly/6Zzes*).

CHAPTER 4

Modernizing .NET Applications to Serverless

The term *serverless* can be a source of confusion in software engineering circles. How can you run a web application without servers? Is it really just a marketing phrase? In a way, yes it is. Serverless computing is the broad term for backend systems that are architected to use managed services instead of manually configured servers. Serverless applications are "serverless" in the same way that a wireless charger for your smartphone is "wireless." A wireless charger still has a wire; it comes out of the charger and plugs into the mains outlet, transferring energy from your wall to your desk. The *wireless* part is only the interface between the charger and your phone. The word "serverless" in serverless computing is used in the same way. Yes, there are servers, but they are all managed behind the scenes by AWS. The servers are the mains cable plugging your otherwise wireless charger into the wall outlet. The other side, the part visible to us as developers, the part that really matters when deploying and running code, that part does not involve any configuration or management of servers and is therefore *serverless*.

You are most likely already using serverless computing for some tasks. Consider three popular types of server:

- Web servers
- Email servers
- File servers

Of these three, the second two are servers that we have been replacing with managed serverless solutions for a long time now. If you have ever sent an email via an API call to Mailchimp, Mailgun, SendGrid, SparkPost, or indeed Amazon's Simple Email Service (SES), then you have used a serverless emailing solution. The days of running an SMTP server either in-house or in the cloud are, for a lot of organizations, already firmly in the past. File servers too are steadily going out of fashion and being replaced by serverless file storage solutions. Many modern web applications rely entirely on cloud native services such as Amazon Simple Storage Service (S3) as their primary storage mechanism for files. The last stone to fall from that list is the web server. In this chapter, we will show you how to replace your .NET web server with a serverless, cloud native implementation and what that means for the way you write your code.

A Serverless Web Server

A web server is a computer, either physical or virtual, that is permanently connected to the internet and is ready to respond to HTTP(S) requests 24 hours a day. The lifecycle of an HTTP request inside a web server involves a lot of steps and executes code written by many different parties in order to read, transform, and execute each request. Right in the middle of that journey is the code written by you, the application developer.

In order to replicate the functionality of a web server, we need a way to run that custom logic on a managed and on-demand basis. AWS offers us a few ways to do this; we will look at "App Runner" on page 140, which is a service that allows us to deploy a fully managed containerized application without having to worry about servers. AWS Fargate is another serverless solution for running web servers on a pay-as-you-go pricing model. These services take your web services and deploy them to the cloud in a serverless way. We can, however, go one step further and break apart the service itself into individual functions that are deployed independently to the cloud. For this we will need Functions as a Service (FaaS).

FaaS solutions, such as AWS Lambda, are stateless compute containers that are triggered by events. You upload the code you want to run when an event occurs and the cloud provider will handle provisioning, executing, and then deprovisioning resources for you. This unlocks two main advantages:

- FaaS allows your code to scale down to zero. You only pay for the resources you use *while your function is executing* and nothing in between. This means you can write applications that follow a true pay-as-you-go pricing model, paying only for each function execution and not for the unused time in between.
- FaaS forces you to think about separation of concerns, and places restrictions on the way you write your application that will generally lead to better code.

The disadvantages are born from the extra effort involved in actually implementing a FaaS solution. Consider this quote from Rich Hickley:

> Simplicity is hard work. But, there's a huge payoff. The person who has a genuinely simpler system—a system made out of genuinely simple parts, is going to be able to affect the greatest change with the least work. He's going to kick your ass. He's gonna spend more time simplifying things up front and in the long haul he's gonna wipe the plate with you because he'll have that ability to change things when you're struggling to push elephants around.
>
> —Rich Hickey, creator of the Clojure programming language

Simplicity as it relates to writing your code for FaaS means thinking in terms of *pure functions* and following the Single Responsibility Principle. A function should take a value object, perform an action, and then return a value object. A good example of a pure function that follows this pattern is a `Reverse()` function for a string:

```
public static string Reverse(string str)
{
    char[] charArray = str.ToCharArray();
    Array.Reverse( charArray );
    return new string( charArray );
}
```

This function fits the two requirements to be called a "pure function":

- It will always return the same output for a given input.
- It has no side effects; it does not mutate any static variables or mutable reference arguments, or otherwise require persistence of state outside the scope of the function.

These are both characteristics that are required for writing functions for FaaS. Since FaaS functions run in response to events, you want to keep the first point true so that the sentence "When X happens, perform Y" remains true for every time event X occurs. You also need to keep your function stateless (the second point). This is both a limitation and a feature of running your function on managed FaaS. Because AWS can and will deprovision resources in between executions of your function, it is not possible to share static variables. If you want to persist data in an FaaS function, you must intentionally persist it to a shared storage area, for example by saving to a database or a Redis cache.

Architecting your code into stateless functions with no side effects like this can be a challenge that requires discipline. It forces you to think about how to write your logic and how much scope each area of your code is really allowed to control. It also forces you to think about separation of concerns.

When multiple FaaS functions are connected together using events and augmented with other serverless services (such as message queues and API gateways), it becomes possible to build a backend application that will be able to perform any function a traditional web API running on a server can. This allows you to write a completely serverless backend application hosted on AWS. And the best bit is, you can do all of this in C#! AWS offers many services you can use as the building blocks for such a serverless application. Let's take a look at some of the components they have to offer.

Choosing Serverless Components for .NET on AWS

We are going to introduce you to some of the most useful serverless services from AWS and how you can use the various packages of the AWS SDK for .NET (*https://aws.amazon.com/sdk-for-net*) to interact with these services in your code. Let's progressively build a serverless web application for the rest of this chapter, adding functionality with each new concept introduced.

Imagine that we run a software development consultancy and are recruiting for the best and brightest C# developers around! In order for them to apply, we want them to visit our website, where they will find an HTML form that allows them to upload their résumé as a PDF file. Submitting this form will send their PDF résumé to our API, where it will be saved to a file server and an email will be sent to our recruitment team, asking them to review it. We'll call this the Serverless C# Résumé Uploader. Figure 4-1 shows a high-level overview of the architecture.

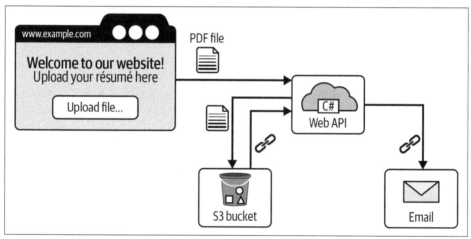

Figure 4-1. Serverless C# Résumé Uploader architecture

The current implementation of our backend uses a web API controller action to accept the PDF file upload, save it to cloud storage, and email our recruitment team. The code looks like this:

```
[ApiController]
[Route("[controller]")]
public class ApplicationController : ControllerBase
{
    private readonly IStorageService _storageService;
    private readonly IEmailService _emailService;

    public ApplicationController(IStorageService storageService,
                                 IEmailService emailService)
    {
        _storageService = storageService;
        _emailService = emailService;
    }

    [HttpPost]
    public async Task<IActionResult> SaveUploadedResume()
    {
        Request.EnableBuffering();
        using var fileStream = new MemoryStream();
        using var reader = new StreamReader(fileStream);
        await Request.Body.CopyToAsync(fileStream); ❶

        var storedFileUrl = await _storageService.Upload(fileStream); ❷

        await _emailService.Send("recruitment@example.com",
            $"Somebody has uploaded a resume! Read it here: {storedFileUrl}"); ❸

        return Ok();
    }
}
```

❶ Read the uploaded file from the request.

❷ Save it to cloud storage.

❸ Send an email to our recruitment team with a link to the file.

The code for IStorageService looks like this:

```
public class AwsS3StorageService : IStorageService
{
    const string BucketName = "csharp-examples-bucket";

    public async Task<string> Upload(Stream stream)
    {
        var fileName = Guid.NewGuid().ToString() + ".pdf"; ❶

        using var s3Client = new AmazonS3Client(RegionEndpoint.EUWest2);
```

```
        await s3Client.PutObjectAsync(new PutObjectRequest()
        {
            InputStream = stream,
            BucketName = BucketName,
            Key = fileName,
        }); ❷

        var url = s3Client.GetPreSignedURL(new GetPreSignedUrlRequest()
        {
            BucketName = BucketName,
            Key = fileName,
            Expires = DateTime.UtcNow.AddMinutes(10)
        }); ❸

        return url;
    }
}
```

❶ Create a unique S3 key name.

❷ Upload the file to S3.

❸ Generate a presigned URL pointing to our new file.[1]

This uses the AWSSDK.S3 NuGet package for saving a file to an AWS S3 bucket. In this example, the bucket is called csharp-examples-bucket[2] and the file will be uploaded and given a unique key using Guid.NewGuid().

The second service in our example is the IEmailService, which uses AWS SES to send an email to our recruitment team. This implementation uses another NuGet package from the AWS SDK called Amazon.SimpleEmail:

```
public class AwsSesEmailService : IEmailService
{
    public async Task Send(string emailAddress, string body)
    {
        using var emailClient = new AmazonSimpleEmailServiceClient(
                                        RegionEndpoint.EUWest1);

        await emailClient.SendEmailAsync(new SendEmailRequest
```

---

1 A presigned URL is a link to an S3 resource that can be used from anywhere to download the contents anonymously (i.e., by entering it into a browser window). The URL is presigned using the authentication permissions of the IAM role that made this request. This effectively allows this you to share access to a secured S3 resource with anyone with whom this presigned URL is shared.

2 S3 bucket names are unique across *all* AWS accounts in a region. So you may find the bucket name you want is unavailable as it is in use by another AWS account. You could avoid this by prefixing the bucket name with the name of your product or organization.

```
        {
            Source = "from@example.com",
            Destination = new Destination
            {
                ToAddresses = new List<string> { emailAddress }
            },
            Message = new Message
            {
                Subject = new Content("Email Subject"),
                Body = new Body { Text = new Content(body) }
            }
        });
    }
}
```

We will be using these two implementations for the rest of the examples in this chapter. As mentioned earlier, by saving the PDF file with S3 and sending our email via SES we are already using serverless solutions for file storage and email services. So let's get rid of this web server too and move our controller action to managed cloud functions.

Developing with AWS Lambda and C#

AWS's FaaS product is called Lambda. AWS Lambda was introduced in 2014 by Werner Vogels, CTO of Amazon, with the following summary that we feel nicely sums up the motivation and value behind AWS Lambda:

> The focus here is on the events. Events may be driven by web services that would trigger these events. You'll write some code, say, in JavaScript, and this will run without any hardware that you have to provision for it.
>
> —Werner Vogels

Since 2014, AWS Lambda has grown enormously in both adoption and features. They've added more and more event options to trigger your functions from, cutting-edge abilities like Lambda@Edge that runs your functions on the CDN server closest to your users (a.k.a. "edge computing"), custom runtimes, shared memory layers for libraries called "Lambda layers," and crucially for us, built-in support for .NET on both x86_64 and ARM64 CPU architectures.

There are a lot of examples provided by AWS for writing Lambda functions in C# and for refactoring existing code so it can be deployed to AWS Lambda. Here is a quick sample to create and deploy a simple Lambda function in C# by taking advantage of the templates found in the Amazon.Lambda.Templates NuGet package. This package includes project templates that can be used with the dotnet new command on the .NET Core CLI:

```
dotnet new -i Amazon.Lambda.Templates
```

```
dotnet new lambda.EmptyFunction --name SingleCSharpLambda
```

This will create a folder called *SingleCSharpLambda* containing a source and a test project for your function. The sample function is in a file called *Function.cs*:

```
[assembly: LambdaSerializer(typeof(Amazon.Lambda.Serialization.SystemTextJson.
        DefaultLambdaJsonSerializer))]

namespace SingleCSharpLambda
{
    public class Function
    {
        public string FunctionHandler(string input, ILambdaContext context)
        {
            LambdaLogger.Log("Hello from" + context.FunctionName);

            return input?.ToUpper();
        }
    }
}
```

The template creates a class with a public function FunctionHandler(input, context). This is the method signature for the entry point to every C# Lambda function in AWS Lambda. The two parameters are the input, the shape of which will be determined to whatever event we hook our Lambda function up to, and the ILambdaContext context, which is generated by AWS on execution and contains information about the currently executing Lambda function.

We've also added a line to print a log message to the previous template function so we can check it executes when we run it on AWS. The static class LambdaLogger here is part of the Amazon.Lambda.Core package, which was added in with our template. You can also use Console.WriteLine() here; AWS will send any call that writes to stdout or stderr to the CloudWatch log stream attached to your function.[3]

Now we can get on and deploy our function to AWS. If you don't already have them installed, now is a good time to get the AWS Lambda Global Tool for .NET (*https://oreil.ly/k0wcz*). A Global Tool is a special kind of NuGet package that you can execute from the dotnet command line:

```
dotnet tool install -g Amazon.Lambda.Tools
```

---

3 CloudWatch is a service from AWS that provides logging and monitoring for your entire cloud infrastructure. AWS Lambda connects to CloudWatch and posts log messages that you can view from the CloudWatch console or integrate into another AWS service further downstream.

Then deploy your function:

```
dotnet lambda deploy-function SingleCSharpLambda
```

If not already set in the *aws-lambda-tools-defaults.json* configuration file, you will be asked for AWS region and the ARN for an IAM role you would like the function to use when it executes. The IAM role can be created on the fly by the `Amazon.Lambda.Tools` tool including all the permissions needed. You can view and edit the permissions for this (or any other) IAM role by visiting the IAM Dashboard (*https://console.aws.amazon.com/iamv2*).

Figure 4-2 shows our example function in the AWS Management Console for the region we deployed to. You can test the function directly in the console from the Test tab on the next screen.

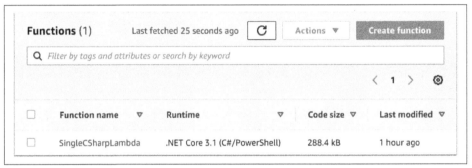

Figure 4-2. Function list in the AWS Lambda console

This test window (shown in Figure 4-3) allows you to enter some JSON to pass into your function in the `input` parameter we defined earlier. Since we declared our input value as being of type *string* in `FunctionHandler(string input, ILambdaContext context)`, we should change this to be any string and we can test the function directly in the Management Console.

Figure 4-3. Testing your deployed Lambda function

The results of your execution are inserted into the page, including an inline "Log output" window, which is also shown in Figure 4-3. This allows you to rapidly find and debug errors in your Lambda function and perform manual testing.

C# résumé example: AWS Lambda

Now that we are familiar with AWS Lambda, let's apply this to our serverless example. We are going to take our web API controller from the C# Résumé Uploader example and turn it into an AWS Lambda function. Any web API controller can be deployed to AWS Lambda with the help of a package from AWS called Amazon.Lambda.AspNetCoreServer.Hosting. This package makes it easy to wrap a .NET controller in a Lambda function called by API Gateway.

API Gateway is a service from AWS that makes building an API composed of Lambda functions possible. It provides the plumbing between HTTP requests and Lambda functions allowing you to configure a set of individual Lambda functions to run on GET, PUT, POST, PATCH, and DELETE requests to API routes you configure in API Gateway. We are using API Gateway in this example to map the route POST: https://our-api/Application to a Lambda function.

To deploy an ASP .NET application to AWS Lambda using this method, install the Amazon.Lambda.AspNetCoreServer package then add a call to AddAWSLambdaHosting() in the services collection of the application.[4] This allows API Gateway and AWS Lambda to act as the web server when running on Lambda:

```
var builder = WebApplication.CreateBuilder(args);

builder.Services.AddRazorPages();

// Add AWS Lambda support.
builder.Services.AddAWSLambdaHosting(LambdaEventSource.HttpApi); ❶

app.MapRazorPages();

var app = builder.Build();
```

❶ This is the only line we need to add.

Just as we did in "Developing with AWS Lambda and C#" on page 91, deploy this Lambda function to AWS using our new class as the entry point. We will have to create a JSON file for settings. If you have Visual Studio and the AWS Toolkit for Visual Studio installed, there are template projects you can try out that demonstrate how this JSON file is configured, so we'd urge you to give those a go. For our example here, however, we are just going to deploy it straight to AWS Lambda:

```
dotnet lambda deploy-function UploadNewResume
```

Figure 4-4 shows the steps dotnet lambda deploy-function will take you through if you do not have all these settings configured in your JSON file. For the IAM role, we need to create a role with the policies in place to do all the things our résumé uploader function will need to do (saving to S3, sending email via SES) along with invoking a Lambda function and creating CloudWatch log groups.

---

4 This method uses the minimal APIs style of configuring and ASP .NET application that was introduced in .NET 6. Amazon.Lambda.AspNetCoreServer does also support .NET applications built on earlier versions of .NET Core; however, the configuration is slightly different and involves implementing Amazon.Lambda.AspNetCoreServer.APIGatewayProxyFunction. More information can be found at Amazon.Lambda.AspNetCoreServer (*https://oreil.ly/gmY9K*).

```
Administrator: Windows PowerShell                                    —  □  ×

PS C:\> dotnet lambda deploy-function UploadNewResume

Created publish archive (D:\Code\CSharpBookExamples\Chapter4Example\PartOne-
Lambda\ServerlessResumeUploader\bin\Release\netcoreapp3.1\ServerlessResumeUploader.zip).

Creating new Lambda function UploadNewResume
Select IAM Role that to provide AWS credentials to your code:
    1) ResumeUploaderLambdaRole
    2) *** Create new IAM Role ***
1
Enter Memory Size: (The amount of memory, in MB, your Lambda function is given)
256
Enter Timeout: (The function execution timeout in seconds)
30
Enter Handler: (Handler for the function <assembly>::<type>::<method>)
ServerlessResumeUploader::ServerlessResumeUploader.LambdaEntryPoint::FunctionHandlerAsync
New Lambda function created
```

Figure 4-4. Execution of `dotnet lambda deploy-function` *in the console*

Next we have to create an API Gateway service to attach our Lambda to the outside
world. Later on in this chapter, we will explore the AWS Serverless Application Model
(SAM)—which is a great way of creating and managing serverless resources such as
API Gateway—using template files that can be checked in to source control. For now,
however, we would recommend creating the API Gateway service using the AWS
Management Console as shown in Figure 4-5.

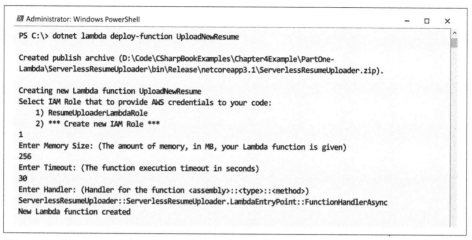

Figure 4-5. Creating an API in the API Gateway console

The AWS Management Console is a great way to explore and familiarize yourself with all the different settings and options of these managed AWS services so when you do come to keep these settings in template files, you have an anchor point in your mind to how everything fits together.

Figure 4-6 shows how we have set up an API Gateway service with a Lambda function proxy that forwards all routes to the AWS Lambda function we just deployed, UploadNewResume. You can test this out either by using the TEST tool in the console (shown on the left in Figure 4-6) or, better yet, by making an actual HTTP POST request with the PDF file in the body to the public URL of your API Gateway service. You can find the URL of API Gateway in the Stages setting in the Management Console. For example, my API Gateway instance has the id xxxlrx74l3 and is in the eu-west-2 region. To upload a résumé to our API, we can execute a POST request to this using curl:

```
curl https://xxxlrx74l3.execute-api.eu-west-2.amazonaws.com/Prod/Application
  --data-binary @MyResumeFile.pdf
```

This will upload our PDF file to API Gateway, which will pass it on to our Lambda function, where our code will save it to S3 and send out an email.

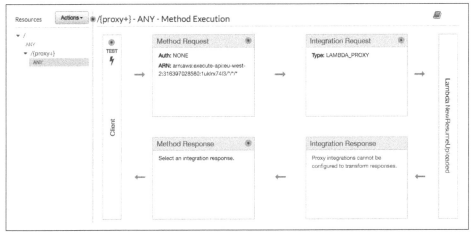

Figure 4-6. API Gateway Lambda proxy setup

All this has been possible by wrapping our API controller in the APIGatewayProxy Function class and deploying to AWS Lambda as a cloud function. Next, we are going to explore what is possible when we add multiple Lambda functions to perform more complex and granular tasks in our applications.

Developing with AWS Step Functions

By this point, we have deployed a web API controller to a Lambda function and hooked it up to API Gateway so it can be called via HTTP requests. Next, let's think about what we can do to really take advantage of our new function as a service execution model. Remember how we spoke about FaaS forcing you to be more intentional about separation of concerns? The function in our example is doing quite a lot. This is often the case with API controller actions in any language, not just C# —they do tend to assume multiple responsibilities at once. Our UploadNewResume() is doing a lot more than simply uploading a résumé; it is emailing the recruitment team, and it is creating a new file name. If we want to further unlock some of the flexibility of serverless and FaaS, we need to split these operations out into their own functions. AWS has a very neat tool for managing workflows involving multiple Lambda functions (and more), and it is called AWS Step Functions.

AWS Step Functions abstracts away the plumbing between steps in your workflow. We can take a look at the controller action from our previous example and see how much of this code is just plumbing:

```
[HttpPost]
public async Task<IActionResult> SaveUploadedResume()
{
    Request.EnableBuffering();
    using var fileStream = new MemoryStream();
    using var reader = new StreamReader(fileStream);
    await Request.Body.CopyToAsync(fileStream); ❶

    var storedFileUrl = await _storageService.Upload(fileStream); ❷

    await _emailService.Send("recruitment@example.com",
        $"Somebody has uploaded a resume! Read it here: {storedFileUrl}"); ❸

    return Ok(); ❹
}
```

❶ Moving bits around between memory streams.

❷ Executing a function on the storage service.

❸ Executing a function on the email service.

❹ Creating an HTTP response with code 200.

This function is doing four things, none of which are particularly complex, however *all* of which make up the business logic (or "workflow") of our backend API. It also does not really respect the Single Responsibility Principle. The function is called SaveUploadedResume(), so you could argue that its single responsibility should be inserting the résumé file into S3. Why then, is it sending emails and constructing HTTP responses?

If you were to write unit tests for this function, it would be nice to simply cover all the cases you would expect to encounter when "saving an uploaded résumé." Instead, you have to consider mocking out email dissemination and the boilerplate needed to execute an API controller action in a unit test. This increases the scope of the function and increases the number of things you need to test, ultimately increasing the friction involved in making changes to this piece of code.

Wouldn't it be nice if we could reduce the scope of this function down to truly having one responsibility (saving the résumé) and split out email and HTTP concerns into something else?

With AWS Step Functions, you can move some or all of that workflow out of your code and into a configuration file. Step Functions uses a bespoke JSON object format called Amazon States Language (*https://oreil.ly/nmxp3*) to build up what it calls the *state machine*. These state machines in AWS Step Functions are triggered by an event and flow through the steps configured in the definition file, executing tasks and passing data along the workflow until an end state is reached.

We are going to refactor our Serverless C# Résumé Uploader to use Step Functions in the next section but suffice to say, one of the major advantages of using Step Functions is the ability to develop the *plumbing* of your application separately from the individual functions. Figure 4-7 is a screenshot from the AWS Step Functions sections in the AWS Management Console with the section "Execution event history" showing the operations this execution of the state machine took to arrive at the end state.

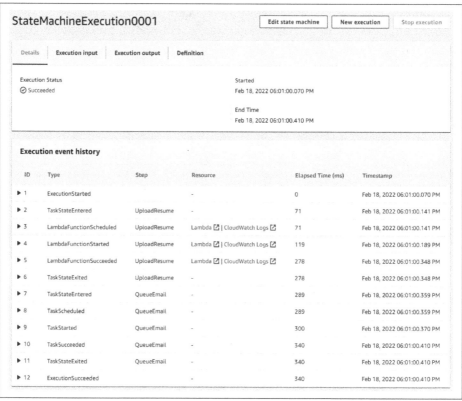

ID	Type	Step	Resource	Elapsed Time (ms)	Timestamp
▶ 1	ExecutionStarted		-	0	Feb 18, 2022 06:01:00.070 PM
▶ 2	TaskStateEntered	UploadResume	-	71	Feb 18, 2022 06:01:00.141 PM
▶ 3	LambdaFunctionScheduled	UploadResume	Lambda ☑	CloudWatch Logs ☑	71	Feb 18, 2022 06:01:00.141 PM
▶ 4	LambdaFunctionStarted	UploadResume	Lambda ☑	CloudWatch Logs ☑	119	Feb 18, 2022 06:01:00.189 PM
▶ 5	LambdaFunctionSucceeded	UploadResume	Lambda ☑	CloudWatch Logs ☑	278	Feb 18, 2022 06:01:00.348 PM
▶ 6	TaskStateExited	UploadResume	-	278	Feb 18, 2022 06:01:00.348 PM
▶ 7	TaskStateEntered	QueueEmail	-	289	Feb 18, 2022 06:01:00.359 PM
▶ 8	TaskScheduled	QueueEmail	-	289	Feb 18, 2022 06:01:00.359 PM
▶ 9	TaskStarted	QueueEmail	-	300	Feb 18, 2022 06:01:00.370 PM
▶ 10	TaskSucceeded	QueueEmail	-	340	Feb 18, 2022 06:01:00.410 PM
▶ 11	TaskStateExited	QueueEmail	-	340	Feb 18, 2022 06:01:00.410 PM
▶ 12	ExecutionSucceeded		-	340	Feb 18, 2022 06:01:00.410 PM

Figure 4-7. Step Functions execution log in the Management Console

C# Résumé Uploader Example: Step Functions

To demonstrate what we can do with AWS Step Functions, let's take the AWS Lambda function we created in the previous part of our Résumé Uploader example and split it out from one, to multiple Lambda functions. The `UploadNewResume` Lambda function can have the single responsibility of uploading the file to S3, then we have a second Lambda to send the email (`EmailRecruitment`). The HTTP part can also be abstracted away entirely and handled by the API Gateway. This gives us much more flexibility to change or optimize our workflow on the backend even after these two functions have been developed, tested, and deployed:

```
[assembly: LambdaSerializer(
    typeof(Amazon.Lambda.Serialization.SystemTextJson.
        DefaultLambdaJsonSerializer))]

namespace ServerlessResumeUploader
{
    public class LambdaFunctions
    {
```

```
    private readonly IStorageService _storageService
                                = new AwsS3StorageService();
    private readonly IEmailService _emailService
                                = new AwsSesEmailService();

❶
    public async Task<StepFunctionsState> UploadNewResume(
        StepFunctionsState state, ILambdaContext context)
    {
        byte[] bytes = Convert.FromBase64String(state.FileBase64);
        using var memoryStream = new MemoryStream(bytes);

        state.StoredFileUrl = await _storageService.Upload(memoryStream);

        state.FileBase64 = null;

        return state;
    }

❷
    public async Task<StepFunctionsState> EmailRecruitment(
        StepFunctionsState state, ILambdaContext context)
    {
        await _emailService.Send("recruitment@example.com",
        $"Somebody uploaded a resume! Read here: {state.StoredFileUrl}\n\n" +
        $"...and check out their GitHub profile: {state.GithubProfileUrl}");

        return state;
    }
  }
}
```

❶ The first Lambda function that takes a file and saves to S3.

❷ The second Lambda that emails our recruitment team a link to the file.

You can see the code for this is very similar to the ApplicationController code we had earlier in this chapter except it has been refactored into two methods on a Lambda Functions class. This will be deployed as two individual AWS Lambda functions that use the same binaries, a fairly common way to deploy multiple Lambda functions that share code. The actual uploading and email sending is again performed by the AwsS3StorageService and AwsSesEmailService; however, we are not using dependency injection anymore.[5]

---

5 It is possible to do dependency injection with AWS Lambda functions in C#, either by handcoding the setup or using third-party libraries. You may often find, however, that the functions are so simple they really do not need to be decorated with it.

Also note that for these two functions the first parameter is now `state` and they are both of the type `StepFunctionsState`. AWS Step Functions executes your workflow by passing a state object between each task (in this case, a task is a function). The functions add to or remove properties from the state. The state for our previous functions looks like this:

```
public class StepFunctionsState
{
    public string FileBase64 { get; set; }

    public string StoredFileUrl { get; set; }
}
```

When this `state` input is passed to the first function, `UploadNewResume()`, it will have the `state.FileBase64` set by API Gateway from the HTTP POST request from our frontend. The function will save this file to S3 then set `state.StoredFileUrl` before passing the state object to the next function. It will also clear `state.FileBase64` from the state object. The state object in AWS Step Functions is passed around between each step and since this base 64 string will be quite large, we can set it to null after reading it to reduce the size of the state object that is passed on.

We can deploy these two functions to AWS Lambda as we did before; however, this time we need to specify the `--function-handler` parameter for each. The *function handler* is the C# function in our code that acts as the entry point to our Lambda, as we saw previously in "Developing with AWS Lambda and C#" on page 91:

```
dotnet lambda deploy-function UploadNewResume
    --function-handler ServerlessResumeUploader::ServerlessResumeUploader.
    LambdaFunctions::UploadNewResume


dotnet lambda deploy-function EmailRecruitment
    --function-handler ServerlessResumeUploader::ServerlessResumeUploader.
    LambdaFunctions::EmailRecruitment
```

If we go into AWS Step Functions we can create a new state machine and connect these two Lambdas together and to API Gateway. The AWS Management Console does give us a graphical user interface to build up these workflows; however, we are engineers, so we are going to write it in Amazon States Language in a JSON file. This also has the crucial benefit of utilizing a plain-text JSON file that we can check into source control, giving us a great *Infrastructure as Code (IaC)* deployment model. The JSON configuration for our simple workflow here looks like this:

```
{
  "Comment": "Resume Uploader State Machine",
  "StartAt": "SaveUploadedResume",
  "States": {
    "SaveUploadedResume": {
      "Type": "Task",
      "Resource": "arn:aws:lambda:eu-west-2:00000000:function:UploadNewResume",
      "Next": "EmailRecruitment"
    },
    "EmailRecruitment": {
      "Type": "Task",
      "Resource": "arn:aws:lambda:eu-west-2:00000000:function:EmailRecruitment",
      "End": true
    }
  }
}
```

The Amazon Resource Name (ARN) of the Lambda function can be found in the AWS Lambda section of the Management Console, and it allows us to reference these Lambda functions from anywhere in AWS. If we copy the previous JSON into the definition of our AWS Step Functions state machine, you can see in the console that it creates a graphical representation of the workflow for us. Figure 4-11 later in this chapter shows what that looks like.

The last step in this example is to connect the start of our state machine to API Gateway. Whereas previously API Gateway was configured to proxy all requests to our AWS Lambda function, we now want to specify the exact route in API Gateway and forward it to our Step Functions workflow. Figure 4-8 shows the setup of a POST endpoint called /applications that has "Step Functions" set as the AWS Service. You can also see in Figure 4-8 that we have set Content Handling to "Convert to text (if needed)". This is an option specific for our résumé uploader example here. Since we will be POSTing the PDF file to our API as raw binary, this option tells API Gateway to convert that to Base64 text for us. This can then be easily added onto our state object (represented by StepFunctionsState.cs shown earlier) and passed around between Lambda functions on our AWS Step Functions workflow.

Figure 4-8. API Gateway configuration for triggering Step Functions

Lastly, we can set up some request mapping in API Gateway to transform the request into a JSON object that tells AWS Step Functions which state machine to execute. That is shown in Figure 4-9 as a mapping template linked to the *application/pdf* content type header.

We now have everything in place to send a file to our API and watch the Step Functions workflow execute:

```
curl https://xxxlrx74l3.execute-api.eu-west-2.amazonaws.com/Prod/Application
  --data-binary @MyResumeFile.pdf
```

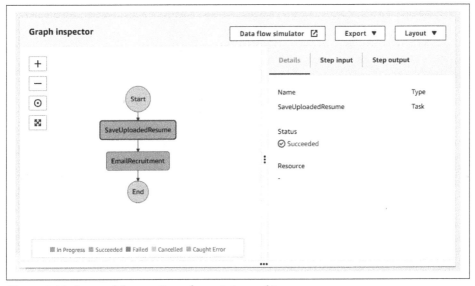

Figure 4-9. Content type mapping for PDF file

If we navigate to the Executions tab of the AWS Step Functions state machine in the Management Console, we will be able to see this upload trigger an execution of our state machine. Figure 4-10 shows a visual representation of the execution as it goes through our two steps; you can see this graph by clicking on the latest execution.

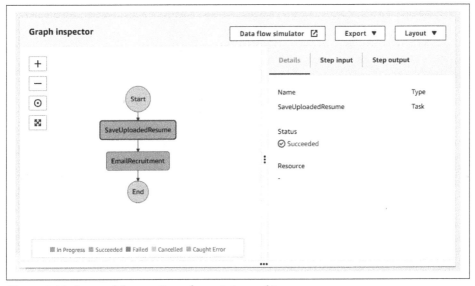

Figure 4-10. Successful execution of our state machine

We will admit, this has seemed like a lot of work just to save a file to S3 and send an email. By this point you might be thinking what is even the point? So we can abstract our workflow into a JSON file? The point of refactoring all of this and deploying to AWS Step Functions is that now we have the starting point for something much more flexible and extensible. We can do some extremely cool things now without having to go anywhere near our two deployed Lambda functions. For example, why not take advantage of AWS Textract to read the PDF file and extract the candidate's GitHub profile? This is what we'll be doing in the next example.

C# Résumé Uploader Example: AWS Textract

This is the kind of functionality that not too long ago would have been a very involved task to code, but with Step Functions and AWS Textract we can add this in very easily without even having to pull extra third-party libraries into our existing code, or even recompile it:

```
public async Task<StepFunctionsState> LookForGithubProfile(
    StepFunctionsState state, ILambdaContext context)
{
    using var textractClient =
            new AmazonTextractClient(RegionEndpoint.EUWest2);❶

    var s3ObjectKey = Regex.Match(state.StoredFileUrl,
            "amazonaws\\.com\\/(.+?(?=\\.pdf))").Groups[1].Value + ".pdf";

    var detectResponse = await textractClient.DetectDocumentTextAsync(
        new DetectDocumentTextRequest
    {
        Document = new Document
        {
            S3Object = new S3Object
            {
                Bucket = AwsS3StorageService.BucketName,
                Name = s3ObjectKey,
            }
        }
    });

    state.GithubProfileUrl = detectResponse.Blocks
            .FirstOrDefault(x => x.BlockType == BlockType.WORD &&
                              x.Text.Contains("github.com"))
            ?.Text;

    return state;
}
```

❶ The AmazonTextractClient is found in the AWSSDK.Textract NuGet package and allows us to easily call AWS Textract.

Textract is one of many machine learning services offered by AWS. They also provide AWS Comprehend for performing natural language processing on text and Amazon Rekognition for tagging images. All of these services are priced on an accessible pay-as-you-go model and can be called from a Lambda function like we are doing here with AWS Textract.

Here we have the code for another C# Lambda function that will take in the same state object we have been using for all our functions and send the PDF file to Textract. The response from this will be an array of text blocks that were extracted from the PDF file. If any of these text blocks contains the string "github.com," we add it into our state object for use by a later Lambda function. This allows us to include it in the email that is sent out, for example:

```
public async Task<StepFunctionsState> EmailRecruitment(StepFunctionsState state,
                                                        ILambdaContext context)
{
    await _emailService.Send("recruitment@example.com",
    $"Somebody uploaded a resume! Read it here: {state.StoredFileUrl}\n\n" +❶
    $"...check out their GitHub profile: {state.GithubProfileUrl}");❷

    return state;
}
```

❶ The stored file URL has still been left in the state object from the first function that saved it to S3.

❷ This new field was added by LookForGithubProfile() when Textract found a GitHub URL in the PDF.

We can deploy our new LookForGithubProfile() function as a third AWS Lambda and add it into our state machine JSON. We have also added an error handler in here that calls off to a function to notify us that there was an error uploading the résumé. There are many different steps and ways to create complex paths in your workflow using Amazon States Language JSON definitions. Figure 4-11 shows all of this together in the AWS Management Console with our definition JSON on the left and a visual representation of our workflow on the right.

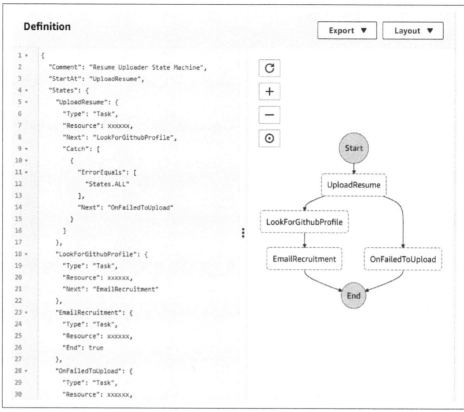

Figure 4-11. Workflow definition and graphical representation in AWS Step Functions

We can also update our architecture diagram to remove the web server shown in Figure 4-1 and make the application completely serverless, as illustrated in Figure 4-12.

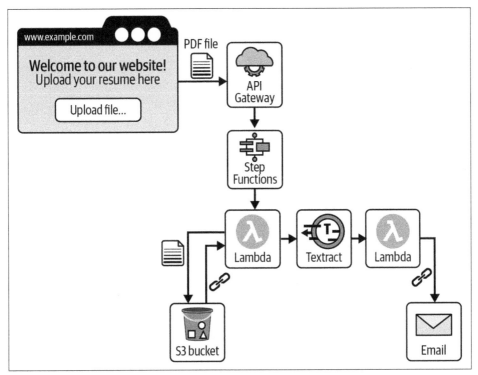

Figure 4-12. Serverless C# Résumé Uploader architecture

Now we have a truly serverless application in which the individual components can be developed, tested, and deployed independently. But what if we don't want to rely on AWS Step Functions to bind all this logic together?

Developing with SQS and SNS

AWS Step Functions are not the only way to communicate between AWS Lambda invocations and other serverless services. Long before AWS Step Functions existed we had message queues and the publisher/subscriber pattern. These are the two services offered by AWS:

Amazon Simple Notification Service (SNS)
    SNS is a distributed implementation of the pub/sub pattern. Subscribers attach themselves to an SNS channel (called a "topic") and when a message is published, all subscribers will instantly be notified. You can have multiple subscribers listening to published messages on any given topic in SNS and it supports several endpoints such as email and SMS, as well as triggering Lambda functions or making HTTP requests.

Amazon Simple Queue Service (SQS)
SQS is AWS's message queue. Instead of being pushed to subscribers, messages sent to SQS are added to the queue and stored there for a duration of time (up to 14 days). Message receivers poll the queue at a rate suitable for them, reading and then deleting the messages from the queue as necessary. SQS queues make it possible to delay actions or batch up messages until the subscriber is ready to handle them.

These two services allow us to think in terms of *messages* and *events*, which are important concepts for building serverless systems. They will allow us to implement a publisher/subscriber pattern in our example system.

C# Résumé Uploader example: SQS

Think about what we can do with our Serverless C# Résumé Uploader application to take advantage of SQS or SNS. We know users can upload their résumé to our API (via API Gateway), which will store it in S3 and then use Textract to read the candidate's GitHub profile. How about instead of immediately emailing our recruitment team, we add a message to a queue? That way we can run a job once every morning and send *one* email for *all* the messages that have built up on the queue during the past 24 hours. This might make it easier for our recruitment team to sit down and read all of the day's résumés at once instead of doing it piecemeal throughout the day. Can we do all of this without having to touch the rest of our code? Without having to rebuild, retest, or redeploy the entire application? Yes, and here's how.

Since we are using AWS Step Functions, we can simply create a task in our definition JSON file that posts a message to an SQS queue. We don't need another Lambda function to do this; instead, we can specify the message body directly in the JSON and then update our state engine definition. Here we have the task called `"QueueEmail"` that posts a message to an SQS queue we have set up called `UploadedResumeFiles`, referenced here by its ARN:

```
{
  "Comment": "Resume Uploader State Machine",
  "StartAt": "SaveUploadedResume",
  "States": {
    "SaveUploadedResume": {
      "Type": "Task",
      "Resource": "arn:aws:lambda:eu-west-2:00000000:function:UploadNewResume",
      "Next": "QueueEmail"
    },
    "QueueEmail": {
      "Type": "Task",
      "Resource": "arn:aws:states:::sqs:sendMessage",
      "Parameters": {
        "QueueUrl": "https://sqs.eu-west-2.amazonaws.com/UploadedResumeFiles",
        "MessageBody": {
```

```
        "StoredFileUrl.$": "$.StoredFileUrl"
      }
    },
    "End": true
  }
 }
}
```

Now, when file uploads trigger the state machine, the `EmailRecruitment` Lambda will not be executed; we will just get a message posted to the queue. All we need to do now is write a new AWS Lambda function to run once a day that will read all the messages from the queue and send an email containing all the file URLs. The code for such a Lambda might look like this:

```
public async Task<string> BatchEmailRecruitment(object input, ILambdaContext c)
{
    using var sqsClient = new AmazonSQSClient(RegionEndpoint.EUWest2);
    var messageResponse = await sqsClient.ReceiveMessageAsync(
        new ReceiveMessageRequest()❶
        {
            QueueUrl = queueUrl,
            MaxNumberOfMessages = 10
        });

    var stateObjects =
        messageResponse.Messages.Select(msg => Deserialize(msg.Body));

    var listOfFiles =
        string.Join("\n\n", stateObjects.Select(x => x.StoredFileUrl));❷

    await _emailService.Send("recruitment@example.com", ❸
        $"You have {messageResponse.Messages.Count} new resumes to review!\n\n"
        + listOfFiles);

    await sqsClient.DeleteMessageBatchAsync(new DeleteMessageBatchRequest() ❹
    {
        QueueUrl = queueUrl,
        Entries = messageResponse.Messages.Select(x =>
                new DeleteMessageBatchRequestEntry()
        {
            Id = x.MessageId,
            ReceiptHandle = x.ReceiptHandle
        }).ToList()
    });

    return "ok";
}
```

❶ Connect to the SQS queue and read a batch of messages.

❷ Concatenate the file URLs from the state objects we posted inside each message.

❸ Send one email with all links.

❹ Delete the messages from the queue—this does not happen automatically.

Triggering this Lambda once per day can be done using AWS EventBridge as shown in Figure 4-13. This "Add trigger" form is accessed from the Function Overview window of our new Lambda function in the AWS Management Console.

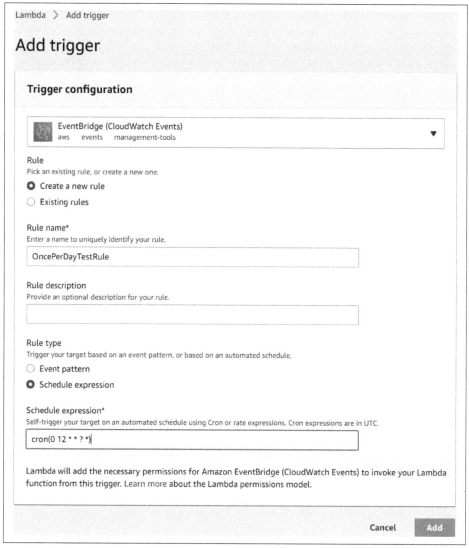

Figure 4-13. Adding a scheduled EventBridge trigger to a Lambda function

Now our system will send out an email once per day, including links to all the résumés on the queue, just as in Figure 4-14.

Figure 4-14. Email sent from our scheduled Lambda function

By adding an SQS queue, we have modified the behavior of our system at runtime and improved the service it provides by collating all the links into one daily email. All of this, however, is still kicked off by an HTTP request to our API. Next, we are going to explore some other types of events that can trigger logic and functions to run in our state engine.

Developing Event-Driven Systems with AWS Triggers

Imagine you speak to someone who has a brilliant idea for an app and wants you to build it for them.[6] You ask them to describe the functionality, and they say something like this:

"When the user uploads a photo I want to notify their followers, and when they send an email to my support mailbox, I want to open a support ticket."

These "when X then do Y" statements are describing an *event-driven system*. All systems are event-driven under the hood; the trouble is that for a lot of backend applications, those events are just HTTP requests. Instead of, "When the user uploads a photo I want to notify their followers," what we usually end up implementing is "When our server receives an HTTP message indicating a user has uploaded a photo, notify their followers."

That's understandable; up until serverless computing came along, the only way you could really implement this was to listen to an HTTP event on your API. But wouldn't it be great if we could remove that extra step and implement our architecture to respond to the *real events as they happen* and not some intermediary implementation detail, such as an HTTP request?

---

6 One of the drawbacks of being a software developer is this tends to happen a lot, whether you ask for it or not.

This is the central tenet behind event-driven serverless systems. You execute functions and trigger workflows on the changes that really make sense to the problems you are trying to solve. Instead of writing an application that listens to an action from a human and then sends an HTTP request to an API to trigger an effect, you let AWS do all that and simply attach the event to the action directly. In the previous example, you could listen to a `s3:ObjectCreated:Post` in S3 and run your code whenever that event occurs, bypassing the API step completely.

C# Résumé Uploader example: event-driven

Let's visit our serverless résumé uploader for one final time. If you look back to Figure 4-12, you can see the PDF file goes from our website to the Step Functions tasks via API Gateway. There is no reason for API Gateway to be there; it is simply an implementation detail to allow our frontend to make an easy HTTP call when it uploads the file. Wouldn't it be nice if we could rid ourselves of this API altogether and have the website upload the file directly to an S3 bucket? This would also allow us to throw away our `UploadNewResume` Lambda function too, and there is no more cathartic feeling in software development than deleting code we no longer need while retaining all the functionality of our system.

By removing the API step and having the frontend upload the file directly into S3, we also open up new possibilities for our system. For example, what if in addition to uploading a résumé on our *website*, we want to accept résumés emailed to *application@ouremail.com*? Using SES it is relatively simple to hook up an email forwarder that will extract an attached PDF file and save it to S3. This would then trigger the same workflow on the backend, because we have hooked our logic up to the S3 event and not some intermediary HTTP API call. The statement "when we see a new PDF file in S3, kick off our workflow" becomes much more natural to the business problem we are solving. It doesn't actually matter anymore how the PDF file gets in there because our system reacts in the same way.

As far as uploading the PDF file directly to S3 goes, we have options. If we already happen to be using AWS Amplify (*https://docs.amplify.aws*)[7] on the frontend, then we can use the storage module and the `"protected"` upload method, restricting access to a path in our S3 bucket based on the Cognito identity of the authenticated user:

```
amplify add storage
```

The frontend JavaScript used to upload a file to S3 would look like this:

```
import Amplify, { Auth, Storage } from 'aws-amplify';

Amplify.configure({ Storage: { AWSS3: {
```

---

[7] AWS Amplify is a frontend framework for mobile and web apps that allows us to quickly build up a UI around serverless AWS services, such as S3 Simple Storage Service.

```
                  bucket: '<bucket-name>'
          } } });

     async function uploadFile(fileName, file) {
         await Storage.put(fileName, file, { level: 'protected',
                 contentType: file.type });
     }
```

Even without AWS Amplify and an authenticated user on the frontend, there is still
a way we can upload directly to the S3 bucket using a presigned URL (*https://oreil.ly/
AXPDg*). The process for this is to create a Lambda function behind an API gateway
that, when executed, will call `AmazonS3Client.GetPreSignedURL()` and return that to
the frontend to use to upload the file. Sure, you still have an API in this scenario, but
the *function* of this API is much more in line with performing one generic task. You
could, after all, use the presigned URL to upload other types of files in the frontend
and hook multiple Step Function workflows to each.

Once you have the frontend uploading files directly into S3 instead of sending them
via a web API, adding a trigger into the S3 bucket can be done directly in the
Management Console on the Properties tab of the S3 bucket configuration, as shown
in Figure 4-15.

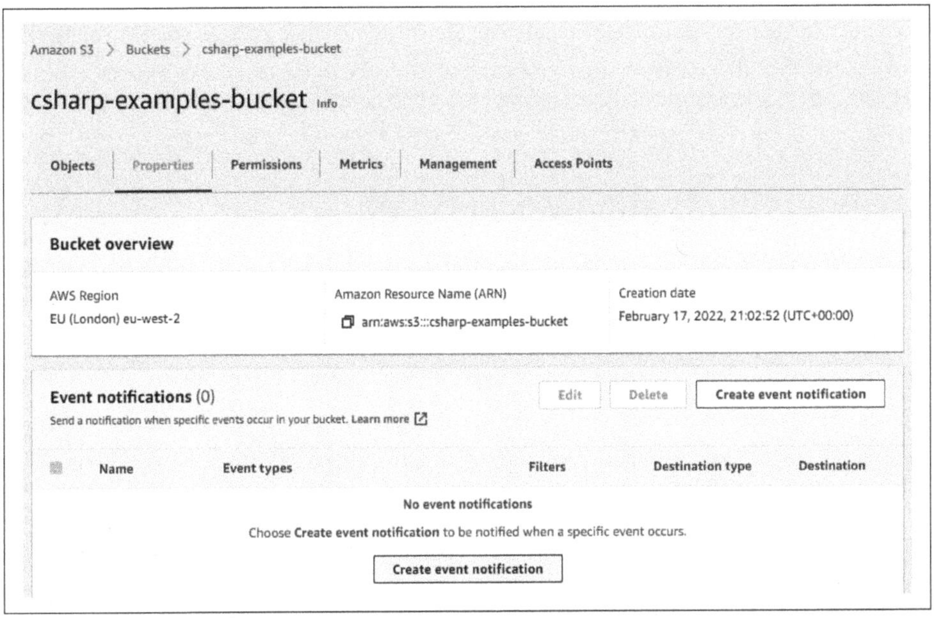

Figure 4-15. Adding an event notification to an S3 bucket

Add the Step Functions state engine as the destination for this event and we arrive at
the final form of our event-driven, serverless, C# Résumé Uploader Service! The final
architecture is shown in Figure 4-16.

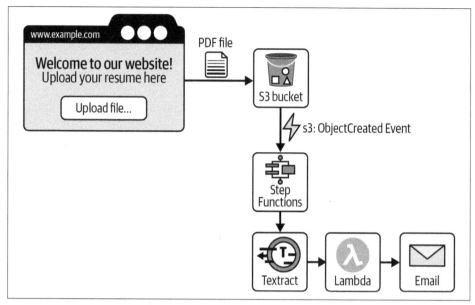

Figure 4-16. Final event-driven architecture of our résumé uploader example

As you can see we now have a concise, descriptive, and *event-driven* system that is dynamic enough to allow us to extend or modify parts of the workflow without risking introducing bugs or issues elsewhere. The last thing to think about is how we manage all these moving parts and easily configure them in one place.

Serverless Application Model (SAM)

So far we have been making all our configuration changes by logging into the AWS Management Console and clicking around the UI. This is fine for experimentation, but is not a method particularly well suited to running a production system. One wrong click and you could cause an outage to part of your application. This is where Infrastructure as Code (IaC) can help.

IaC is the process of configuring your serverless infrastructure through machine readable definition files. CloudFormation is an IaC tool used across AWS that allows you to keep your entire cloud configuration in either YAML or JSON files. Virtually everything in your AWS can be modeled in CloudFormation templates, from DNS settings to S3 bucket properties to IAM roles and permissions. When a setting needs changing, you change the value in a CloudFormation template and tell AWS to apply the change to your resources. The most obvious advantage of this is that you can check your template JSON/YAML file into version control and have each change code reviewed, audited, and tested in a sandbox/staging environment, just like with any other code change.

One drawback of CloudFormation, however, is it can be quite complicated and verbose. Due to the sheer number of settings that are available for you to modify in your AWS resources, CloudFormation templates can become unwieldy when trying to configure a serverless system composed of multiple Lambda functions, message queues, and IAM roles. There are various tools that add an abstraction layer around CloudFormation and aid in configuring serverless systems. Tools such as Serverless Framework and Serverless Application Model (SAM) have been created to solve this problem.

You can think of SAM as a layer over the top of CloudFormation that brings the most pertinent settings for serverless applications to the front. You can find the full specification for SAM online at AWS SAM Documentation (*https://oreil.ly/4fEfH*), but to give you an overview, here is part of the SAM YAML file for our C# Résumé Uploader system:

```
AWSTemplateFormatVersion: '2010-09-09'
Transform: AWS::Serverless-2016-10-31
Description: Resume Uploader Serverless C# Application.
Resources:
  SaveUploadedResumeLambda:
    Type: AWS::Lambda::Function
    Properties:
      Handler: ServerlessResumeUploader::ServerlessResumeUploader.
      LambdaFunctions::SaveUploadedResume
      Role: arn:aws:iam::0000000000:role/ResumeUploaderLambdaRole
      Runtime: dotnetcore3.1
      MemorySize: 256
      Timeout: 30
  LookForGithubProfileLambda:
    Type: AWS::Lambda::Function
    Properties:
      Handler: ServerlessResumeUploader::ServerlessResumeUploader.
      LambdaFunctions::LookForGithubProfile
      Role: arn:aws:iam::0000000000:role/ResumeUploaderLambdaRole
      Runtime: dotnetcore3.1
      MemorySize: 256
      Timeout: 30
```

You can see how we have defined the SaveUploadedResumeLambda and LookForGithubProfileLambda Lambda functions, indicated where in our C# code the entry point is, and configured them with memory, timeout, and permissions settings for execution.

With your infrastructure configured in SAM files like this, you can easily deploy new environments for testing or staging. You benefit from code reviews and you get the ability to create an automated deployment pipeline for your *resources* just like with your application code.

Conclusion

Serverless computing allows you to build intricate, yet flexible and scalable solutions that operate on a pay-as-you-go pricing model and can scale down to zero. Personally, we use a serverless execution model whenever we need to build something quickly to validate an idea, solve a business problem, or where budget is a concern. Because you only pay for what you use, a serverless architecture centered on AWS Lambda can be an extremely low-cost way to build a minimum viable product (MVP) or deploy the backend for a mobile app. AWS offers a whopping 1 million Lambda executions per month for free, which can easily be enough to get a startup out of the idea phase or beta test a product. The other services we have introduced in this chapter all have extremely generous free tiers, allowing you to experiment with ideas and architectures without breaking the bank.

That being said, going serverless will not automatically cause your system to be cheaper to run. You will need to be considerate of designing applications that make unnecessarily large numbers of AWS Lambda calls. Just because two functions *can* be two separate Lambdas doesn't always mean they *should* be from a cost and performance point of view. Experiment and measure. Functions as a Service can also be expensive at higher volumes if your application is not architected to make efficient use of each invocation. Because you pay per execution, at very high volumes you may find the costs soaring well past what it would have been to simply run a dotnet process on EC2 or Elastic Beanstalk. The costs of serverless should always be weighed up against the other advantages such as scalability.

Flexibility is another enormous advantage of serverless architectures, as the example in this chapter has shown. In each step we have radically changed the architecture of a part of our Serverless C# Résumé Uploader by making very small changes—most of the time without even having to redeploy the rest of the application. This separation between the moving parts of your system makes growth much easier and unlocks diversification of talent within your development team. There is nothing in a serverless architecture that specifies what version, technology, or even programming language the individual components are written in. Have you ever wanted to try your hand at F#? With a system built on AWS Lambda, there is nothing stopping you from writing the latest feature in an F# Lambda and slotting it into your serverless architecture. Need to route some HTTP calls to a third-party API? You can proxy that directly from API Gateway if you need to, without having to create the interface and the "plumbing" in your code. By adopting IaC tools such as SAM (or third-party frameworks such as Serverless Framework and Terraform), you can automate changes to your infrastructure and run code reviews, pull requests, and automate testing pipelines on the infrastructure configuration itself. A pull request for a serverless system will often be composed of two changes: a simple, easy to review AWS

Lambda and an entry into the SAM/Terraform/CloudFormation template showing how that Lambda integrates with the rest of the system.

Critical Thinking Discussion Questions

- What could be the advantage of using a functional programming style when building FaaS services on AWS?
- A friend tells you AWS Lambda is slightly slower than another open source framework for FaaS, so they won't use it. What more considerable advantage on AWS could they be missing out on by not using AWS Lambda?
- Why is the execution event history in AWS Step Functions one of the most critical features of the service?
- Describe an architecture in which Amazon SQS is a crucial component in a global-scale platform.
- What are the critical differences between SQS and SNS?

Exercises

- Build an AWS Lambda function that pulls messages from an SQS queue trigger.
- Build an AWS Lambda function that accepts messages from an SNS topic.
- Build an AWS Lambda function that prints the names of files placed in a bucket via an S3 trigger.
- Build an AWS Step Function that accepts the payload "hello" in one AWS Lambda and returns the payload "goodbye" in a second AWS Lambda function.
- Use AWS CloudShell and invoke an AWS Lambda function or AWS Step Function using the AWS CLI.

## CHAPTER 5

Containerization of .NET

One way to think about containers is as a technology revolution. Think about the internal combustion engine, which went a long way toward transforming the way society used transportation. But now, a new transformation is taking place with the popularity of electric vehicles. They are creating a new way to drive! The same idea applies to the subject of containers when compared to virtual machines—you'll see what we mean in a moment.

Machines used for transportation have undergone multiple shifts throughout the centuries as technology has improved.[1] Currently, the next wave of innovation in engines is around electric vehicles. Electric vehicles are faster, have more torque, more range, and allow for new ways of fueling that do not require access to fuel depots since they can charge by the sun or the electric grid. Electric vehicles create a new way to fuel a car, like charging while parked at home, at work, or on a road trip. Deeply coupled with electric vehicles is work on building autonomous or semiautonomous cars. New technologies enable new ways to work.

A similar progression has occurred with computing over the decades, as shown in Figure 5-1.[2] Computing has morphed into smaller and more portable computing units, currently manifested as containers. In turn, these new computing units enable new ways to work. Containers provide a standard way to package your application's code, configurations, and dependencies into a single entity. Containers run within the

---

1 In his book *How Innovation Works: And Why It Flourishes in Freedom* (HarperCollins), Matt Ridley makes the point that "The story of the internal-combustion engine displays the usual features of an innovation: a long and deep prehistory characterized by failure; a shorter period marked by an improvement in affordability characterized by simultaneous patenting and rivalries."

2 Isaacson points out that an enormous driver for the creation of personal computers was the desire for more time on a mainframe. (Walter Isaacson. *The Innovators: How a Group of Hackers, Geniuses, and Geeks Created the Digital Revolution*. New York: Simon & Schuster, 2014.)

host operating system but run as lightweight, resource-isolated processes, ensuring quick, reliable, reproducible, and consistent deployments.

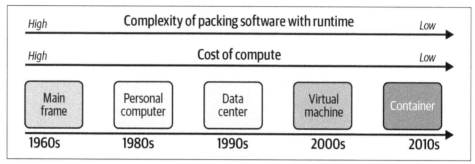

Figure 5-1. Technological progression of compute

Before we can dig into using container services on AWS, we first need to discuss containers a bit more, starting with an overview of both containers and Docker, an open platform for designing, delivering, and executing applications. First, let's look at containers in more depth.

Introduction to Containers

The key innovation of a container is the ability to package the runtime needed for the software solution alongside the code. As a result of modern container technology, a user can run a docker run command to run a solution and not worry about installing any software. Similarly, a developer can look inside a git repository and inspect the code and the runtime necessary to run it by looking at the Dockerfile as shown in Figure 5-2. In this example, GitHub serves as the central "source of truth" where each component necessary to deploy an application is in the repository. The Dockerfile defines the runtime. The Infrastructure as Code (IaC) describes the cloud configuration, such as networking and loadbalancing. The build system config file specifies the process for software project builds and deploys.

 A great example of the advantage of containers is using a Docker one-liner to run Docker Hub SQL Server (*https://oreil.ly/OuNbY*). The following example shows how to start an mssql-server instance running as the SQL Express edition:

```
docker run -e "ACCEPT_EULA=Y" \
    -e "SA_PASSWORD=ABC!1234!pass" \
    -e "MSSQL_PID=Express" \
    -p 1433:1433 -it \
    -d mcr.microsoft.com/mssql/server:2019-latest
```

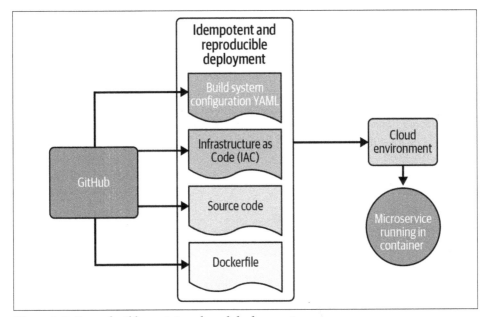

Figure 5-2. Reproducible container-based deployment

A virtual machine inherits the legacy of the physical data center. In one sense, a virtual machine is a copy of the physical data center compute technology. But if you look at a container, it's an entirely new way of thinking and working. The infrastructure definition, the runtime definition, source code, and build server configuration can all be in the same project. As a result of this new way of working, there is new transparency for the lifecycle of a software development project.

> Not all projects keep the IaC, build configuration, Dockerfile, and source code in the same repository. These assets can live in multiple repositories as well as a single repo.

If you look at a virtual machine, it's opaque what is inside it in terms of installed software and configuration. Another considerable downside of the virtual machine is start-up time, as it can take several minutes to start up a virtual machine.[3] If you're going to deploy a microservice or a web app using load balancers and virtual machines, you have to design around these limitations. With a container-based

---

3 According to AWS (*https://oreil.ly/zuKS9*), it typically takes "a few minutes for an instance reboot to complete."

service, you can count on deploying thousands of container instances in seconds with ECS,[4] so there's a considerable advantage to deploying things via containers.

Let's look at another way of getting started with containers—the desktop versus the cloud. The Docker environment is an ideal environment for local experimentation with the desktop. It allows you to upload or download containers that will enable you to start using standalone containers or use Kubernetes workflows, as shown in Figure 5-3. The Dockerfile uses a base, read-only image stored in the container registry. The local development workflow involves building a writeable new container where a developer will build, test, run, and finally deploy the container to a container registry by pushing it there.

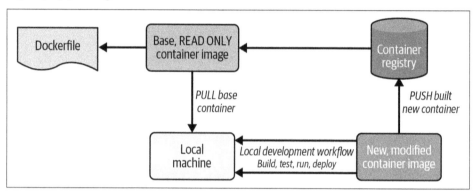

Figure 5-3. Container workflow

It's a great place to play around with your ideas before moving to the cloud. Similarly, a developer can download containers built by the domain experts at AWS and execute them in their local environment.[5]

Once you've decided what you want to do and toyed around a bit locally, naturally, you can move into an AWS environment and start interacting with these containers in a cloud native manner. Starting with AWS Cloud9 is a great way to experiment with containers. You can build the containers in the cloud development environment, save the environment, and then deploy that container to ECR. You can also experiment with containers by launching a virtual machine and then doing the build process on that virtual machine.

---

4 You can learn more about advanced capabilities of container launch times in this AWS blog post (*https://oreil.ly/tmh5o*).

5 An excellent example of this workflow is the AWS Lambda Runtime Interface Emulator (*https://oreil.ly/17yhY*). According to AWS, "The Lambda Runtime Interface Emulator is a proxy for Lambda's Runtime and Extensions APIs, which allows customers to locally test their Lambda function packaged as a container image."

Yet another option is to develop locally using Docker tools and Visual Studio. Let's discuss Docker next.

Introduction to Docker

Docker is an open source platform for managing the lifecycle of containers. It allows a developer to package and develop applications into Docker container images, defined by Dockerfiles, and run containerized applications developed externally or locally. One of the more popular aspects of Docker is its container registry, Docker Hub, which allows collaboration with containers.

There are container image formats beyond the Docker container image format (*https://oreil.ly/IsKxP*). Another container image format is Open Container Initiative (OCI) Specification (*https://oreil.ly/IetNb*).

What problem do Docker containers (*https://oreil.ly/HF9zX*) solve? The OS, runtime, and code package together in the built container image. This action solves an incredibly complicated problem with a long history. A famous meme goes, "It works on my machine!" While this is often said as a joke to illustrate the complexity of deploying software, it is also true that without containers packaging the runtime together with the code, it is tough to verify a local development solution will behave the same when distributed to production. Containers solve this exact problem. If the code works in a container, the container configuration file checks in as any other type of code into the source code repository.

It is common for modern application best practices to include IaC that provisions the environment alongside the container. In this blog post about Amazon internal best practices (*https://oreil.ly/dPm35*), the author notes that for containerized applications, it is considered the best practice to deploy code changes and microservice infrastructure changes through the same CI/CD release pipeline.

Containers have been around for quite some time but in different forms. One of the modern forms of containers was Solaris Containers, released in 2004. It allowed you to telnet to a powered-off machine capable of responding to commands through a Lights Out Management (LOM) card, which told it to boot. It would then "kickstart" a machine with no operating system into booting from the network, then via ssh and through the vim text editor, create new containers, which also booted off the network.

Since then, containers have continued to improve and enable additional workflows, such as continuous delivery and packaging code and runtime together. Docker is the most popular container format. In Figure 5-4, notice how the ecosystem plays out in practice. There are two primary components of Docker: Docker Desktop (*https://oreil.ly/gfcmt*) and Docker Hub (*https://oreil.ly/iNGPb*). With Docker Desktop, the local development workflow includes access to a Linux container runtime, developer tools, the Docker app itself, and an optional Kubernetes installation. In the case of Docker Hub, there is both private and public container repository, automated build of container images, collaboration features like teams and organizations, and certified images.

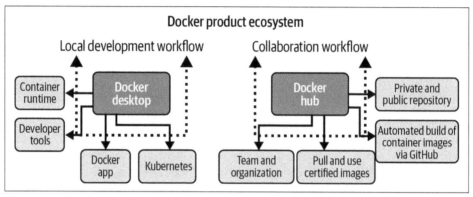

Figure 5-4. Docker ecosystem

A further innovation with modern containers is the concept of inheriting from a *base image*. A base image allows you to leverage developers' expertise from many different domains such as Python, .NET, or Linux to build your container on top of their base image. Additionally, they save a developer time and effort in putting an entire image together from scratch.

Next, let's dive a bit deeper into the Docker ecosystem.

Docker Ecosystem

Docker operates by providing a definitive way to run your code. Multiple AWS services work with Docker (*https://aws.amazon.com/docker*) container images. These services include Amazon ECS (Amazon Elastic Container Service) (*https://aws.amazon.com/ecs*), and Amazon ECR (Elastic Container Registry) (*https://aws.amazon.com/ecr*), a secure container image repository. Also worth noting is Amazon EKS (Elastic Kubernetes Service) (*https://aws.amazon.com/eks*), a managed container service that enables Kubernetes applications, and AWS App Runner, a PaaS for containerized applications, which is discussed later in the chapter, and finally AWS Lambda.

The desktop application contains the container runtime, which allows containers to execute. It also orchestrates the local development workflow, including the ability to use Kubernetes (*https://github.com/kubernetes/kubernetes*), which is an open source system for managing containerized applications that came out of Google.

Next, let's discuss how Docker Hub interacts with Docker Desktop and other container development environments. Just as the `git` (*https://git-scm.com*) source code ecosystem has local developer tools like Vim (*https://www.vim.org*), eMacs (*https://www.gnu.org/software/emacs*), Visual Studio Code (*https://code.visualstudio.com*), or Xcode (*https://developer.apple.com/xcode*) that work with it, Docker Desktop works with Docker containers and allows for local use and development.

When collaborating with `git` outside of the local environment, developers often use platforms like GitHub (*https://github.com*) or GitLab (*https://about.gitlab.com*) to communicate with other parties and share code. Docker Hub (*https://hub.docker.com*) works similarly. Docker Hub allows developers to share Docker containers that can serve as the base image for building new solutions and pull down complete solutions like a SQL server image.

These base images, built by experts, are certified to be high quality, i.e., the official ASP.NET Core Runtime (*https://oreil.ly/nx7Qm*) from Microsoft. This process allows a developer to leverage the right expert's expertise on a particular software component and improve their container's overall quality. This concept is similar to using a library developed by another developer versus writing it yourself.

 Like a software library, a Dockerfile allows you to bind your implementation to an existing version with the additional capability of running in an encapsulated environment.

Next, let's dig a little deeper into how Docker containers compare to virtual machines.

Containers Versus Virtual Machines?

Table 5-1 provides a high-level breakdown of the differences between a container and a virtual machine.

Table 5-1. Containers versus virtual machines

Category	Container	Virtual machine
Size	MBs	GBs
Speed	Boot in milliseconds	Boot in minutes
Composability	Source code as file	Image-based build process

Note that there are other containers besides Docker containers, including Windows and Linux alternatives. Docker is the most popular format and for the sake of this chapter, assume all references to containers going forward will be Docker containers.

The core advantage of containers is that they are smaller, composable, and faster to launch. Where virtual machines do well is in scenarios that require a copy of the paradigms of the physical data center. An example of this workflow would be moving a web application running in a physical data center without changing the code to a cloud-based virtual machine. Let's look at some real-world examples where containers helped a project run smoothly:

Developer shares local project
> A developer can work on a .NET web application that uses `Blazor` (an example covered later in the chapter). The Docker container image handles the installation and configuration of the underlying operating system. Another team member can check out the code and use `docker run` to run the project. This process eliminates what could be a multiday problem of configuring a laptop correctly to run a software project.

Data scientist shares Jupyter notebook with a researcher at another university
> A data scientist working with Jupyter-style notebooks (*https://jupyter.org*) wants to share a complex data science project with multiple dependencies on C, Julia, Fortran, R, and Python code. They package up the runtime as a Docker container image and eliminate the back-and-forth over several weeks when sharing a project like this.

A machine learning engineer load tests a production machine learning model
> A machine learning engineer builds a new ML model and deploys it to production. Previously, they were concerned about accurately testing the new model's accuracy before committing to it. The model recommends products to paying customers to purchase additional products they may like. If the model is inaccurate, it could cost the company a lot of revenue. Using containers to deploy the ML model in this example, it is possible to deploy the model to a fraction of the customers. They can start at only 10% at first, and if there are problems, the model is quickly reverted. If the model performs well, it can promptly replace the existing models.

Finally, other scenarios for containers include building microservices, doing continuous integration, data processing, and containers as a service (CaaS). Let's dive into some of these topics in the next section.

Developing with AWS Container Compatible Services

There are multiple ways a .NET developer can deploy containers on AWS, including AWS Lambda, Amazon ECS, Amazon EKS, and AWS App Runner. A good starter point to dive deeper into the latest container services is the AWS containers documentation (*https://aws.amazon.com/containers*). Among other things, it covers a high-level overview of current container services offered at AWS and everyday use cases.

Which abstraction is best depends on what level of the shared responsibility model a developer wants.[6] Next, let's dive into these container scenarios using a fully cloud native workflow with Cloud9 and AWS container services.

Using AWS Container Services for .NET with Cloud9

A space station is a spaceship that sits in the Earth's low orbit and allows astronauts to spend time in space, do research in labs, or recover for a future trip to a new destination. Similarly, if you are a cloud developer, the best place to develop for the cloud is the cloud!

Cloud9 is a cloud-based development that includes deep integration with AWS and works in a browser. This technology radically departs from traditional software engineering development practices since it opens up many new ways to work.

Here are a few reasons why Cloud9 is so good for cloud development:

Close proximity to AWS resources
> If you are in a coffee shop, it could be challenging to copy files back and forth to the cloud, but if you use a web browser IDE, the response time doesn't matter since the IDE is sitting next to the servers it communicates with within AWS. This advantage comes in handy with building containers because you can quickly push container images to the Amazon ECR.

Near-identical development environment to production
> Something else that comes in handy is the ability to develop code in the same operating system as it runs in. Cloud9 runs the latest version of Amazon Linux, so there are no deployment surprises.

Specialized Cloud IDE
> Cloud9 has specialized IDE functionality that only exists in the AWS Cloud IDE. Examples include the ability to navigate S3 buckets, invoke AWS Lambda functions, and pair programs with other developers who have access to your AWS account.

---

6 AWS offers multiple levels of shared responsibility (*https://oreil.ly/MEQRN*) depending on the service.

To get started, create a new Cloud9 environment by searching for it in the AWS Console, selecting the service, and giving the instance's name a helpful description, as shown in Figure 5-5. It is worth pointing out that underneath the hood, an EC2 instance runs Cloud9, and you can access it via the AWS EC2 Console to make modifications like increasing storage size or changing networking.

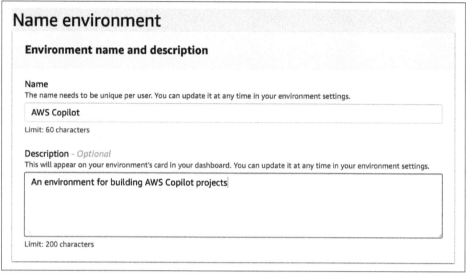

Figure 5-5. Launch Cloud9

Next, configure a machine with a decent amount of power since you build containers with this environment as shown in Figure 5-6.

 It is worth mentioning that because Cloud9 has no additional cost (*https://oreil.ly/LVHeF*), the cost driver is EC2. Choose an appropriate instance size to save on costs.

Once the Cloud9 environment loads next, you need to install .NET 6 (*https://oreil.ly/8JRNY*):

```
sudo rpm -Uvh \
https://packages.microsoft.com/config/centos/7/packages-microsoft-prod.rpm
sudo yum -y update
sudo yum install dotnet-sdk-6.0
```

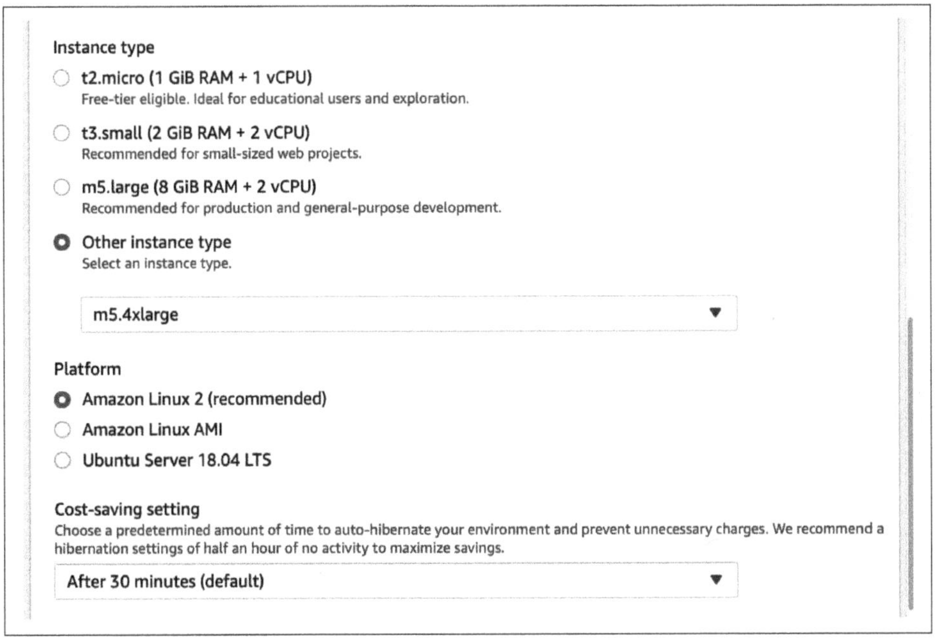

Figure 5-6. Select Cloud9 instance

Next, it is good to test the environment by creating a simple Console Application:

```
dotnet new console -o hello \
    && cd hello \
    && dotnet run

//Output of command below
The template "Console App" was created successfully.

Processing post-creation actions...
Running 'dotnet restore' on /home/ec2-user/environment/hello/hello.csproj...
  Determining projects to restore...
  Restored /home/ec2-user/environment/hello/hello.csproj (in 122 ms).
Restore succeeded.

Hello, World!
```

This test command works using the **dotnet** command-line interface, which allows for a new "Console App" without Visual Studio.

Containerized .NET 6 on Lambda

Another service supported by containers is AWS Lambda. A good reference point is an AWS Lambda Dockerfile (*https://gallery.ecr.aws/lambda/dotnet*). This document contains instructions on how to build AWS Lambda that targets the .NET 6 runtime. Another great resource is the official .NET 6 support on AWS (*https://oreil.ly/BSuv3*). Check out the chapter on serverless for more insights into building AWS Lambda.

To build containers, first, the Cloud9 environment needs resizing. Let's tackle that next.

Resizing

AWS Cloud9, when provisioned, has a minimal disk, and it can quickly get full when working with containers. It is good to resize your environment and clean up old container images you don't need. You can refer to the Bash script by AWS that allows you to resize Cloud9 (*https://oreil.ly/kcDFE*) easily.

You can find a copy of the script here (*https://oreil.ly/m4wgR*). To run it, you execute the following command, which resizes the instance to 50 GB:

```
chmod +x resize.sh
./resize.sh 50
```

After running this on your system, you'll see the following output. Notice that the mount point /dev/nvme0n1p1 now has 41G free:

```
ec2-user:~/environment/dot-net-6-aws (main) $ df -h
Filesystem        Size  Used Avail Use% Mounted on
devtmpfs          32G      0   32G   0% /dev
tmpfs             32G      0   32G   0% /dev/shm
tmpfs             32G   536K   32G   1% /run
tmpfs             32G      0   32G   0% /sys/fs/cgroup
/dev/nvme0n1p1    50G   9.6G   41G  20% /
tmpfs            6.3G      0  6.3G   0% /run/user/1000
tmpfs            6.3G      0  6.3G   0% /run/user/0
```

Next, let's build a containerized .NET 6 API.

Containerized .NET 6 API

Another way to develop .NET 6 is to build a microservice that deploys with a container service like AWS ECS or AWS App Runner. Both methods offer an efficient way to deploy an API with minimal effort. To get started, first create a new web API project in Cloud9:

```
dotnet new web -n WebServiceAWS
```

Running this in your Cloud9 environment generates the following output:

```
ec2-user:~/environment/dot-net-6-aws (main) $ dotnet new web -n WebServiceAWS
The template "ASP.NET Core Empty" was created successfully.
Processing post-creation actions...
Running 'dotnet restore' on ...WebServiceAWS/
Determining projects to restore...
Restored /home/ec2-user/environment/dot-net-6-aws/WebServiceAWS/
Restore succeeded.
```

Let's change the default code generated from the dotnet tool by adding a slightly fancier route to understand further the process of building containerized APIs. You can find more information about routing at ASP.NET Core here (*https://oreil.ly/bkU8x*). Note how similar this code looks to other high-level languages like Node, Ruby, Python, or Swift in the following example:

```
var builder = WebApplication.CreateBuilder(args);
var app = builder.Build();
app.MapGet("/", () => "Home Page");
app.MapGet("/hello/{name:alpha}", (string name) => $"Hello {name}!");
app.Run();
```

Now you can run this code by changing it into the directory using dotnet run:

```
cd WebServiceAWS && dotnet run
```

The output looks something like this in AWS Cloud9. Note how helpful it is to see the full content root path for your Cloud9 environment, making it easy to host multiple projects and switch back and forth between working on them:

```
ec2-user:~/environment/dot-net-6-aws (main) $ cd WebServiceAWS && dotnet run
Building...
info: Microsoft.Hosting.Lifetime[14]
      Now listening on: https://localhost:7117
info: Microsoft.Hosting.Lifetime[14]
      Now listening on: http://localhost:5262
info: Microsoft.Hosting.Lifetime[0]
      Application started. Press Ctrl+C to shut down.
      Content root path: /home/ec2-user/environment/dot-net-6-aws/WebServiceAWS/
```

You can see the output in Figure 5-7; note how you can toggle terminals side-by-side alongside the code.

This test works using the dotnet command-line interface. There are two separate curl commands: the first curl command invokes the homepage, and the second curl command invokes the route /hello/aws.

 The "HTTP" URL works in both curl commands, but "HTTPS" would return an invalid certificate issue.

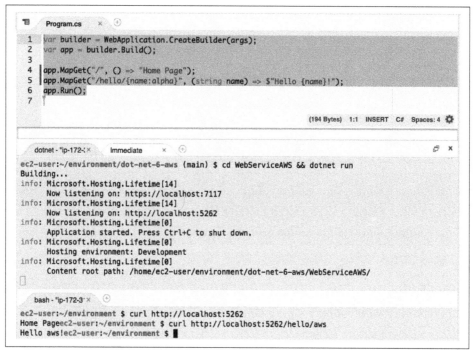

Figure 5-7. Cloud9 with ASP.NET

With the project working locally, let's move on to containerizing our code.

Containerize the Project

Now let's convert our project to using a container registered with the Amazon ECR. Once in the registry, our code is deployed to services that support containers. Our example is AWS App Runner, but it could also be Amazon ECS, Amazon EKS, or Amazon Batch, among the many container services on AWS. To do this, create a Dockerfile in the project folder:

```
FROM mcr.microsoft.com/dotnet/sdk:6.0 AS build ❶
WORKDIR /src
COPY ["WebServiceAWS.csproj", "./"]
RUN dotnet restore "WebServiceAWS.csproj"
COPY . .
WORKDIR "/src/."
RUN dotnet build "WebServiceAWS.csproj" -c Release -o /app/build
FROM build AS publish
RUN dotnet publish "WebServiceAWS.csproj" -c Release -o /app/publish
FROM mcr.microsoft.com/dotnet/aspnet:6.0 AS base
WORKDIR /app
EXPOSE 8080
ENV ASPNETCORE_URLS=http://+:8080
```

```
WORKDIR /app
COPY --from=publish /app/publish .
ENTRYPOINT ["dotnet", "WebServiceAWS.dll"] ❷
```

❶ Note how this container pulls in a .NET 6 runtime, configures the correct ports, and builds the project.

❷ Finally, it creates an entry point for the .dll.

Now build this container with the following command:

```
docker build . -t web-service-dotnet:latest
```

You can look at the container by using docker image ls. The output should look something like this:

```
web-service-dotnet  latest  3c191e7643d5   38 seconds ago   208MB
```

To run it, do the following:

```
docker run -p 8080:8080 web-service-dotnet:latest
```

The output should be similar to the following result:

```
listening on: {address}"}}
{"EventId":0,"LogLevel":"Information","Category"..}
{"EventId":0,"LogLevel":"Information","Category"...
...{contentRoot}"}}
```

Now invoke it via curl: curl http://localhost:8080/hello/aws as shown in Figure 5-8. Note how AWS Cloud9 provides a simple yet powerful cloud-based development environment with specialized features for developing on the AWS platform.

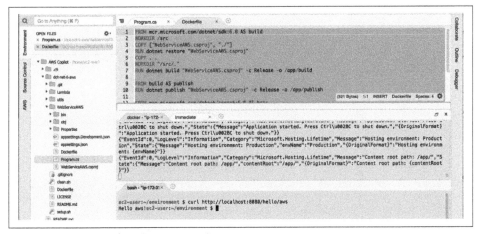

Figure 5-8. Containerized .NET 6 Web API

Next, let's discuss ECR and how it enables many new workflows on AWS.

Amazon Elastic Container Registry

An essential component in the new world of containers is a container registry optimized for the cloud you use. It securely allows the speedy deployment of deeply integrated cloud services. Amazon Elastic Container Registry (ECR) has the core services necessary for robust container strategies, as shown in Figure 5-9.

Figure 5-9. Amazon ECR

ECR enables workflows like developing in Cloud9 (or CloudShell), then automatically pushing a container to ECR (Elastic Container Registry) through AWS Code-Build. This build process triggers a continuous delivery pipeline to AWS App Runner, as shown in Figure 5-10.

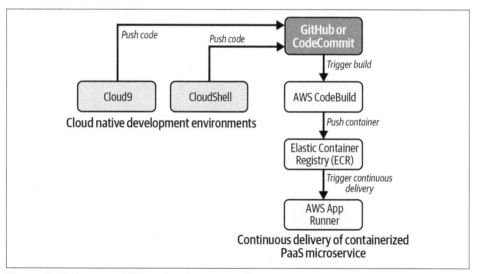

Figure 5-10. Amazon ECR to App Runner architecture

Create a new ECR repo by navigating to the AWS Console and searching for ECR. You can then create a new repo as shown in Figure 5-11 to use this ECR service.

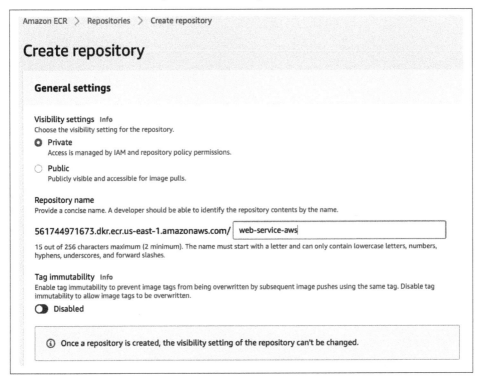

Figure 5-11. Create ECR repo

Next, click on the repo (located in the top-right corner of the web-service-aws repo page) to find the command necessary to push this container to ECR, as shown in Figure 5-12.

 These commands can easily integrate into an AWS CodeBuild pipeline for continuous delivery later by adding them to a *buildspec.yml* file and creating a new AWS CodeBuild pipeline that communicates with a source repo such as GitHub or AWS CodeCommit.

Next, run the ECR push commands in your local AWS Cloud9 environment. They will look similar to Figure 5-12. We named this repository web-service-aws, which then reflected in the build commands to push to ECR.

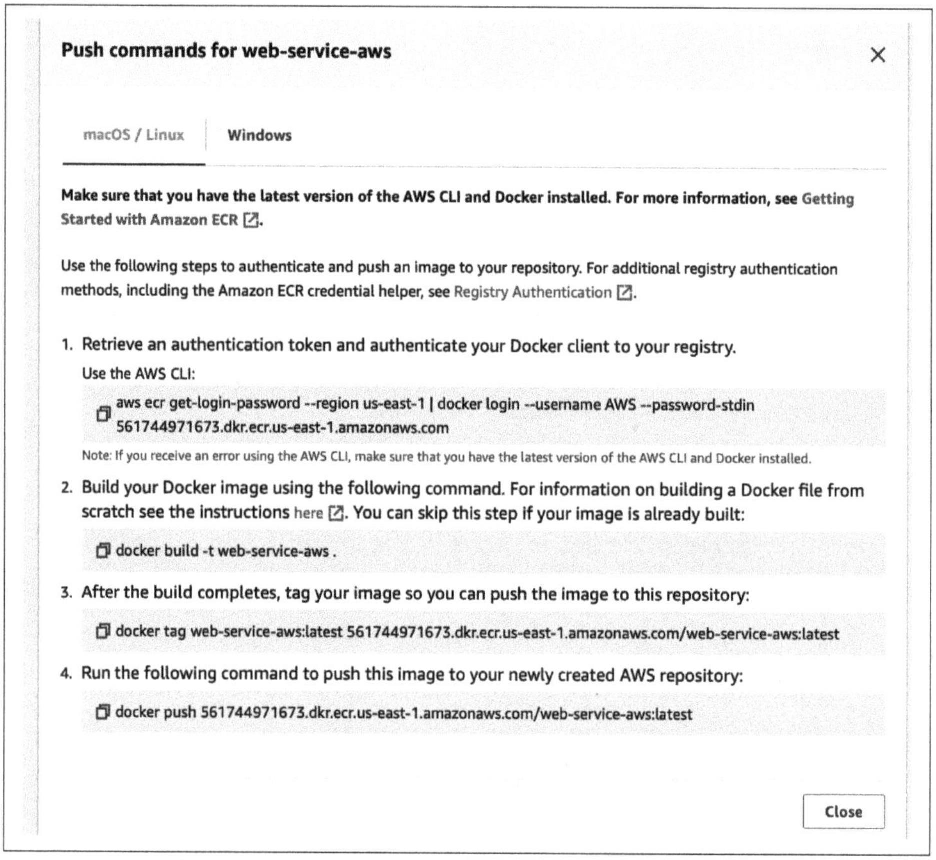

Push commands for web-service-aws   ✕

macOS / Linux | **Windows**

Make sure that you have the latest version of the AWS CLI and Docker installed. For more information, see Getting Started with Amazon ECR [↗].

Use the following steps to authenticate and push an image to your repository. For additional registry authentication methods, including the Amazon ECR credential helper, see Registry Authentication [↗].

1. Retrieve an authentication token and authenticate your Docker client to your registry.
   Use the AWS CLI:

   ```
   aws ecr get-login-password --region us-east-1 | docker login --username AWS --password-stdin
   561744971673.dkr.ecr.us-east-1.amazonaws.com
   ```
   Note: If you receive an error using the AWS CLI, make sure that you have the latest version of the AWS CLI and Docker installed.

2. Build your Docker image using the following command. For information on building a Docker file from scratch see the instructions here [↗]. You can skip this step if your image is already built:

   ```
   docker build -t web-service-aws .
   ```

3. After the build completes, tag your image so you can push the image to this repository:

   ```
   docker tag web-service-aws:latest 561744971673.dkr.ecr.us-east-1.amazonaws.com/web-service-aws:latest
   ```

4. Run the following command to push this image to your newly created AWS repository:

   ```
   docker push 561744971673.dkr.ecr.us-east-1.amazonaws.com/web-service-aws:latest
   ```

                                                                              Close

Figure 5-12. Push to ECR repo

Now check out the image as shown in Figure 5-13.

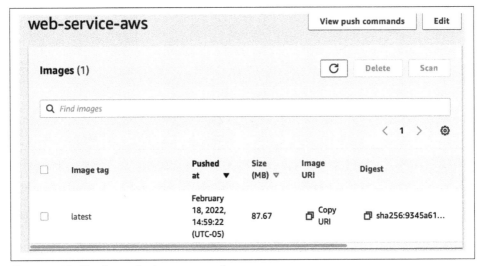

Figure 5-13. Check out the image created

 Note that the AWS App Runner service name is not required to link to either the container's name or the repository in ECR.

With ECR hosting our container, let's discuss using a service that can deploy it automatically.

App Runner

AWS App Runner is a compelling PaaS offering because it takes a complex problem, creates a secure microservice, and trivializes it, as shown in Figure 5-14. It makes it convenient for the developer by allowing a developer to deploy a container directly from ECR. Further, it will listen to the ECR repository, and when a new image deploys there, it triggers the deployment of a new version of AWS App Runner.

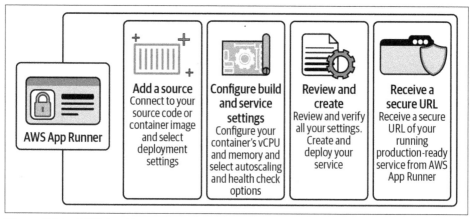

Figure 5-14. AWS App Runner

It requires very little work to take a containerized .NET 6 web API that lives in Amazon ECR and deploy it as a microservice with AWS App Runner. First, open the AWS App Runner and select the container image you built earlier, as shown in Figure 5-15.

Figure 5-15. Select ECR image

Next, select the deployment process, either manual or automatic, as shown in Figure 5-16. Automatic is typically what a developer building a production application wants because it will set up continuous delivery using ECR as the source of truth. Manual deployment may be the best option when initially trying the service out.

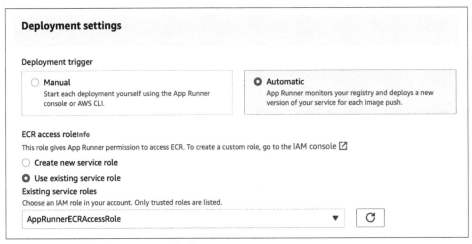

Deployment settings

Deployment trigger

○ **Manual**
Start each deployment yourself using the App Runner console or AWS CLI.

● **Automatic**
App Runner monitors your registry and deploys a new version of your service for each image push.

ECR access role Info
This role gives App Runner permission to access ECR. To create a custom role, go to the IAM console ☑

○ **Create new service role**
● **Use existing service role**
Existing service roles
Choose an IAM role in your account. Only trusted roles are listed.

| AppRunnerECRAccessRole | ▼ | C |

Figure 5-16. Select App Runner deployment process

Notice that there is an existing App Runner that we use in the deployment process that gives App Runner the ability to pull images from ECR. If you haven't set up an IAM role yet, you will need to create a new service role by selecting that checkbox instead. You can refer to the official App Runner documentation (*https://oreil.ly/EEHs2*) for a detailed walk-through of your setup options.

Now select the port the container exposes; this will match the port of the .NET 6 application Dockerfile configuration. In our case, it is 8080, as shown in Figure 5-17.

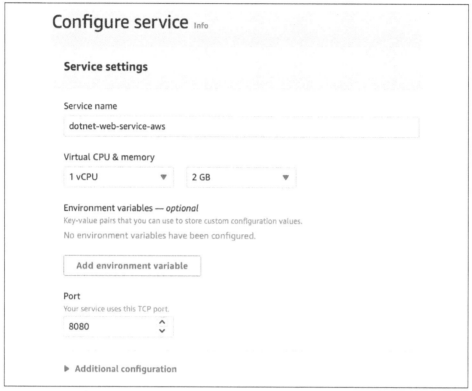

Configure service Info

Service settings

Service name

dotnet-web-service-aws

Virtual CPU & memory

1 vCPU ▼   2 GB ▼

Environment variables — *optional*
Key-value pairs that you can use to store custom configuration values.
No environment variables have been configured.

Add environment variable

Port
Your service uses this TCP port.

8080

▶ Additional configuration

Figure 5-17. Select App Runner port

Notice that this configuration used the default settings. You may want to configure many options, including setting environmental variables, health check configurations, and autoscaling configurations. You can refer to the latest documentation (*https://oreil.ly/q6zg8*) for detailed information on how to do these actions.

Finally, observe the service after creating it as shown in Figure 5-18. This step shows us that the service is deploying, and we can watch step by step as it becomes active by observing the event log.

Figure 5-18. Observe AWS App Runner service

After the service has initially deployed, you can "re-deploy" the application manually by selecting the deploy button. In the case of ECR, this will manually deploy the latest image in the repository. Likewise, any new push to ECR will trigger a redeployment of that image because of the automatic deployment configuration enablement.

Once the service runs, hop over to AWS CloudShell and run the following `curl` command in a CloudShell or Cloud9 terminal to invoke the API as shown in Figure 5-19. You can also invoke the API from any terminal that supports the `curl` command and a web browser.

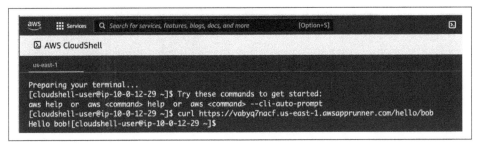

Figure 5-19. `curl` running service

You can also watch a walk-through of a containerized .NET 6 application from scratch on YouTube (*https://oreil.ly/qdD9B*) or O'Reilly (*https://oreil.ly/K7GHw*). The source code for this project in this repo (*https://github.com/noahgift/dot-net-6-aws*).

Managed Container Services with Amazon ECS

An important consideration when dealing with containers is where they run. In the case of your desktop or a cloud development environment like Cloud9, it is simple enough to launch a container and experiment with it using tools like Docker Desktop. Deployment gets more complex, though, in the real world, and this is where AWS-managed container services play a considerable role in creating robust deployment targets.

The two options on the AWS platform that provide a comprehensive end-to-end solution for managing containers at scale are Amazon Elastic Kubernetes Service (Amazon EKS) and Amazon Elastic Container Service (Amazon ECS). Let's discuss the homegrown Amazon solution, ECS, in detail next.

Amazon ECS is a fully managed container orchestration service and a central hub of compute options, as shown in Figure 5-20. Starting with ECR, which stores built container images, the ECS service allows for application definition using container images coupled with compute options. Finally, ECS scales your application seamlessly using AWS best practices like elasticity and availability.

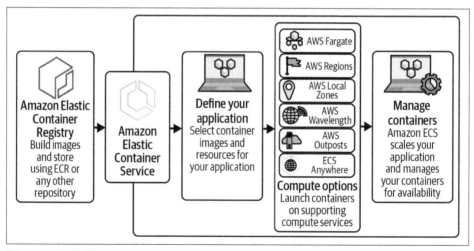

Figure 5-20. ECS

There are two common ways of deploying to ECS for .NET developers. The first is AWS Copilot (*https://oreil.ly/LYFrv*) and the second is the AWS .NET deployment tool (*https://oreil.ly/uBdJZ*). The newer .NET deployment tool has the advantage that it can also deploy to App Runner and Beanstalk.

Further, ECS supports three essential use cases. Let's spell these out:

Hybrid scenario
> Build a container anywhere and run it anywhere with Amazon ECS Anywhere.

Batch processing scenario
> Orchestrate batch processing across AWS services, including EC2, Fargate, and Spot Instances.

Scale web scenario
> Build and deploy scalable web applications built with Amazon best practices.

> Amazon ECS supports Linux as well as Windows containers (*https://oreil.ly/BehOC*). Note the following essentials on Windows containers: First, they support tasks that use the EC2 and Fargate launch types. Also, not all task definition parameters for Linux containers are available. Finally, Windows container instances require more storage space than Linux containers.

The best possible way to get started with ECS is through the .NET deployment tool AWS .NET deployment tool for the .NET CLI (*https://oreil.ly/IdeWu*). Let's enumerate the key features of this tool:

Serverless deploy
> This tool creates a deployment to AWS Elastic Beanstalk or Amazon ECS via AWS Fargate (*https://aws.amazon.com/fargate*).

Cloud native to Linux deploy
> This implementation deploys cloud-native .NET applications built on .NET Core 2.1 and later targeting Linux.

Deploys utility .NET applications
> Many .NET utilities have deployment capabilities, including ASP.NET Core web apps, Blazor WebAssembly apps, long-running service apps, and scheduled tasks.

> AWS Fargate is a technology that you can use with Amazon ECS to run containers without managing servers or clusters of Amazon EC2 instances. With this technology, you no longer have to provision, configure, or scale clusters of virtual machines to run containers.

Let's use `dotnet aws deploy` to deploy to ECS Fargate. We can leverage both AWS Cloud9 and Blazor (*https://oreil.ly/5W2FA*) for this. First, let's update the tool to ensure the latest version of the deployment tool is enabled. Since this tool is under active development, it is a best practice to update it often using the following command:

```
dotnet tool update -g aws.deploy.tools
```

Now observe the entire software development lifecycle as shown in Figure 5-21.

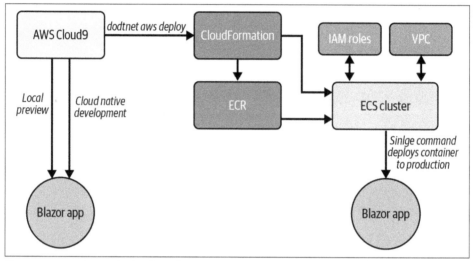

Figure 5-21. ECS and Cloud9 software development lifecycle

To create a new Blazor application, use the following command:

```
dotnet new blazorserver -o BlazorApp -f net6.0
```

Next, change into the Blazor directory:

```
cd BlazorApp
```

You can run the application on port 8080 via the following `dotnet` command:

```
dotnet run --urls=http://localhost:8080
```

Select the preview functionality with the application running as shown in Figure 5-22 to view it as a web page in the IDE.

Figure 5-22. Blazor in Cloud9

> Note that AWS Cloud9 uses ports 8080, 8081, or 8082 for preview
> (*https://oreil.ly/bZQi8*).

Now that we know the application works locally, let's change the Index.razor page to the following content before deploying to AWS by editing in the Cloud9 IDE:

```
@page "/"
<PageTitle>Index</PageTitle>
<h1>Hello, AWS dotnet aws deploy!</h1>
Welcome to your new app.
```

Additionally, create a Dockerfile in the project directory with the following content. This step allows for customization of the runtime for ECS:

```
FROM mcr.microsoft.com/dotnet/sdk:6.0 AS build
WORKDIR /src
COPY ["BlazorApp.csproj", "./"]
RUN dotnet restore "BlazorApp.csproj"
COPY . .
RUN dotnet publish "BlazorApp.csproj" -c Release -o /app/publish
FROM mcr.microsoft.com/dotnet/aspnet:6.0 AS base
WORKDIR /app
```

```
EXPOSE 80
EXPOSE 443
WORKDIR /app
COPY --from=build /app/publish
ENTRYPOINT ["dotnet", "BlazorApp.dll"]
```

Finally, with these steps out of the way, it is time to deploy to ECS Fargate using the following command in a new Cloud9 terminal:

```
dotnet aws deploy
```

When prompted, you will see several options and should select the number associated with ASP.NET Core App to Amazon ECS using Fargate, as shown in the following (truncated) code output. The numbers could be different depending on the conditions of your environment, so select the number associated with Fargate.

```
Recommended Deployment Option
1: ASP.NET Core App to Amazon ECS using Fargate...
```

For the following prompts, you should select "Enter" to use the default options except Desired Task Count: 3, which you should change to a single task or 1. This process will initiate the container push to ECR and the subsequent deployment to ECS.

 Note a common problem when working with containers in a cloud-based development environment is running out of space. One brute force way of solving this problem is periodically deleting all local container images using the command docker rmi -f $ (docker images -aq).

Once the deployment finishes, we can test the application using the URL generated from the deploy command, as shown in Figure 5-23.

Figure 5-23. Blazor deployed to ECS Fargate

You can watch a complete walk-through of this deployment process on YouTube (*https://youtu.be/Xs9vGM3U2Ek*) or the O'Reilly Platform (*https://oreil.ly/ScFrj*). The source code for the example is available on GitHub (*https://oreil.ly/v9O1N*).

With the deployment successfully tested, it would be good to clean up your stack by first listing the deployments with the following command: `dotnet aws list-deployments`. Next, you can delete the stack `dotnet aws delete-deployment <stack-name>`.

 One item to be aware of in deploying to Blazor to Fargate is that you will need to make one of the following changes to deploy without errors:

- Create a single task instead of three (which is the default).
- Turn on stickiness in the EC2 Target Group (*https://oreil.ly/vELfc*).

Now that our ECS example is complete, let's wrap up the chapter and discuss the next steps.

Conclusion

New technology opens up new ways to solve problems. Cloud computing enables near-infinite computing and storage through virtualization, allowing more sophisticated technologies to build on it. One of those technologies is containers, and it has many advanced service integrations available on AWS.

Nonintuitively, new technologies often open up new ways to work. We covered how AWS Cloud9 offers a new and exciting way to work with containers due to deep integration with the AWS ecosystem. This deep integration includes access to highly performant compute, storage, and networking beyond what a typical home or work desktop offering can provide. You may find that Cloud9 is a trusty complement to a traditional Visual Studio workflow and allows you to do some development tasks more efficiently.

There is no better investment for a .NET developer than mastering containers. This chapter went through the foundations of containers and serves as a foundation for building more complex solutions later in the book. In the next chapter, we expand on many of these topics by tackling DevOps on AWS. DevOps topics covered include AWS Code Build, AWS Code Pipeline, and how to integrate with third-party servers like GitHub Actions, TeamCity, and Jenkins. Before reading that chapter, you may want to go through the critical thinking discussions and exercise discussions.

Critical Thinking Discussion Questions

- How can you manage the size of container images?
- What is the best AWS container service for small start-ups?
- What is the best AWS container service for large companies that use containers extensively for batch computing?
- What is the advantage of using Amazon Linux 2 to deploy .NET 6?
- What is the disadvantage of using Amazon Linux 2 to deploy .NET 6?

Exercises

- Take the containerized project built in this chapter and deploy it via continuous delivery through AWS CodeBuild.[7]
- Build your own AWS Lambda container that targets .NET 6 and deploy it to AWS.
- Use Cloud9 to invoke an AWS Lambda function you deploy.
- Build another container that uses .NET 6 and Amazon Linux 2 and push it to ECR.
- Build a Console App command-line tool that targets .NET 6 and uses the AWS SDK to call AWS Comprehend and push this to a public ECR repo.

---

7 You can refer to the *buildspec.yml* file (*https://github.com/noahgift/dot-net-6-aws*) for ideas.

## CHAPTER 6

DevOps

There is a collective realization amongst industry professionals that cloud computing enables new workflows. For example, cloud-native solutions like serverless computing open new ways to architect solutions in an event-driven manner. Likewise, the underlying elastic capabilities of cloud computing enable virtualized storage, networking, and computing. DevOps, a blend of practices combining software development and operations best practices, is one ideal methodology to harness these new workflows.

This chapter's central focus is identifying the importance of DevOps to utilize cloud computing fully. It covers getting started on DevOps for AWS and principles supporting DevOps rooted in Japanese culture.

Getting Started with DevOps on AWS

An ideal way to get started with DevOps on AWS is with a definition of how AWS sees DevOps (*https://oreil.ly/UAhEl*): "the combination of cultural philosophies, practices, and tools that increases an organization's ability to deliver applications and services at high velocity." In practice, this means that AWS provides managed services that support a high-velocity workflow enabled by DevOps.

Underneath the surface of DevOps is a definite historical trend of organizational best practices supporting the rise of DevOps. Let's discuss these concepts next.

What Are the Principles Behind DevOps?

At the heart of DevOps is the Japanese word *Kaizen*, meaning "improvement" or "change for the better." In *The Toyota Way*, Second Edition (O'Reilly), Jeffrey K. Liker mentions that post-World War II Toyota developed a lean manufacturing system that incorporated this Kaizen philosophy. Ultimately, this philosophy led to Toyota being one of the leaders in automobile manufacturing quality.

One of the core principles of the Toyota Production System is that assembly line workers will stop the moving production line to fix abnormalities. Another way to describe this process is Plan-Do-Check-Act, or PDCA cycle, which is shown in Figure 6-1. First, a problem needs identification; next, you try out a solution, analyze the results, implement the fix if it solves the problem, or repeat the entire PDCA process.

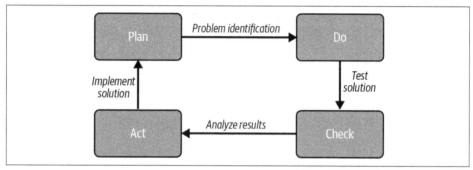

Figure 6-1. Plan-Do-Check-Act lifecycle

Essentially, PDCA is the scientific method implemented as a manufacturing business practice.

 According to *Encylopedia Britannica*, the scientific method (*https://oreil.ly/MP7G4*) is a "mathematical and experimental technique employed in the sciences. More specifically, it is the technique used in the construction and testing of a scientific hypothesis."

Related to both Kaizen and the scientific method is the 5 Whys technique in debugging the root cause of a problem. This technique works in the following manner. First, you identify a problem. Next, you ask "why" when you receive an answer, you ask why again, until ultimately, by the fifth time, you get to the root cause of the issue and have a solution to fix it. The origin of 5 Whys has a historical lineage to the Toyota Production System, and it works well with the concept of continuously improving a system. In Figure 6-2, a real scenario on AWS goes through the five stages of debugging.

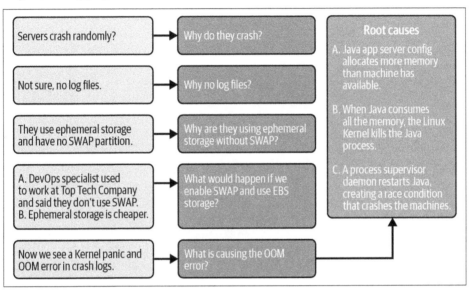

Figure 6-2. Using 5 Whys to debug a production system

 Children are intuitively very good at the 5 Whys technique, which is why they ask simple, practical questions such as, "Why is the sky blue?" followed by the next question. An incredible way to get in the right mindframe for using the 5 Whys technique is to ask questions the way a child would ask them.

Notice that the series of questions eventually leads to a reasonably straightforward fix, i.e., configure machines differently, i.e., use EBS storage, enable a swap partition, and configure the memory constraints of the Java process to match the resources on the server.

As you can see, DevOps isn't something invented overnight. DevOps derives from centuries of improvements in critical thinking, from the scientific method centuries ago to, more recently, Kaizen and the Japanese automobile industry. At the heart of DevOps is the ancient concept of the scientific method, i.e., asking why. The Japanese automobile industry refined this into the methodology of asking why coupled with continuous improvement in manufacturing. DevOps is the further refinement of this continuous improvement manufacturing methodology in the software engineering domain, which is now ideally suited to cloud-native development. Now that we know where DevOps came from, let's discuss the best practices on the AWS platform.

AWS DevOps Best Practices

An ideal place to start with AWS best practices is the "Introduction to DevOps on AWS" (*https://oreil.ly/dfLzx*) AWS whitepaper. Inside there are six best practices listed:

Continuous integration (CI)

The heart and soul of DevOps is a continuous integration system. Developers periodically merge changes into a central source control repository where automated tests run on the code. You can see the workflow around CI in Figure 6-3. A developer in one environment, perhaps a laptop or Cloud9 workspace, pushes changes to the source code repository, triggers the build, tests the code, and allows it to merge. Later, a second developer pulls these improvements into their checkout in a new local environment. Note the tie-in to the concept of Kaizen here, or continuous improvement, since each time the build server tests changes, the system can improve the quality of the source code.

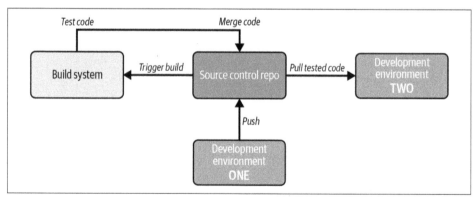

Figure 6-3. Continuous integration workflow

Continuous delivery (CD)

Continuous delivery builds on the concepts of continuous integration by automatically testing software pushed into the repository and preparing the software for release to any number of environments. In Figure 6-4, you'll see the foundation established by CI. Now, with the addition of IaC, which automatically deploys the infrastructure alongside the existing software, the entire system can seamlessly deploy to a new environment because the whole process is automated. In a CD workflow, containers are a complementary aspect of the deployment since they work side by side with the deployment of the code and infrastructure. Kaizen again plays a role in deploying improvements automatically. Each commit to the source code repository adds improvements to the system, and since changes are easy to make, it encourages frequent minor enhancements.

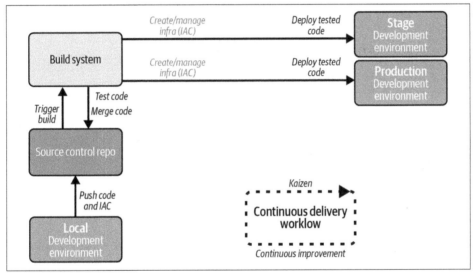

Figure 6-4. Continuous delivery workflow

Infrastructure as Code (IaC)

IaC is a software development best practice that describes treating the provisioning and management of Infrastructure as Code checked into a repository. Looking at Figure 6-5, the IaC workflow can do many valuable actions beyond initially creating the infrastructure. Some of the use cases of IaC include making idempotent changes and cleaning up experiments efficiently by deleting the entire stack.

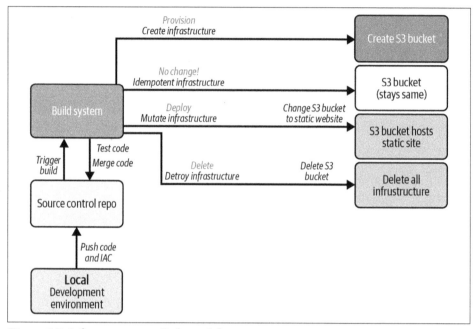

Figure 6-5. Infrastructure as Code workflow

 Idempotent is a word frequently used with DevOps because it is essential to be able to do the same action repeatedly and always have the same state. An outstanding example of an idempotent deployment process is IaC that creates an S3 bucket with read-only permissions. No matter how often this code runs, the result will be the same: an S3 bucket with read-only permissions.

The concept of idempotent actions is essential in DevOps because an automated agile workflow depends on automation actions that have the same effect no matter how often they run. A fantastic example of the mathematical foundations of idempotency is multiplying a series of numbers by zero. The result is always zero, no matter what number you multiply by zero.

Monitoring and logging

Data science for software systems is a unique way to think about monitoring and logging. It is essential to use data about the infrastructure and deployed application to determine what actions are necessary to maintain a deployed application. In Figure 6-6, servers send system- and application-level logging, metrics, and data from monitoring agents to AWS CloudWatch, where the data is centralized and distributed to dashboards, alerts, search, and automated insights.

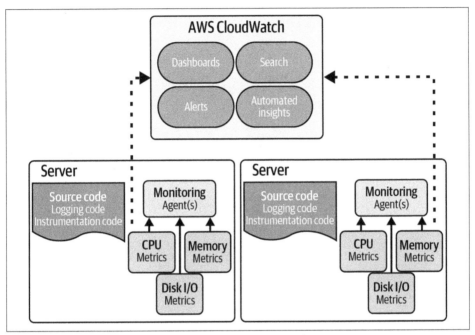

Figure 6-6. Monitoring and logging is data science for software systems

Communication and collaboration

DevOps is a behavior, not a specific task to check off a list. As a result, when teams work together to implement DevOps practices through communication and collaboration, an optimal outcome results. In Figure 6-7, we see that communication embeds in every step of the DevOps lifecycle, from code itself and the conversation around it, to the alerts from production systems that emit into a chat channel. Note also the possible human interactions on pull requests, pushing to production, and monitoring the application in production.

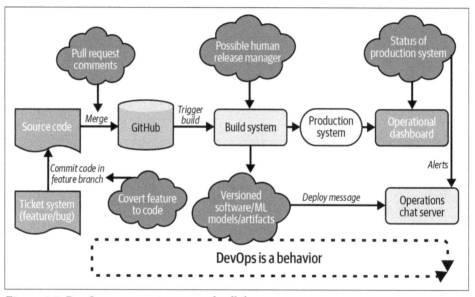

Figure 6-7. DevOps communication and collaboration

Security

Security needs integration at every level of building a software system. Additionally, the continuous integration and delivery systems need strict access control governance as they deliver software to production. In Figure 6-8, notice multiple layers of security in an adequately architected system on the AWS cloud. This system includes firewall rules layered into a VPC to prevent unauthorized network access and policy control that leverages the principle of least privilege to secure the system. Encryption for data in transit and rest hardens the environment against leaked data. Finally, auditing all security events via AWS CloudTrail and two-factor authentication for access to the AWS console adds even more protection.

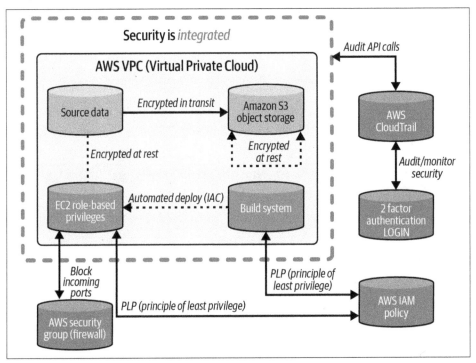

Figure 6-8. DevOps security integration

These core DevOps principles are essential to consider when architecting a modern solution on the AWS Cloud. Let's dive deeper into specific CI/CD (continuous integration and continuous delivery) services on the AWS platform.

Developing with CI/CD on AWS

Several AWS-managed services deal with CI/CD, but two critical services are AWS CodeBuild (*https://aws.amazon.com/codebuild*) and CodePipeline (*https://aws.amazon.com/codepipeline*). Let's dive into how they both work.

AWS Code Deploy Services

AWS CodePipeline, AWS CodeBuild, AWS CodeCommit, and AWS CodeDeploy are deeply integrated services on AWS and include complementary workflows. AWS CodePipeline is a continuous integration and continuous delivery (CI/CD) managed service that fully automates software releases. AWS CodeBuild is a fully managed build service that handles the components of a build process, including testing, building, and releasing packages. AWS CodeDeploy is a managed service that automates the code deployment to any instance, including EC2 instances or on-premise servers. Finally, AWS CodeCommit is a fully managed code hosting service similar to GitHub or GitLab.

Let's take a look at the AWS CodePipeline in Figure 6-9 and notice how it flows from left to right: source, then build, then test, then staging, then production. This workflow encapsulates the lifecycle of a project in the real world running on AWS.

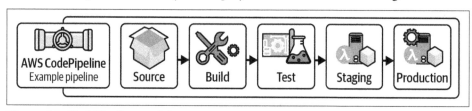

Figure 6-9. CodePipeline workflow

Next, if you open the AWS Console and type in **CodePipeline**, the interface that pops up is, as shown in Figure 6-10, mapping these same real-world steps to distinct stages in the process of deploying software on the AWS platform.

Developer Tools

CodeDeploy

▶ **Source** • CodeCommit

▶ **Artifacts** • CodeArtifact

▶ **Build** • CodeBuild

▼ **Deploy** • CodeDeploy

    Getting started

    Deployments

    Applications

    Deployment configurations

    On-premises instances

▶ **Pipeline** • CodePipeline

▶ **Settings**

Figure 6-10. CodePipeline interface

Since we already briefly covered continuous delivery of a .NET 6 application using AWS CodeBuild in Chapter 5, let's take a different look at how we could be continuously deploying a Hugo website (*https://gohugo.io*) using AWS CodeBuild. AWS is a common deployment target for hosting a static website via Amazon S3, Amazon Route 53, and Amazon CloudFront, as shown in Figure 6-11. AWS CodeBuild works very well as the deployment mechanism for these sites. You can log into AWS Code-Build, set up a new build project, and tell it to use a *buildspec.yml* (*https://oreil.ly/KNRop*).

 Hugo is a unique static website hosting technology written in the Go programming language (*https://go.dev*) that builds pages at <1ms per page. You don't need to use Go to use Hugo; you can write websites in the Markdown language (*https://oreil.ly/uF0Tk*). The speed to build websites and the ease of writing pages in Markdown make Hugo a superior technology for S3 static websites.

Once GitHub gets a change event, CodeBuild runs the install in a container:

1. It grabs the specific version of Hugo noted in the *buildspec.yml*.

2. It builds the Hugo pages. Thousands of Hugo pages can be rendered in subseconds because of the speed of Go.

3. The HTML pages sync to Amazon S3.

Because this sync process runs inside of AWS, it is also speedy.

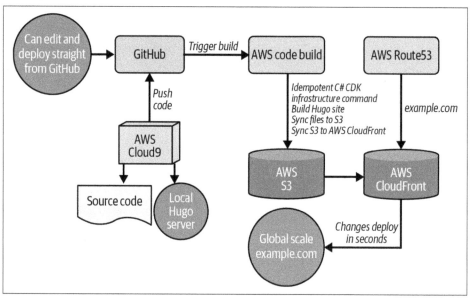

Figure 6-11. Hugo continuous deploy on AWS

Following is a more templated version of an AWS *buildspec.yml*, and you can swap out templated values with ones that work for your project:

```
version: 0.1

environment_variables:
  plaintext:
    HUGO_VERSION: "0.42"

phases:
  install:
    commands:
      - cd /tmp
      - wget https://github.com/gohugoio/hugo/releases/\
      download/v${HUGO_VERSION}/hugo_${HUGO_VERSION}_Linux-64bit.tar.gz
      - tar -xzf hugo_${HUGO_VERSION}_Linux-64bit.tar.gz
      - mv hugo /usr/bin/hugo
      - cd -
```

```
        - rm -rf /tmp/*
  build:
    commands:
      - rm -rf public
      - hugo
  post_build:
    commands:
      - aws s3 sync public/ s3://<yourwebsite>.com/ --region us-west-2 --delete
      - aws s3 cp s3://<yourwebsite>.com/\
      s3://<yourwebsite>.com/ --metadata-directive REPLACE \
        --cache-control 'max-age=604800' --recursive
      - aws cloudfront create-invalidation --distribution-id=<YOURID> --paths '/*'
      - echo Build completed on `date`
```

> You can watch a complete walk-through of Hugo continuous delivery on YouTube here (*https://oreil.ly/UjqS0*), and also follow along with notes on Hugo on the Pragmatic AI Labs website (*https://oreil.ly/saRAN*).

Now that we have more insight into the pure AWS build solution, let's discuss how third-party build servers work with .NET on AWS.

Integrating Third-Party Build Servers

Not only can you use AWS build servers to build and deploy .NET to AWS, but there is beautiful support for third-party build servers, including Jenkins (*https://www.jenkins.io*), Azure DevOps (*https://oreil.ly/wwt7c*), and GitHub Actions (*https://docs.github.com/en/actions*). Let's mainly focus on GitHub Actions since it is the most widely used managed build service.

> You can watch a walk-through of setting up a C# xUnit project with GitHub Actions on YouTube (*https://youtu.be/6OkcNWGA6FY*).

In building solutions with GitHub Actions, an ideal place to make code solutions is with GitHub CodeSpaces (*https://oreil.ly/YH0i2*), as shown launching in Figure 6-12. The code for the repository lives here (*https://oreil.ly/BlklG*), and by selecting the green Code button, we can launch a 16-core workspace that has a clean Visual Studio interface.

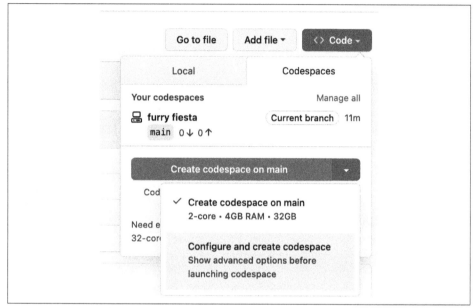

Figure 6-12. GitHub CodeSpaces

 GitHub CodeSpaces is a paid service that allows development in a web-based development environment. If your organization does not have access to this service, an alternative is AWS Cloud9, which has many similar features, but with the advantage of deep AWS integration.

Notice that we created a file inside the path *.github/workflows* called *dotnet.yml*, which contains the entire workflow to build and test our project as shown in Figure 6-13.

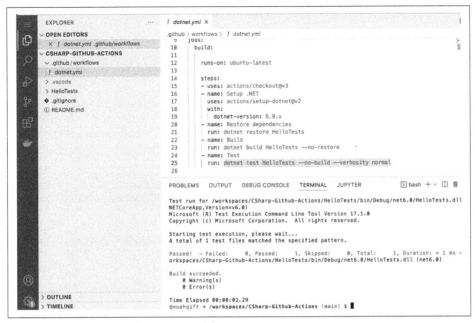

Figure 6-13. GitHub CodeSpaces workflow

The *dotnet.yml* shows that the key steps are to restore the dependency, build the project, and then test the project:

```
name: .NET
on:
  push:
    branches: [ "main" ]
jobs:
  build:
    runs-on: ubuntu-latest
    steps:
    - uses: actions/checkout@v3
    - name: Setup .NET
      uses: actions/setup-dotnet@v2
      with:
        dotnet-version: 5.0.x
    - name: Restore dependencies ❶
      run: dotnet restore
    - name: Build ❷
      run: dotnet build --no-restore
    - name: Test ❸
      run: dotnet test --no-build --verbosity normal
```

❶ Restore dependencies.

❷ Build the project.

❸ Test the project.

To create the structure for the project, first, create a directory and cd into it:

```
mkdir HelloTests && cd HelloTests
```

Next, use dotnet new xunit to create the project. Finally, paste the following code block inside your source code file. Let's walk through what the code does:

```
using Xunit;

namespace MyFirstUnitTests
{
    public class UnitTest1
    {
        [Fact] ❶
        public void PassingTest()
        {
            Assert.Equal(4, Add(2, 2));
        }
        int Add(int x, int y) ❷
        {
            return x + y;
        }
    }
}
```

❶ The [Fact] block is the unit test that tests the `add` function

❷ There is an "inline" method, Add, which we run tests on.

To run this project, you perform the following actions:

1. Install the dependencies: dotnet restore.

2. Build the project: dotnet build --no-restore.

3. Test the project: dotnet test --no-build --verbosity normal.

You can see the final output in Figure 6-14 showing a successful run of GitHub Actions. What is extremely useful about this entire workflow is how easy it is to add steps for a project, like deploying to AWS. A helpful blog post on AWS shows a detailed example of how to deploy code to AWS from GitHub Actions (*https://oreil.ly/ jNRng*).

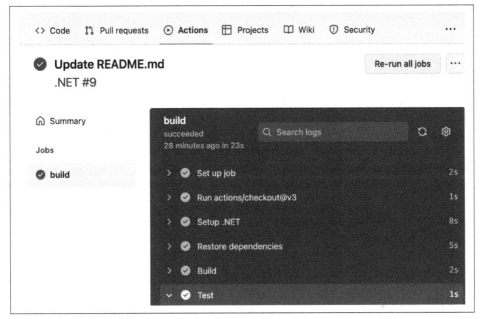

Figure 6-14. GitHub Actions build process

 It is also worth noting that many AWS services or tools have automatic pipelines built in:

AWS App Runner
AWS App Runner (*https://oreil.ly/mIA74*) has a feature for automatic deployments from GitHub. When you connect App Runner to your code repository or container image registry, App Runner can automatically build and deploy your application when you update your source code or container image.

AWS Copilot
AWS Copilot (*https://oreil.ly/YQVjZ*) can provision multiple deployment environments for you, such as testing and production environments. Additionally, Copilot can set up a CI/CD pipeline to automatically deploy.

Integration with Partner Products

It is worth noting that there are many great options for third-party partner products, including Jenkins, TeamCity, Azure DevOps, and Terraform. A great place to highlight integrations with AWS CodeDeploy is the "Integration with partner products and services" section of the AWS documentation (*https://oreil.ly/cof1J*). Here are standout highlighted resources:

Jenkins

Jenkins is an open source Swiss Army knife of build systems, and AWS provides outstanding support. One key advantage of Jenkins is the ability to mount a network filesystem on AWS and integrate that with your build and deploy process. You can read about how to set up CI/CD pipelines with Jenkins (*https://oreil.ly/es2pf*) with AWS App2Container as well as use AWS CodeBuild with Jenkins (*https://oreil.ly/MEAe7*).

TeamCity

TeamCity is a classic build system that many experienced and new .NET developers love. A team using TeamCity can use the AWS CodeDeploy Runner plugin (*https://oreil.ly/RisFO*) to deploy directly to AWS.

Azure DevOps

AWS App2Container has integration with Microsoft Azure DevOps (*https://oreil.ly/sKTWK*). The AWS Toolkit for Azure DevOps (*https://aws.amazon.com/vsts*) allows you to deploy .NET code to AWS without leaving the existing build/release pipeline.

Terraform

HashiCorp has integration with AWS CodeDeploy (*https://oreil.ly/NhcdI*), allowing developers to not only use Terraform CDK in C# (*https://www.terraform.io/cdktf*), but also products like Consul (*https://oreil.ly/MoiAW*).

Now that you understand how to integrate tests with third-party partner integrations, including GitHub Actions, let's discuss IaC.

Developing with IaC on AWS

IaC is code that defines the infrastructure and maintains it. Ultimately, containers and IaC are complementary technologies on the AWS platform. Notice in Figure 6-15 that GitHub contains the essential elements of a project, including the build system file, the IaC file, the source code, and the Dockerfile.

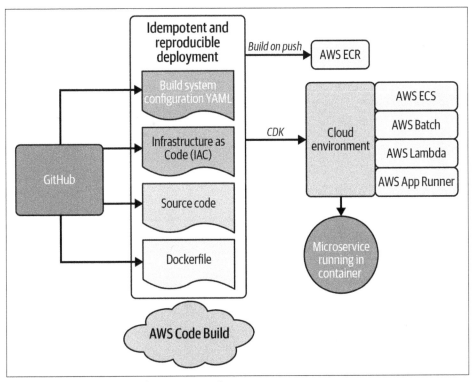

Figure 6-15. AWS-flavored containerized DevOps

In many scenarios, you could have all elements of a containerized microservice defined in a single repository, making it easy to debug and build locally or in a new environment. IaC enables part of this workflow. Let's talk about how an AWS IaC solution called Cloud Development Kit (CDK)) helps with this.

Working with AWS CDK in C#

AWS CDK (*https://aws.amazon.com/cdk*) is open source and supported by AWS. It provides many benefits, including faster development and rich examples (*https://oreil.ly/xrLwb*). The unit of deployment (*https://oreil.ly/mG6iD*) in the AWS CDK is called a *stack*. For example, to create two stacks representing a "development" and "production" environment, use the following C# code:

```
var app = new App();

new MyFirstStack(app, "dev");
new MySecondStack(app, "prod");

app.Synth();
```

To synthesize one stack, you run cdk synth dev. Behind the scenes, this then creates the CloudFormation template (*https://oreil.ly/UtxOT*).

 It is worth noting that constructs (*https://oreil.ly/l2j1s*) are fundamental building blocks of AWS CDK apps and contain everything necessary to build a resource, say an S3 bucket. The Construct Hub (*https://constructs.dev*) includes over 600 .NET CDK constructs and is a recommended resource for building solutions efficiently and with AWS's best practices behind you.

You can see the concepts defined in Figure 6-16. At the core of CDK is the idea of writing code that then turns into infrastructure since the infrastructure is a virtual resource. Notice that the C# language compiles down to CloudFormation (*https://oreil.ly/pBAiY*), which then provisions resources.

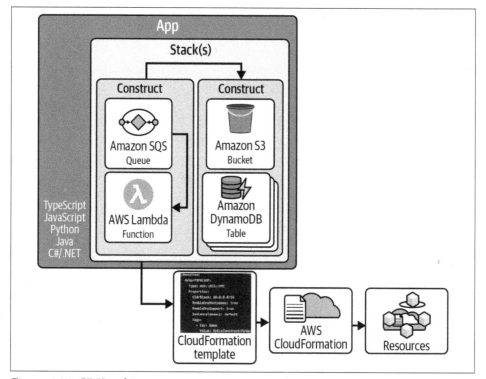

Figure 6-16. CDK architecture

AWS CloudFormation (*https://oreil.ly/lfNIR*) is a form of IaC that lets you manage AWS resources by treating infrastructure as code written in JSON or YAML. Some developers prefer CDK over regular CloudFormation because it takes less code to build the same solution. Further, you can create solutions in your favorite language, such as C#. This blog post (*https://oreil.ly/CMBVE*) is a perfect example of what you can do with CloudFormation and .NET.

In practice, a developer can use one of two approaches with CDK. The first approach is to write CDK in C#, and there is a rich toolchain of examples, including many exciting examples on the .NET Workshop page (*https://oreil.ly/acwT1*). A second approach is to use a high-level abstraction that generates the CDK code for you, like `dotnet aws deploy`.

One example of this approach comes from the AWS Deploy Tool to deploy a Blazor WebAssembly application (*https://oreil.ly/O9AfD*). The key idea is that you must run `dotnet aws deploy`.

For example, in your development environment, you can do the following:

1. Install or update the `dotnet` AWS deploy tool: `dotnet tool install -g aws.deploy.tools`.

2. Create a new Blazor WebAssembly application: `dotnet new blazorserver -o BlazorApp --no-https && BlazorApp`.

3. Finally, deploy by running the command `dotnet aws deploy`.

You can refer to the latest documentation on GitHub (*https://oreil.ly/RUgOb*) to check out the latest options for using this deployment process.

There are IaC solutions beyond just CDK. One of the more popular is Terraform (*https://www.terraform.io/cdktf*), which has a CDKTF or Cloud Development Kit for Terraform with C# support. Another solution provider is Pulumi, and you can find a great example of how to publish a C# Lambda, here (*https://oreil.ly/3y4NQ*).

As a final point, it is essential to point out that some AWS tools automatically create and deploy CDK projects. Examples include the AWS deployment tool for .NET CLI (*https://oreil.ly/ZmsmQ*) and AWS Toolkit for Visual Studio—Publish to AWS feature (*https://oreil.ly/jXtPb*). Additionally, with CDK deployment projects (*https://oreil.ly/WHjKB*), you can add additional AWS resources like Amazon SQS queues, Amazon DynamoDB tables, and more.

Now that we have an overview of Infrastructure as Code, let's wrap up everything we covered in this chapter.

Conclusion

This chapter covered the historical origin of DevOps, including this history of continuous improvement in the Japanese automobile industry. At the heart of modern DevOps is an embrace of the cloud. Cloud computing enables even deeper coupling of automation, testing, and speed of deployment. One example of this integration is IaC, which is the perfect vehicle for DevOps workflows. DevOps also enables optimal human interaction at key points of the lifecycle of software engineering, from code reviews via pull requests to working with a release manager on a production software release to finally monitoring the production system.

Another topic we covered is how AWS thinks of DevOps and the best practices of DevOps on AWS. We then used build systems like AWS CodeBuild and third-party systems like GitHub Actions. AWS has tight integration of each component and can replace any third-party tool if your organization chooses or integrates with them.

Finally, we ended the chapter with IaC, an essential tool for DevOps automation of infrastructure. We showed how you could do a one-line command to deploy static websites to AWS S3 using the AWS .NET deployment tool. This tool's ability to wrap up CDK and make it part of the automation lifecycle is extremely powerful.

This chapter's big takeaway is that AWS takes DevOps seriously and provides a whole set of managed services and best practices to enable you to build maintainable and agile solutions. Next up in Chapter 7, we cover logging, monitoring, and instrumentation for .NET, which builds upon the foundational knowledge we covered on DevOps. Before heading to that chapter, try some critical thinking questions and examples to cement your DevOps understanding further.

Critical Thinking Discussion Questions

- What is your definition of DevOps, and how can you use it to enhance organizational outcomes?
- What is the advantage of using the .NET AWS CDK framework (*https://oreil.ly/6xBjV*) to define cloud application resources on AWS?
- Which AWS deployment strategy (*https://oreil.ly/MRqXj*) most closely aligns with where your organization works best?
- Why is it essential to use AWS CloudTrail (*https://oreil.ly/aa2ID*) for any AWS deployment?

- What could be an advantage of using AWS CodeCommit versus a third-party source code hosting service?

Exercises

- Use AWS CodeBuild to deploy a static S3 site using AWS CDK in C# (*https://oreil.ly/TK8X2*).
- Set up a continuous integration workflow for a .NET 6 project using GitHub Actions that tests code automatically upon check-in.
- Set up a continuous integration workflow for a .NET 6 project using AWS Code Build.
- Find an example CDK application in the csharp (*https://oreil.ly/JIHP3*) repo and deploy it to your AWS environment.
- Continuously deploy your own Hugo website and blog about .NET on AWS using your own homegrown CMS.

## CHAPTER 7

Logging, Monitoring, and Instrumentation for .NET

Back in 2007, when people were setting up their Nintendo Wii and dreaming of owning Apple's revolutionary new touchscreen cellphone, James was working his first job as a graduate software engineer. Not in web-based SaaS applications where he works today, however, but starting an engineering career writing industrial control software for production lines, oil rigs, cruise liners, and the military. Of all the weird and exciting projects James had a chance to work on back then, the most fun was designing the control system software for a roller coaster. Let us tell you how that worked.

This was a theme park ride with several cars on wheels going around a typical roller coaster track. Each car carried four people and there were between three and five cars going around the track simultaneously at any one time. The cars would be sent off from the station, making their way up the chain-driven incline to the top of the track, then rolling down under gravity to make an intense, exciting, and most importantly *safe* ride.

The code that operated the roller coaster was incredibly simple: the software read an input for the "GO" button being pressed by a ride operator. This then commanded the brakes to release, sending the car from the station into the starting blocks of the incline. There, with no further control inputs from the software, the car would be picked up by the chain-lift mechanism, carried up to the top of the ramp, and then sent off around the track. The brakes, hidden under the track along the platform, would then be re-armed, ready to catch the car and stop it gently on return.

With multiple cars hurtling around a roller coaster track at the same time, however, it is not hard to see what could go wrong. What if one of them got stuck? What if a car didn't have enough momentum to make it to the top of an incline or a fault on the track caused it to slow down or stop? With multiple cars on the track this can present a very real danger, potentially even risking human life. If one car stopped, we had to stop all the cars on the ride until an engineer could be sent out to fix the issue. For this reason, we had sensors and emergency brakes all over the track. We had code to detect cars entering "blocks" around the track in the same way a railroad signaling system works to prevent collisions. We had multiple sensors placed in a row to measure the speed of the cars at multiple points around the track.[1] Every speed sensor, motion detector, emergency brake, *backup* emergency brake, all of this had to be coded in the software. The volume of all this code greatly surpassed that which we had to actually operate the ride. Ninety-five percent of the code that runs on the control system of a roller coaster is monitoring, logging, alarming, and triggering emergency brakes.

Your distributed cloud-based system is a roller coaster. The amount of code you need to perform the main function may be small, but the number and variety of things that can go wrong is large, and you may end up adding a lot more complexity into your system to account for the rare instances of something going wrong, in order to maintain a high level of service to your users.

In this chapter, we are going to look at what we can build, configure, or simply enable in AWS that will improve our ability to monitor a cloud-based application. The majority of the services we will visit are not .NET specific; however, AWS does provide .NET SDKs for many of the tools we are about to cover. This helps you dig deep into your C# source code to identify the cause of an error or performance bottleneck. We will start by introducing the most important page you will visit on the Management Console when it comes to logging and monitoring: CloudWatch.

AWS CloudWatch

AWS CloudWatch (*https://aws.amazon.com/cloudwatch*) is a service (or rather a collection of services) from AWS that allow you to monitor, analyze, and act on events generated by your AWS resources. If you have some code deployed to and running on AWS, you will probably be able to monitor it using CloudWatch. Figure 7-1 shows the four core pillars of AWS CloudWatch: Collect, Monitor, Act, and Analyze. These pillars work together to allow you to iteratively improve the availability and scalability of your system.

---

1 The weight of the riders can greatly affect the speed of a roller coaster car under gravity. If you see four grown adults in a kiddie roller coaster car it might look funny, but the increased momentum that car will have coming back into the station can really test the strength of the braking system.

Figure 7-1. The four pillars of AWS CloudWatch

You *Collect* log events emitted by your AWS services, *Monitor* them with dashboards and metrics, *Act* on exceptional cases using alarms, and periodically *Analyze* your application(s) in order to make architectural improvements. These four pillars are shown in a line in Figure 7-1; however, it is more accurately thought of as a feedback loop. Analysis of your logs and metrics will allow you to improve what logs are collected and fine-tune when to trigger alarms, thus guiding you to make changes to your resources. The benefit of this is to ensure your system is running with the most efficient amount of headroom. You will be able to allocate enough resources to keep your performance within a desired range, but not so much that it becomes unnecessarily expensive to run.

Collecting CloudWatch Logs

CloudWatch collects and stores log messages from the services you have deployed to AWS. Many AWS services natively publish CloudWatch log messages with information about the execution of that service. You can also manually set up log collection or, as we will demonstrate in this chapter, you can programmatically post log messages using the AWS .NET SDK.

Some of the AWS services that natively publish logs to CloudWatch include:

API Gateway
Can be configured to send errors, request and response parameters, payloads, and execution traces.

Elastic Beanstalk
Application and system log files from your Elastic Beanstalk application can be read in CloudWatch.

AWS CodeBuild
Sends full verbose build logs for all your cloud builds.

Amazon Cognito
Authentication and user management metrics can be sent to CloudWatch.

Route 53
Amazon's Domain Name System (DNS) service can be configured to log DNS queries, amongst other things.

AWS Lambda
> Lambda functions are automatically set up to send metrics and execution logs to CloudWatch.

Simple Notification Service (SNS)
> Mobile text messaging (SMS) deliveries from SNS are automatically logged.

These are just a few examples; a vast majority of AWS services do publish log messages, either completely automatically, or with a little configuration. For a full list of AWS services that can publish logs to CloudWatch, visit the AWS documentation page "AWS services that publish logs to CloudWatch" (*https://oreil.ly/dlbYK*). Next we are going to explore logging from some of these services in more detail.

Logs from AWS Lambda functions

In the example for "Developing with AWS Lambda and C#" on page 91, we created a new AWS Lambda function using the .NET CLI:

```
dotnet lambda deploy-function SingleCSharpLambda
```

If you followed this you may have noticed that as well as creating the function, the CLI also creates an IAM execution role under which the Lambda function will execute. If you navigate to this execution role in the IAM Management Console, you can see that one of the default permissions policies added to the role is called AWSLambdaBasicExecutionRole.[2] This role is managed by AWS and is there to grant any new Lambda function the permission to be able to create a log group, create a stream, and then post log messages to CloudWatch. Figure 7-2 shows the policy JSON that is included in this policy.

Any service that posts log messages to AWS CloudWatch must be running under an IAM role that grants these permissions. Through their names, these permissions introduce us to three important concepts in CloudWatch logging.

---

[2] Despite being called "AWSLambdaBasicExecutionRole," this is actually not a role but a *policy*—a permissions set that can be applied to a role to grant or deny access to certain resources.

Figure 7-2. CloudWatch permissions that are added to every new Lambda function

Groups, streams, and events

CloudWatch stores log messages (or "events") in streams, and then groups each set of streams by the service or instance that sent them. For example, if we were logging messages from the execution of a Lambda function, then each stream of events on one Lambda invocation will be written to the same *log stream*. Multiple concurrent invocations of the Lambda function would create separate log streams; however, these would still be grouped under the same *log group*. The log group corresponds, in this case, to the individual Lambda function. So in your CloudWatch console you will have a log group for each Lambda, EC2 instance, S3 bucket, CodeBuild project, or any service you are logging from. Under each log group will be multiple streams, each containing multiple messages. Figure 7-3 shows the log messages from one invocation of an AWS Lambda function. You can browse the groups, streams, and logs through the Logs section in the CloudWatch Management Console. It is also possible to view CloudWatch logs directly in Visual Studio if you have the AWS Toolkit for Visual Studio installed. Navigate to CloudWatch Logs in the AWS Explorer window, right-click on a log group, and select View Log Stream.

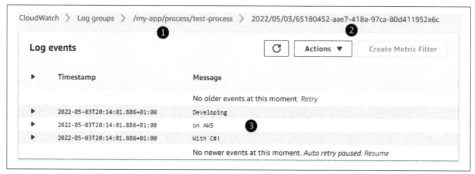

Figure 7-3. (1) CloudWatch log groups, (2) log stream, and (3) log event messages

Now we have a bit of familiarity with how CloudWatch log events are stored and accessed, let's see how we can take advantage of this to use CloudWatch to save custom log messages from our application.

Sending Logs from C#

Out of the box AWS Lambda will forward any calls made to `Console.WriteLine()` to CloudWatch, but you can also push logs directly to CloudWatch from our C# application with the help of the AWSSDK.CloudWatchLogs NuGet package, part of the AWS SDK for .NET. With the package installed, create a new .NET 6 Console Application to log a test message, as shown in Example 7-1.

Example 7-1. Program.cs

```
using TestCloudWatchLogPublishing;

await using (var logger = await CloudWatchLogger.CreateNew())
{
    logger.WriteLine("Developing");
    logger.WriteLine("on AWS");
    logger.WriteLine("With C#!");
}
```

Since we haven't yet created the `TestCloudWatchLogPublishing.CloudWatchLogger` class, this will fail to compile, but you can see all we are doing here is creating a new instance of a logger and writing a couple of log lines. The `using` block in this example is there as a handy way of scoping our logger instance over a few lines of code. The messages will be batched up and then flushed (sent to CloudWatch) when the `DisposeAsync()` method is called on the last line.[3]

---

3 The IAsyncDisposable interface was introduced in C# 8.0 and allows us to call asynchronous code in a DisposeAsync() method by adding "await" before our "using" statement.

Here is the code for our `TestCloudWatchLogPublishing.CloudWatchLogger` class that batches up and sends the log messages to AWS CloudWatch:

```csharp
using Amazon.CloudWatchLogs;
using Amazon.CloudWatchLogs.Model;

namespace TestCloudWatchLogPublishing;

public class CloudWatchLogger : IAsyncDisposable
{
    const string LogGroup = "/my-app/process/test-process";  ❶

    private readonly AmazonCloudWatchLogsClient _client;
    private readonly string _logStreamName;
    private readonly List<InputLogEvent> _logs = new List<InputLogEvent>();  ❷

    public CloudWatchLogger(AmazonCloudWatchLogsClient client, string name)
    {
        _client = client;
        _logStreamName = name;
    }

    public async static Task<CloudWatchLogger> CreateNew()
    {
        var client = new AmazonCloudWatchLogsClient();

        var logStreamName = DateTime.UtcNow.ToString("yyyy/MM/dd/")
                            + Guid.NewGuid().ToString();  ❸

        await client.CreateLogStreamAsync(new CreateLogStreamRequest  ❹
        {
            LogGroupName = LogGroup,
            LogStreamName = logStreamName
        });

        return new CloudWatchLogger(client, logStreamName);
    }

    public void WriteLine(string message)
    {
        _logs.Add(new InputLogEvent
        {
            Message = message,
            Timestamp = DateTime.Now
        });
    }

    public async ValueTask DisposeAsync()
    {
        await _client.PutLogEventsAsync(new PutLogEventsRequest  ❺
        {
            LogEvents = _logs,
```

```
            LogGroupName = LogGroup,
            LogStreamName = _logStreamName
        });
    }
}
```

❶ The log group name in our example is simply hardcoded. We will most likely want to create a new log group during the deployment of this code to AWS, reading it perhaps through an environment variable.

❷ Log messages will be written to this list and then "flushed" when the class is disposed.

❸ Log streams should have a unique name. We are prefixing this with the date so it can be easily sorted.

❹ A new log stream is created for each instance of our logger class.

❺ All batched log messages are sent to CloudWatch here, using the PutLogEvents Async() method from the AWS SDK.

Running this Console App gives the output shown back in Figure 7-3 when we view the logs in the AWS Management Console (*https://oreil.ly/067XH*).

 When running .NET applications locally, the AWS SDK will look for your AWS credentials in a series of places in order to connect to AWS and post the log messages to CloudWatch. On Windows environments there is a JSON file called the *SDK Store* located in *%USERPROFILE%\AppData\Local\AWSToolkit\RegisteredAccounts.json* or you can use the shared AWS credentials file. For information on all the available options for configuring your local connection to AWS visit this documentation page (*https://oreil.ly/O57Zy*).

In the preceding example, we used CloudWatchLogger directly but, due to AWS Lambda's ability to forward calls to Console.WriteLine() to CloudWatch, we can also use any of the popular logging packages for .NET that write to the console, and then allow AWS Lambda to forward that to CloudWatch for us.

For example, here is a configuration for Serilog that adds a `Serilog.Sinks.Console` logging sink, which AWS Lambda will send to CloudWatch:

```
{
  "Serilog": {
    "Using": [ "Serilog.Sinks.Console" ],
    "MinimumLevel": "Debug",
    "WriteTo": [
      { "Name": "Console" }
    ],
    "Properties": {
      "Application": "SerilogLoggingInLambda"
    }
  }
}
```

We can save this JSON to our *appsettings.json* file and with Serilog and the Serilog.Sinks.Console package installed, our Lambda function will send logs to CloudWatch.

You can find plugins for using other popular third-party logging libraries on the GitHub repository for AWS Logging .NET0 (*https://oreil.ly/PYPL1*).

Metrics

So far we have only looked at log messages that capture a single event in time. This is great for debugging the execution of your application and capturing specific events, but for long-term monitoring and analysis of your system, we need to also capture metrics.

A *metric* is the measure of a specific data point over a given period of time. For example, you might have an application that logs the response time for each HTTP request it processes, and you decide to measure the *average* response time *per minute*. This measure of average HTTP response time per minute is a metric, and it allows you to plot a time-series like the example shown in Figure 7-4. You can create and explore suggested metrics in the CloudWatch Management Console under Metrics → All Metrics.

It is also possible to publish custom metric data points from your C# code using the `AmazonCloudWatchClient` class, found in the AWSSDK.CloudWatch NuGet package.[4]

---

4 AWSSDK.CloudWatch and AWSSDK.CloudWatchLogs are two different packages with different clients; you will need both of these packages if you need to publish custom log messages *and* custom metric data points to CloudWatch.

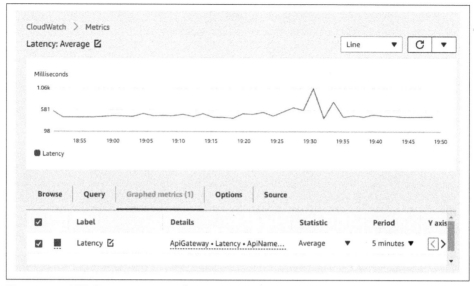

Figure 7-4. API Gateway average latency metric

Example 7-2 sends the number of processes currently running on your local machine to CloudWatch:

Example 7-2. Program.cs

```
using Amazon.CloudWatch;
using Amazon.CloudWatch.Model;
using System.Diagnostics;

var client = new AmazonCloudWatchClient();

await client.PutMetricDataAsync(new Amazon.CloudWatch.Model.PutMetricDataRequest
{
    Namespace = "MyApplication",
    MetricData = new List<MetricDatum>
    {
        new MetricDatum
        {
            MetricName = "ProcessCount",
            Value = Process.GetProcesses().Length,
        }
    }
});
```

You can see the results of repeatedly running this in Figure 7-5. Note that CloudWatch automatically created the namespace "MyApplication" and the metric "ProcessCount" for us.

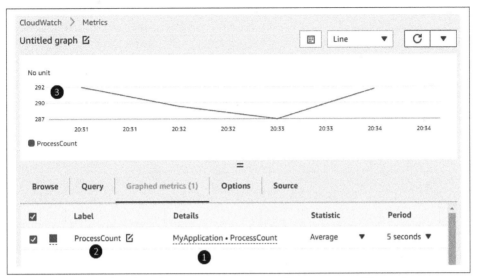

Figure 7-5. (1) Results of sending a custom metric with namespace, (2) metric name, and (3) the number of running processes

So now that we have metrics going into CloudWatch, where do we go from here? Next, we are going to look at how we can build CloudWatch dashboards to visually monitor our system at a glance. Following on from that, we will look at how we can set up alarms to trigger when a metric passes a certain threshold.

Monitoring with CloudWatch Dashboards

Dashboards allow you to monitor your AWS resources at a glance. You can monitor multiple resources across your entire AWS account at once by creating custom dashboards, picking out key metrics that you want to be able to monitor quickly and efficiently. CloudWatch generates *automatic* dashboards for your AWS services, and you can use these as a starting point to create your own.

Navigate to CloudWatch → Dashboards → Automatic Dashboards in the Management Console to view the available automatic dashboards. You can add widgets from the automatic dashboards onto a new, custom dashboard, or you can view and tweak the underlying metrics query by selecting "view in metrics" in the context menu of each widget. Figure 7-6 shows the custom dashboard generated for our Simple Storage Service (S3) buckets. You can see trends for bucket size and number of objects.

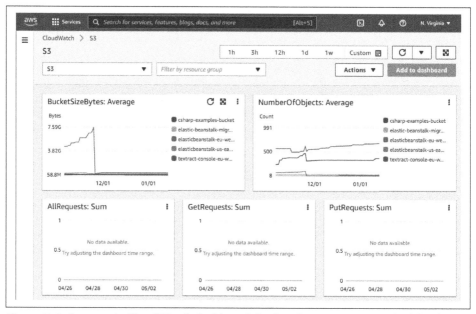

Figure 7-6. Automatic CloudWatch dashboard for Simple Storage Service (S3) buckets

Dashboards allow you to visualize changes to your metrics over time, but what about if you want to actually perform some action when a metric hits a certain value? In Figure 7-6, you can see the BucketSizeBytes value for one of our S3 buckets was creeping up slowly over a long period of time (the sawtoothed line that drops suddenly on the first chart). Well, if we wanted we could set an upper limit to how many bytes we are comfortable storing in this S3 bucket, for cost reasons perhaps, and then perform some action if the bucket size exceeds this limit. For that, we use CloudWatch alarms.

CloudWatch alarms

We introduced this chapter by talking about the monitoring software that keeps a roller coaster running safely. In industrial control software, such as with roller coasters, if an input is read outside some predetermined threshold for more than a set number of seconds, it will trigger an alarm. In an industrial application, these alarms will be connected to physical alarms that emit a loud audible tone alerting nearby operators to the condition being out of bounds. This could be a temperature setpoint being too low or too high for several seconds, or a discrete input such as a laser beam being broken. In the context of your distributed AWS system, you can configure alarms to trigger when your metrics go outside of the limits you have deemed "normal." Alarms are there to trigger actions, either manually by a systems administrator, or automatically by triggering a function inside your system.

In CloudWatch, you can configure an alarm on any single metric, an expression derived from multiple metrics, or even other alarms. An alarm can be in one of three possible states:

OK
> The metric for this alarm is within the defined bounds, and the alarm is not triggered.

IN ALARM
> The metric is outside the defined bounds, and the alarm is triggered.

INSUFFICIENT_DATA
> There is not enough data (yet) to determine the alarm state.

Let's add an alarm to the custom metric we created in Figure 7-5. To do this, navigate to CloudWatch in the Management Console and create the alarm, selecting MyApplication → Metrics with no dimensions → ProcessCount as the metric to monitor. In the example in Figure 7-5, we had between 287 and 292 processes being reported in our custom metric, so we could set our alarm threshold to 290, which will make it easy to test. On the next screen select "Create a new topic" to have AWS create a new Simple Notification Service (SNS) topic. We introduced SNS in "Developing with SQS and SNS" on page 109; it is a service that allows publishers and subscribers to create and listen to events, respectively. For the purposes of this alarm, we will be publishing a message to SNS when the alarm is triggered, that is, when the ProcessCount metric goes above our threshold of 290.

Figure 7-7 shows this alarm after we have created it and waited a few minutes for it to have enough data to leave the *INSUFFICIENT_DATA* state. You can see from this graph that we have a horizontal line at 290, indicating this is the threshold above which our alarm will trigger.

Figure 7-7. CloudWatch alarm monitoring our custom metric

We said at the start of this section that you can also configure an alarm to trigger on multiple metrics. That can be achieved with metric math, which we dig into next.

Metric math

Metrics are data points that change over time and, as such, you can perform arithmetic operations on them over the same time period. CloudWatch enables a whole host of different expressions you can use to combine multiple metrics into one. There are too many to cover in this book; however, a full list of functions and expressions can be found here (*https://oreil.ly/2oYRC*).

Using these arithmetic functions on our metrics, we can create *new* metrics that can be both added to a dashboard and used to trigger alarms. In Figure 7-8, we have created a new expression by combining the ProcessCount from our earlier example, with another custom metric that records the CPU usage of our local machine. This allows us to create a new metric for *Average CPU Per Process*, entered into the customizable "Label" field in the table in Figure 7-8.

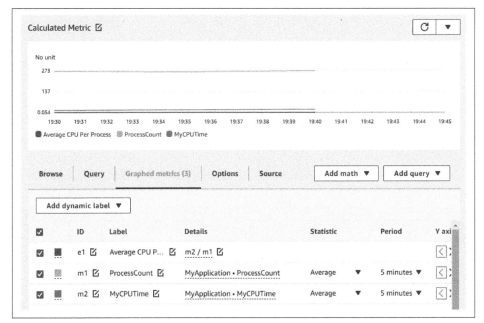

Figure 7-8. Average CPU per process metric created using metric math

We created this expression from the Add Math context menu option above the metrics table and selected "Start with empty expression." The expression in this example is m2 / m1 where m1 and m2 are the default identifiers given to our two custom metrics in the list. You can view/change this metric ID by editing the "ID" field in the table in Figure 7-8.

By using metric math, we can create complex graphs and alarm conditions to monitor any parameter inside our system we like. There is even an IF(condition, trueValue, falseValue) condition available in metric math that allows us to do things such as filter out data points from a time series. Perhaps we want to filter out the first 10 minutes of data points after a system reboot, or during a software update. This is possible by building up new metric expressions using metric math in AWS CloudWatch.

CloudWatch anomaly detection

It is also possible to trigger CloudWatch alarms using a feature called *anomaly detection*. This is a machine learning algorithm that continuously monitors your metric and determines a normal baseline by means of a range of *expected values*. The alarm can then be triggered if the metric deviates too far outside this range. The model used by CloudWatch's anomaly detection can asses hourly, daily, and weekly patterns using the historical values of your metric. This allows it to generate a range of expected values even for metrics that naturally change to follow a regular pattern over time—

such as metrics related to usage patterns of your application. To create a CloudWatch alarm based on anomaly detection, look out for the Anomaly detection option under the Alarm → Graphed Metrics → Conditions section of the alarm configuration in the CloudWatch console (*https://oreil.ly/Ag1Tq*).

Next, we are going to move on from metrics and look at tracing the execution path of your code using a service from AWS called X-Ray.

Distributed Tracing with X-Ray

AWS X-Ray is a service that offers end-to-end tracing for your cloud-hosted applications, giving you insights into the way your code is executing. You can set up X-Ray tracing for HTTP requests for example, and view the execution path through any downstream service calls this HTTP request results in. This gives you the ability to debug your application as it is running in the cloud, helping you understand the root causes of any issues. You can also use AWS X-Ray to find performance bottlenecks in the execution path of your code.

In order to leverage the tools AWS X-Ray provides, you need to set up your services to publish trace events to X-Ray. X-Ray tracing events can be configured automatically for a lot of native AWS services such as AWS Lambda and DynamoDB. Enabling tracing on a Lambda function is a simple case of toggling the "Active tracing" switch in the Management Console for any Lambda function (shown in Figure 7-9).

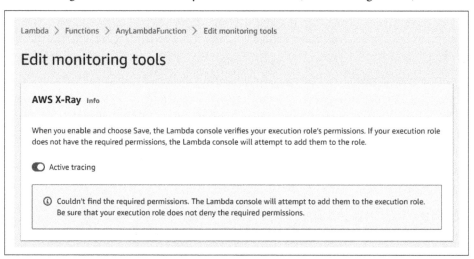

Figure 7-9. X-Ray can be enabled in the configuration settings for many native AWS services

If you have your infrastructure controlled by an Infrastructure as Code (IaC) frame-work such as "Serverless Application Model (SAM)" on page 116, you can enable active tracing in your configuration so it is set when you deploy changes to your resources. Here is the SAM configuration to enable X-Ray on a Lambda function; we have added `Tracing:Active` to the properties object:

```
AWSTemplateFormatVersion: '2010-09-09'
Transform: AWS::Serverless-2016-10-31
Description: My Lambda function with X-Ray active tracing enabled
Resources:
  MyLambdaFunction:
    Type: AWS::Lambda::Function
    Properties:
      Handler: MyApp::MyApp.Function::Handler
      Runtime: dotnet6
      Tracing: Active
```

Not all AWS services can be enabled like this; however, for these we do have options to use the SDK for .NET.

Setting Up X-Ray Using the SDK for .NET

While enabling X-Ray for native services such as AWS Lambda is a simple case of toggling a switch (as shown in Figure 7-9), if your code is instead running inside an EC2 container (including Elastic Beanstalk) or on App Runner, then you will need to configure some things yourself. You will need to install or enable the X-Ray daemon, which runs in the background on your EC2 instance collecting X-Ray trace messages, batching them up, and forwarding them on to AWS X-Ray. You will also need to use the X-Ray SDK for .NET in your C# code to send traces to the daemon.

On an EC2 instance, you can download and install the X-Ray daemon to run auto-matically when you launch the instance by running:

```
#!/bin/bash
curl https://s3.us-east-2.amazonaws.com/aws-xray-assets.us-east-2/
xray-daemon/aws-xray-daemon-3.x.rpm -o /home/ec2-user/xray.rpm
sudo yum install -y /home/ec2-user/xray.rpm
```

If you are using Elastic Beanstalk, you can enable it in the Management Console under Configuration → Software Settings → X-Ray daemon. There is also an option on the publish page in the AWS Toolkit for Visual Studio. Check "Enable AWS X-Ray Tracing Support" when publishing your application to Elastic Beanstalk and the AWS Toolkit will enable the daemon for you.

You can also run the X-Ray daemon process locally on your development machine. You can find instructions for running the daemon locally on Windows, Linux, Mac OS, and even in a Docker container by visiting the X-Ray setup guide (*https://oreil.ly/ Spc0P*).

Once the daemon is installed on your EC2 instance, you will be able to use the X-Ray SDK in your application to send trace messages to X-Ray. To do this, start by installing the NuGet package AWSXRayRecorder, then add the following three lines to the *Program.cs* of your .NET 6 web application:

```
using Amazon.XRay.Recorder.Core;
using Amazon.XRay.Recorder.Handlers.AwsSdk;

AWSXRayRecorder.InitializeInstance(); ❶

AWSSDKHandler.RegisterXRayForAllServices(); ❷

// ...

app.UseXRay("ElasticBeanstalkAppExample"); ❸

app.Run();
```

❶ Initializes the AWS X-Ray recorder for this application.

❷ Add this line if you are using the AWS SDK to make calls to other AWS services inside your application. This will allow X-Ray to trace requests through these downstream services.

❸ Add X-Ray tracing to the routes in your web application. The name "Elastic-BeanstalkAppExample" will be used to identify this application in X-Ray.

Adding these three lines will send trace messages to X-Ray for each HTTP request that comes into your web application. You will be able to measure the duration of the request, including any synchronous calls to downstream AWS services. X-Ray has a concept it calls "segments," which are measurable portions of the execution path of your code. The entire HTTP request is the parent "segment," and any downstream calls that are made as a part of this request will be "subsegments" inside. You can also configure your own subsegments using the X-Ray SDK, allowing you to measure timings for custom parts of your code. In the following example, we have set a subsegment for the duration of the code inside the controller action. We are then invoking an AWS Lambda function from our code called TracedLambdaFunction. X-Ray will also create a subsegment for that Lambda invocation.

Example 7-3. Program.cs

```
[HttpPost]
public async Task<IActionResult> InvokedMyTracedLambda()
{
    AWSXRayRecorder.Instance.BeginSubsegment("Executing Controller Action");

    var lambdaClient = new AmazonLambdaClient(Amazon.RegionEndpoint.EUWest2);
    await lambdaClient.InvokeAsync(new Amazon.Lambda.Model.InvokeRequest
    {
        FunctionName = "TracedLambdaFunction"
    });

    AWSXRayRecorder.Instance.EndSubsegment();

    return Ok();
}
```

We will be able to view the trace results for this example in the X-Ray traces section of the CloudWatch Management Console. Figure 7-10 shows the trace results for this controller method. You can see the Lambda function execution took 2.45 seconds to return. The controller action subsegment we set up with AWSXRayRe corder.Instance.BeginSubsegment(...) took 2.67 seconds, and the entire HTTP request was 2.76 seconds.

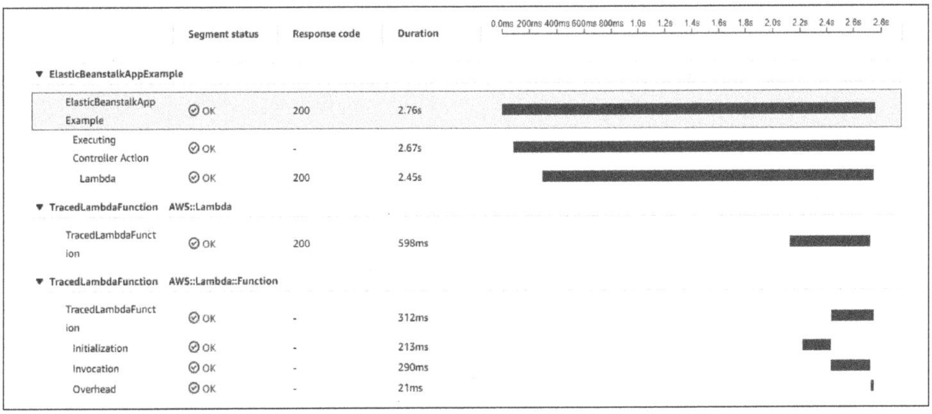

	Segment status	Response code	Duration	0.0ms 200ms 400ms 600ms 800ms 1.0s 1.2s 1.4s 1.6s 1.8s 2.0s 2.2s 2.4s 2.6s 2.8s
▼ ElasticBeanstalkAppExample				
ElasticBeanstalkApp Example	⊘ OK	200	2.76s	
Executing Controller Action	⊘ OK	-	2.67s	
Lambda	⊘ OK	200	2.45s	
▼ TracedLambdaFunction AWS::Lambda				
TracedLambdaFunct ion	⊘ OK	200	598ms	
▼ TracedLambdaFunction AWS::Lambda::Function				
TracedLambdaFunct ion	⊘ OK	-	312ms	
Initialization	⊘ OK	-	213ms	
Invocation	⊘ OK	-	290ms	
Overhead	⊘ OK	-	21ms	

Figure 7-10. Trace view of our web application controller call

With X-Ray tracing you can quickly find performance bottlenecks in your code and refactor or rearchitect your code paths accordingly. There is another feature of X-Ray that is enabled by adding tracing to your applications and services, and that is the *Service Map.*

X-Ray Service Map

The Service Map is now found under the X-Ray traces section of the AWS Cloud-Watch Management Console, and it is a visualization of all your X-Ray enabled services and how they interact.[5] Figure 7-11 shows the Service Map for the previous example. You can see we have our web application ElasticBeanstalkAppExample that makes a call off to the Lambda function `TracedLambdaFunction`. Because we used the X-Ray SDK and called `AWSSDKHandler.RegisterXRayForAllServices()` in our web application, X-Ray was able to determine that this Lambda invocation was called from within the .NET web application we deployed to Elastic Beanstalk.

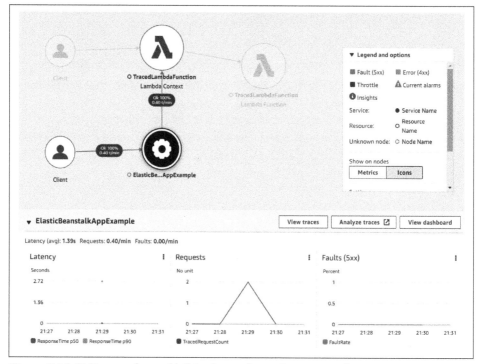

Figure 7-11. X-Ray can be enabled in the configuration settings for many native AWS services

You can click on the services in the Service Map interface to trace the execution path(s) through them and see performance metrics such as latency and 5xx error rates. In Figure 7-11, we have the "ElasticBeanstalkAppExample" selected.

---

5 Service Map was previously accessed through a product AWS calls "Service Lens," so you may find it referenced as a part of that in documentation online.

Next we are going to look at using X-Ray with OpenTelemetry, an open source observability framework that provides a common framework for instrumentation across multiple cloud providers, including AWS.

OpenTelemetry and App Runner

For all the previous services we have been using the X-Ray SDK and/or simply taking advantage of built in X-Ray tracing functionality, such as with AWS Lambda. It is also possible to use X-Ray with OpenTelemetry to send tracing information to X-Ray without as much vendor lock-in. This is the solution if you want to take advantage of X-Ray tracing from within a containerized application, such as one running on Amazon ECS or Amazon EKS.

With the OpenTelemetry SDK added in your codebase, the AWS Distro for Open-Telemetry (*https://aws.amazon.com/otel*) can be used to then instrument your .NET application and send the metrics to X-Ray. You can find more information about setting up OpenTelemetry for your .NET Core/6+ application by visiting Getting Started with the .NET SDK on Traces Instrumentation (*https://oreil.ly/xGe4T*).

Resource Health and Synthetics Canaries

If you have explored around the CloudWatch Management Console by now, you may have visited the Application monitoring section. Under this topic are several services from AWS that help us monitor our resources. Let's take a quick look at two of these: Resource Health and Synthetics Canaries.

The Resource Health view was previously a part of ServiceLens and shows you health and performance data for all your running EC2 hosts. You can customize your view by selecting from three dimensions: CPU Utilization, Memory Utilization, and Status Check. The Management Console window will show blocks of colored squares for each EC2 host in the current region. This gives you an easy-to-read and accessible view of the alarm status of most or all of your hosts.[6]

Synthetics Canaries is another great tool tucked away under the Application monitoring section of CloudWatch. A "canary" in systems monitoring is an active monitoring technique that uses a script or other scheduled task to regularly probe the status of a system.[7]

---

6 You can view up to 500 hosts in one view using the Resource Health window.

7 The term "canary" has a rather dark past. In the days before electronic gas detectors, and indeed also before animal welfare rights, canary birds would be taken into coal mines in a cage and hung up in the area being worked in. If the bird succumbed to toxic fumes down in the mine, the workers would notice the expiry of the poor bird and take it as a sign to raise the alarm and evacuate.

You can create several types of canary in AWS using the templates (or "blueprints") provided:

- Heartbeat monitoring
- API canary
- Broken link checker
- Canary recorder
- GUI workflow builder
- Visual monitoring

The idea behind a synthetic canary is to replicate behavior that approximates the real usage your application will be asked to perform for its users. So, for example, an API canary can be configured to make series requests to your API that mirror what a frontend would do under normal operation.

Synthetics can be easily integrated with X-Ray by selecting "Trace my service with AWS X-Ray" when creating your canary. Refer back to "Distributed Tracing with X-Ray" on page 190 for configuration and familiarity with X-Ray.

Using AWS CloudTrail for Security Auditing

So far in this chapter we have been looking at AWS CloudWatch for logging monitoring of your deployed services in order to find and fix issues. Before we leave the topic of logging and monitoring, however, let's just have a quick look at what AWS has to offer for the auditing of your account itself.

CloudTrail is a service from AWS that records all requests to the AWS APIs in your account and logs them against the user that made the request. These API requests can be made from anywhere, including through the AWS CLI, the Management Console, or from an SDK such as the AWS SDK for .NET (see "AWS SDK for .NET documentation" on page 11). You can even monitor requests made by another AWS service in CloudTrail. CloudTrail has its own section in the AWS Management Console, so to access it and view your audit logs, search for "CloudTrail" in the search bar.

For Google Chrome users, you can move focus to the search bar at any time while navigating the AWS Management Console by using ALT+S (Option+S on a Mac). Another handy feature of the Management Console is the favorites "star" next to each service in the search results. Clicking this causes a link to that service to appear permanently in the header bar of the Management Console window and persists as you navigate around the various AWS services.

To get started with CloudTrail, click "Create a Trail" and run through the setup to configure attributes for your trail, primarily a name and S3 bucket in which to store the logs. You can choose to monitor any or all of these event types:

Management events
> Operations performed on your AWS resources, for example attaching a policy to an IAM role or creating a subnet in EC2.

Data events
> Actions performed on an instance of a resource. Data events include deleting, creating, or updating S3 objects, DynamoDB records, and executing Lambda functions.

Insights events
> AWS logs these events when it detects unusual activity on your account. They monitor write operations on the AWS API and use mathematical models to spot abnormal levels of operations and/or errors.

Once you have created a trail, AWS will begin logging records to the S3 bucket and you will be able to view and analyze your audit logs in the Management Console.

Practical Example: A CloudWatch Circuit Breaker

In this chapter, we have explored some of the features available in AWS CloudWatch. We have looked at collecting logs, metrics, tracing, and sending custom metric data from your C# application to CloudWatch. We have also looked at monitoring dashboards and setting up alarms to trigger when a metric goes outside a predetermined threshold. Let's tie all this together with an example that spans many of the concepts covered in this chapter. For this example, we will be implementing the circuit breaker pattern using serverless AWS components and CloudWatch.

> The circuit breaker is a well-established architectural pattern for handling failures in one part of your application, introducing logic to fall back to a secondary behavior when a failure is detected. This has the benefit of preventing a failure from propagating to downstream components and allows you to maintain a certain level of service to your application users even in the event of one component failing. You can watch an animated example of how this pattern is implemented on YouTube (*https://youtu.be/e5pnfD0rudY*).

In order to implement the circuit breaker pattern on AWS, we will first need an application in which we might have a failure. For this example, we have a website that wants to display the latest currency exchange rate to all our visitors. The exchange rate, in this case from USD to GBP, will come from an external API that we will call every time somebody loads our web page. Exchange rates fluctuate as currencies are traded around the world, so by making this API call every time the page loads we can be sure we are showing our website visitors the most up-to-date rate. Figure 7-12 shows how we make this exchange-rate lookup call from our website. The call is proxied through an instance of API Gateway that we control and passed directly through to the third-party service we are using to retrieve the latest rate.

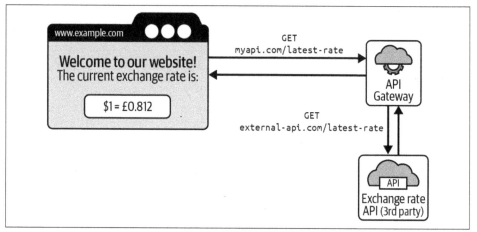

Figure 7-12. External API calls being proxied through API Gateway to our website

The CloudFormation template to set up a simple API Gateway proxy to a third-party API like this would be:

```
Resources:
  ExchangeRateApi:
    Type: AWS::ApiGatewayV2::Api
    Properties:
      Name: ExchangeRateApi
      ProtocolType: HTTP

  ExternalERServiceIntegration:
    Type: "AWS::ApiGatewayV2::Integration"
    Properties:
      ConnectionType: INTERNET
      IntegrationType: HTTP_PROXY
      IntegrationMethod: GET
      IntegrationUri: https://api.example.com/exchange-rate/
      PayloadFormatVersion: 1.0
      ApiId: !Ref ExchangeRateApi
      RequestParameters:
```

```
      "overwrite:header.apikey": "{{API-KEY}}"

LatestRoute:
  Type: 'AWS::ApiGatewayV2::Route'
  Properties:
    ApiId: !Ref ExchangeRateApi
    RouteKey: 'GET /latest'
    AuthorizationType: NONE
    Target: !Join
      - /
      - - integrations
        - !Ref ExternalERServiceIntegration
```

What Could Go Wrong?

Calling this third-party API every time a visitor loads our web page is great for displaying the most up-to-date value; however, we are now heavily dependent on the availability of an API we do not own or control. What happens if this third-party service goes down or begins to respond slowly? As it stands, the response time of our API call is directly proportional to the response time of the external API. If this external API begins responding incredibly slowly, so will our API gateway call, and our users will have to wait for their exchange rate to appear on the website. Perhaps they will even end up seeing a timeout error instead of the USD to GBP rate that they expect. So what can we do?

Using CloudWatch we can monitor the latency of this endpoint, and set up an alarm to trigger when the external API begins to respond slowly. Head over to the CloudWatch Management Console and create a new alarm for the *latency* metric on our API Gateway resource, as shown in Figure 7-13.

You may need to enable "Detailed route metrics" in API Gateway to get the latency for each route as shown in Figure 7-13.

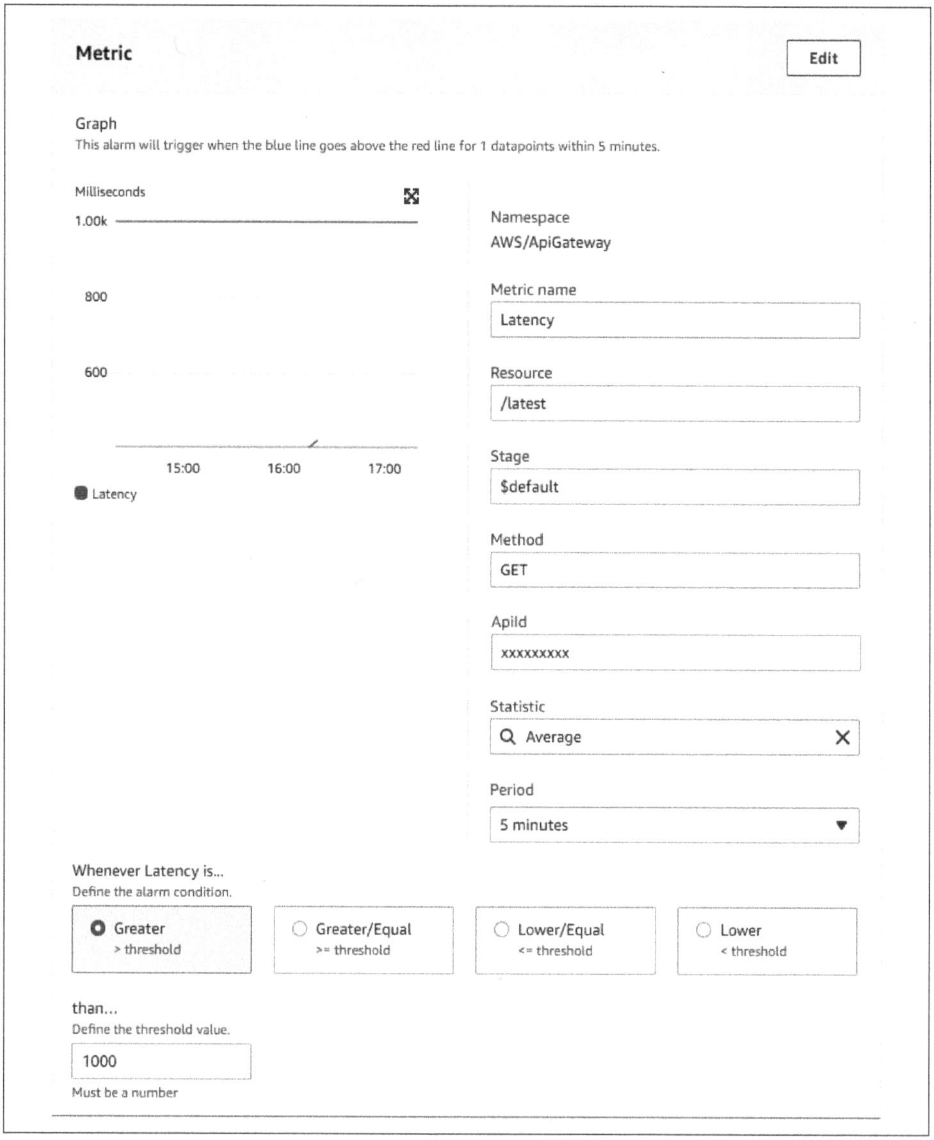

Metric   Edit

Graph
This alarm will trigger when the blue line goes above the red line for 1 datapoints within 5 minutes.

Milliseconds

1.00k ————————————————————————

800

600

```
        15:00      16:00      17:00
```
● Latency

Namespace
AWS/ApiGateway

Metric name
Latency

Resource
/latest

Stage
$default

Method
GET

ApiId
xxxxxxxxx

Statistic
Q Average   ✕

Period
5 minutes   ▼

Whenever Latency is...
Define the alarm condition.

● Greater	○ Greater/Equal	○ Lower/Equal	○ Lower
> threshold	>= threshold	<= threshold	< threshold

than...
Define the threshold value.

1000

Must be a number

Figure 7-13. Configuring a new alarm on the latency of our API Gateway resource

For the notification action of our alarm, we will set up an SNS topic and link it to a Lambda function called `TriggerCircuitBreaker`. We will create this Lambda function next.

Breaking the Circuit

Now we have a way to detect the external API's latency increasing, we need to decide what to do to keep our application running. For our example website, we have made the business decision that in the event that the exchange rate lookup API is not responding quickly enough we will return a *cached* exchange rate from our distributed memory cache. Perhaps we have another Lambda function that runs on a schedule and saves the current exchange rate to this cache periodically. For our distributed cache we can use Amazon ElastiCache (*https://aws.amazon.com/elasticache*), which allows us to use both Redis and Memcached, two extremely popular open source in-memory stores. In Figure 7-14, you can see we have configured our API Gateway with a second "fallback" integration that invokes a Lambda function to retrieve the most recent exchange rate from the cache.

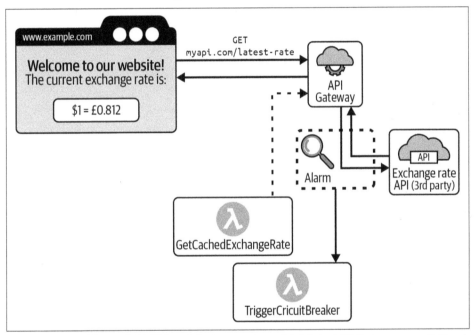

Figure 7-14. Additional AWS Lambda integration added into API Gateway as a fallback

Our circuit breaker could operate by detecting high latency on the third-party API and switching our API Gateway to use this fallback integration. This would not affect our website as the API calls from the frontend are still coming into the gateway, but instead of proxying those calls to our third-party service, we will be sending them to the Lambda function GetCachedExchangeRate.

Making this switch in API Gateway can be done from a simple C# Lambda function, using the `AmazonApiGatewayV2Client` from the NuGet package AWSSDK.ApiGatewayV2:

```
using System.Threading.Tasks;
using Amazon.ApiGatewayV2;
using Amazon.ApiGatewayV2.Model;
using Amazon.Lambda.Core;
using Amazon.Lambda.Serialization.SystemTextJson;

[assembly: LambdaSerializer(typeof(DefaultLambdaJsonSerializer))]

namespace TriggerCircuitBreaker
{
    public class Function
    {
        public async Task FunctionHandler(object input, ILambdaContext context)
        {
            const string apiGatewayId = "abcabc";
            const string exchangeRateRouteId = "defdef";
            const string fallbackIntegrationId = "xyzxyz";

            var apiGatewayClient = new AmazonApiGatewayV2Client();

            await apiGatewayClient.UpdateRouteAsync(new UpdateRouteRequest
            {
                RouteId = exchangeRateRouteId,
                ApiId = apiGatewayId,
                Target = $"integrations/{fallbackIntegrationId}"
            });
        }
    }
}
```

Here we have hardcoded the IDs for our API Gateway instance, route, and integration; however, these could of course be read in from environment variables or looked up at runtime using methods on the `AmazonApiGatewayV2Client`.

Resetting the Tripped State

What we have achieved here through switching the integration in API Gateway is we have provided our users with *some* information on the website. It may not be the latest exchange rate but it should be recent enough and, crucially, we have guarded against an unpredictably slow third-party API. The next thing to consider is how we reset our circuit breaker when the API is no longer experiencing high latency.

The circuit breaker pattern offers a solution for resetting once the initial condition has been resolved, and that is by periodically testing our external API in what the pattern calls a "half open state." We can create yet another Lambda function to do this:

```csharp
using System.Collections.Generic;
using System.Diagnostics;
using System.Net.Http;
using System.Threading.Tasks;
using Amazon.CloudWatch;
using Amazon.CloudWatch.Model;
using Amazon.Lambda.Core;
using Amazon.Lambda.Serialization.SystemTextJson;

[assembly: LambdaSerializer(typeof(DefaultLambdaJsonSerializer))]

namespace ProbeExchangeRateEndpoint
{
    public class Function
    {
        public async Task FunctionHandler(object input, ILambdaContext context)
        {

            var watch = Stopwatch.StartNew();

            var response = await new HttpClient()
                        .GetAsync("https://external-api.com/latest-rate");

            response.EnsureSuccessStatusCode();

            watch.Stop();

            var cloudWatch = new AmazonCloudWatchClient();
            await cloudWatch.PutMetricDataAsync(new PutMetricDataRequest
            {
                Namespace = "CircuitBreakerExample",
                MetricData = new List<MetricDatum>
                {
                    new MetricDatum
                    {
                        MetricName = "ExchangeRateProbeLatency",
                        Value = watch.ElapsedMilliseconds
                    }
                }
            });

        }
    }
}
```

Here we have a function that makes the API call to our third-party exchange rate API and measures the response time. This is then sent back to CloudWatch as a custom metric called "ExchangeRateProbeLatency." We can then set up a second alarm to track this new metric using a *Lower than* threshold. In the alarm configuration window in CloudWatch, there is also a "Datapoints to alarm" setting that we can take advantage of. Setting this (shown in Figure 7-15) will result in our alarm being triggered if 10 API calls to our probe fall below our maximum allowed latency.

▼ Additional configuration

Datapoints to alarm
Define the number of datapoints within the evaluation period that must be breaching to cause the alarm to go to ALARM state.

| 10 | out of | 10 |

Missing data treatment
How to treat missing data when evaluating the alarm.

| Treat missing data as missing ▼ |

Figure 7-15. Datapoints to alarm configuration

Finally, here is our entire example as a flow diagram in Figure 7-16. We are using an EventBridge rule to schedule calling the `ProbeExchangeRateEndpoint` Lambda function until the latency has reduced back down to an acceptable level.

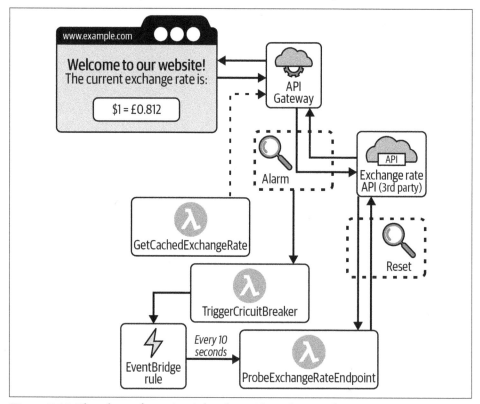

Figure 7-16. Flowchart of our circuit breaker with probing and reset

Conclusion

No system is architected or configured to perfection. Systems evolve over time and as the scale of your application changes you will need to make changes to the way your services talk to each other. This is especially true for growing systems that start small with only a handful of users, and grow, sometimes exponentially, to serve thousands of users all across the world. Architectural decisions that made sense when an application was small can end up hindering performance as adoption increases. You will also learn more about the usage patterns of your services as you scale as more users provide more detailed insight into how your application is used and where the bottlenecks will emerge.

It is therefore vitally important to have logging, monitoring, and instrumentation in place so you can observe these changes happening and respond to them quickly, efficiently, and with the greatest amount of useful data at your disposal. For operations engineers, site reliability engineers, DevOps, and security engineers, AWS CloudWatch is an extremely powerful set of tools that can give you the data you need if some time is invested in getting the most out of it.

For the final chapter of this book, we are going to be jumping back into our application code and exploring more deeply the AWS SDK for .NET. We will also be looking at some of the tooling for Visual Studio that can make interacting with AWS feel much more natural and integrated with your development workflow.

Critical Thinking Discussion Questions

- Why would an engineering manager say logging, monitoring, and instrumentation are essential to software engineering?
- What is another way to describe the four pillars of AWS CloudWatch?
- What are the three of four most important metrics you should look at when building and deploying AWS Lambda services?
- What real-world problems does a service like X-Ray solve?
- How could security auditing using AWS CloudTrail help prevent a ransomware attack at your company?

Exercises

- Build a C# Console App that queries AWS CloudTrail.
- Write custom CloudWatch logging into an AWS CodeBuild job that builds a .NET project.
- Log the incoming API Gateway POST requests for a .NET web service to AWS CloudTrail.
- Log the incoming Elastic Beanstalk POST requests for a .NET web service to AWS CloudTrail.
- Build a C# Console App that finds anomalies in AWS CloudTrail events.

CHAPTER 8

Developing with AWS C# SDK

Throughout this book we have utilized many ways to interact with AWS from your development machine. We have been using the AWS Management Console (*https://aws.amazon.com/console*), and we have been using the AWS CLI both through Cloud9 and locally by installing the CLI locally to our machine. In this last chapter, we will take a look at some tools and integrations that offer a third way to integrate with and control your AWS services, through integrated development environments (IDEs) you will most likely already be familiar with: Visual Studio and Visual Studio Code. Both of these IDEs have extensions for AWS that allow you to interrogate your AWS resources, and we will be covering both in this chapter.

After looking at some of the features of the UI toolkits for AWS, we will also be taking a closer look at the AWS C# SDK. We have been using the SDK extensively throughout this book, so you should be familiar with the basics, but there is a lot more this collection of NuGet packages has to offer.

Lastly, we are going to round off this book by exploring some of the artificial intelligence (AI) services in AWS and how we can utilize these in .NET. So let's jump straight in and talk about the AWS Toolkit for Visual Studio and how you can set up your Visual Studio workflow so that deployment to AWS feels seamless.

Using AWS Toolkit for Visual Studio In Depth

The AWS Toolkit is an extension that supplements the Visual Studio interface with various AWS-related functionality. The aim of the toolkit is to make Visual Studio feel as natively integrated into AWS as it does out of the box with Microsoft's own cloud services. With the toolkit installed you will be able to quickly deploy your code to a multitude of AWS services with the same "publish" workflow you are probably already familiar with.

The toolkit adds menu options, context menu options, project templates, and an AWS Explorer window, all of which we will cover in this chapter.

Configuring Visual Studio for AWS Toolkit

We briefly covered installation of the toolkit in "Using Visual Studio with AWS and AWS Toolkit for Visual Studio" on page 17, so just to recap: you can find the toolkit extension in the Visual Studio Marketplace (*https://oreil.ly/CuWwr*), or through AWS's web page for AWS Toolkit for Visual Studio (*https://aws.amazon.com/visualstudio*), the latter of which also contains links to guides and documentation that can help you in getting the most out of AWS in Visual Studio.

There are three versions of the toolkit that span five versions of Visual Studio, so be sure to download the correct *.msi* installer file for your version of Visual Studio:

- AWS Toolkit for Visual Studio 2013–2015
- AWS Toolkit for Visual Studio 2017–2019
- AWS Toolkit for Visual Studio 2022

The examples in this book will be using AWS Toolkit for Visual Studio 2022; however, screens for earlier versions of Visual Studio are not radically dissimilar.

Once you have installed the extension and opened up Visual Studio, you will be presented with the Getting Started page as shown in Figure 8-1.

Before we can connect to AWS from Visual Studio, we need to configure the toolkit with some AWS credentials so it can make API calls to AWS services on our behalf. The toolkit uses the access key and secret key(s) from your AWS credentials file, stored against a profile. You can find your AWS credentials files under *~/.aws/credentials* (Linux or macOS) or *%USERPROFILE%\.aws\credentials* (Windows), with the profile name in square brackets. For example:

```
[default]
aws_access_key_id = <your-access-key>
aws_secret_access_key = <your-secret-key>
```

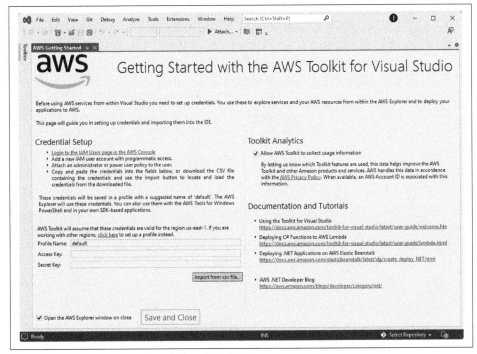

Figure 8-1. Getting started with the AWS Toolkit

If you already have credentials stored on your machine, then you can skip this step as the toolkit will pick them up inside Visual Studio. If you do not have credentials stored, then you can create an IAM user and download credentials, then import into the Credential Setup section in Figure 8-1.

Once you have credentials stored on your machine, you can begin exploring the AWS Toolkit features inside Visual Studio, and what better place to start than the AWS Explorer, accessible from the new Tools → AWS Explorer menu option (Figure 8-2).

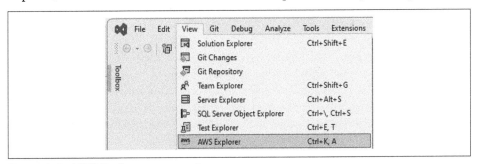

Figure 8-2. AWS Explorer menu option

We introduced the AWS Explorer at the start of this book; you can see an example of the Explorer window in Figure 1-14 under "Using Visual Studio with AWS and AWS Toolkit for Visual Studio" on page 17. Alongside AWS Explorer, the toolkit installs a handful of AWS-specific project templates and blueprints. These serve as an excellent way to both accelerate the creation of a new project and as a means of experimentation with different AWS deployment models for your code.

Project Templates from AWS

Select from one of the newly installed project templates by choosing "AWS" in the *Project type* filter, as shown in Figure 8-3. The project templates are for applications built on AWS Lambda, like many of the examples we have covered in this book.

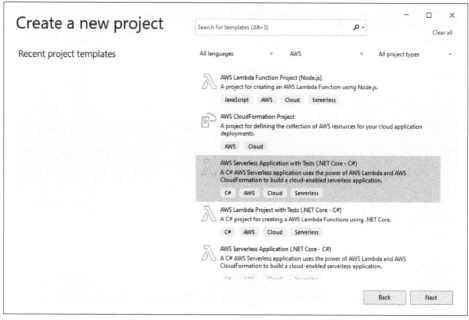

Figure 8-3. Project templates in Visual Studio

If we select this template, "AWS Serverless Application with Tests (.NET Core - C#)," then we will be presented with another selection where we can choose from one of what AWS calls "blueprints" on the next screen. These blueprints are ways to further configure your template project to best reflect the project you are creating. In this case (Figure 8-4), we selected Serverless Application in the preceding step, so we are offered several different blueprints for a serverless application.

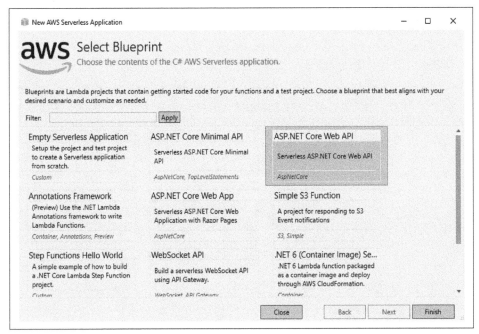

Figure 8-4. AWS project blueprints

Choose the ASP.NET Core Web API blueprint and click "Finish" to create the project we will use in the next example.

Publishing to AWS from Visual Studio

With our serverless ASP.NET Core Web API project created from the blueprint, let's open up the Solution Explorer and visit some of the files that have been created:

serverless.template
> This file is the Serverless Application Model (SAM) template for our resources. This file allows us to configure our infrastructure from one file, which can be checked into version control. We covered SAM in "Serverless Application Model (SAM)" on page 116.

AWSServerless1.Tests
> This test project has been created, including a single unit test in *ValuesControllerTests.cs* to serve as a starting point for writing unit tests for our API. The test project included in this AWS blueprint uses xUnit (*https://xunit.net*), which has been brought in as a NuGet dependency.

aws-lambda-tools-defaults.json

This stores the publish settings for our project. Settings added in the next step will be saved to this file as defaults, so you do not need to re-enter them each time.

The new project that was created from this blueprint is ready to publish immediately—we don't need to make any changes. We can use the AWS Toolkit to publish this serverless project directly from Visual Studio. To do this, open the context menu by right-clicking on the project name and selecting one of the "Publish to AWS…" options. As you can see in Figure 8-5, the AWS Toolkit has added two new menu items you can use to publish your project.

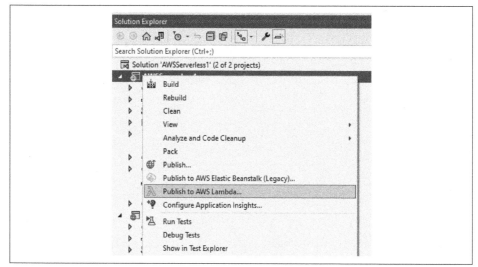

Figure 8-5. New publish options added by the toolkit

However you choose to publish your application, the toolkit will use the *serverless.template* file described previously to create a CloudFormation stack for your project and then build and push your code to AWS.

AWS Toolkit for Visual Studio Code

The rise of Visual Studio Code has been nothing short of meteoric. From public release in 2016 to being used by over 70% of professional software developers (*https://oreil.ly/KJeur*) in 2022, it is clear that Visual Studio Code has supplanted other IDEs for development across the industry. C# developers often turn to Visual Studio Code as a lightweight alternative to Visual Studio, and so in 2019 AWS announced the release of their AWS Toolkit for Visual Studio Code (*https://oreil.ly/spYbP*).

The VS Code toolkit includes a version of the AWS Explorer found in Visual Studio, allowing you to browse and interact with your AWS services from a new "AWS" menu option under the side bar. Figure 8-6 shows how the AWS Explorer in VSCode allows you to browse and interact with your resources.

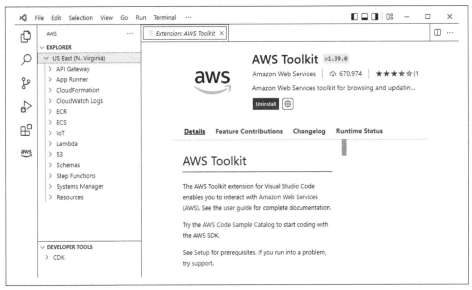

Figure 8-6. AWS Explorer in Visual Studio Code

Installing the toolkit is as simple as searching "AWS Toolkit" in the extensions marketplace from within Visual Studio Code (Ctrl+Shift+X on Windows, or ⌘-Shift-X on macOS).

As with the AWS Toolkit for Visual Studio, the VS Code extension uses your AWS credential profiles stored under *~/.aws/credentials* (Linux or macOS) or *%USERPRO-FILE%\.aws\credentials* (Windows). You can select which profile to use by opening the Command Palette (Ctrl+Shift+P on Windows, or ⌘-Shift-P on macOS) and selecting AWS: Choose AWS Profile. This will bring up the option to select a profile or, if you don't have any profiles saved, set one up from within Visual Studio Code.

Alongside the AWS Explorer (Figure 8-6), the AWS Toolkit for Visual Studio Code also provides an array of AWS commands you can invoke from the Command Palette. Simply search for "AWS:" to bring up all the commands with this prefix. A few of these are shown in Figure 8-7.

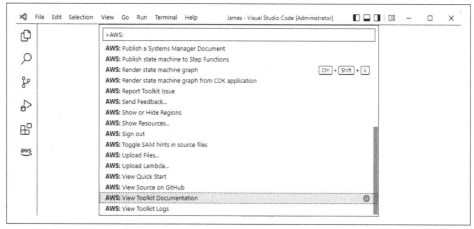

Figure 8-7. AWS commands in VS Code

This brings us to the end of our overview of the AWS Toolkits for both Visual Studio and Visual Studio Code. Next, let's take a quick look at the AWS Toolkit for Rider.

AWS Toolkit for Rider

The last AWS Toolkit extension to be aware of is that provided for JetBrains Rider. The AWS Toolkit for Rider (*https://aws.amazon.com/rider*) provides similar functionality to the toolkits for the other IDEs we have seen here, including an AWS Lambda project template that integrates into Rider's New Project dialog and creates a simple Hello World project and test project.

The AWS Toolkit for Rider also supports running an AWS Lambda locally inside a Docker container, allowing you to debug AWS Lambda from within Rider. We also have a new Deploy Serverless Application context menu item on the *template.yaml* file in your solution that allows you to deploy your Lambda function from within Rider.

Next in this chapter, we are going to take a closer look at the AWS SDK for .NET, and jump back into some C#.

Key SDK Features

The AWS SDK for .NET (*https://aws.amazon.com/sdk-for-net*) is a collection of over 300 NuGet packages that make it easy to call AWS services from applications running on .NET. The SDK libraries can be imported into any .NET project and used from your code to make authenticated calls to the various AWS APIs.

You can explore more tools, libraries, and other resources on the .NET on AWS on GitHub (*https://github.com/aws/dotnet*) page, which contains links to GitHub repositories for all the open source tools maintained by AWS including the AWS SDK for .NET

All the SDK libraries follow a common pattern of service clients that wrap API calls to AWS. These are implemented in the SDK using strongly typed request and response classes available for use in your C# code. An example of one of these client classes is the `AmazonS3Client` from the AWSSDK.S3 (*https://oreil.ly/xuwoj*) package:

```
var s3Client = new AmazonS3Client(Amazon.RegionEndpoint.USEast1);

await s3Client.CopyObjectAsync(
        sourceBucket,
        sourceKey,
        destinationBucket,
        destinationKey
);
```

Here we are invoking the `copy-object` on an AWS Simple Storage Service (S3) bucket to copy one key to another key. We start by creating a new instance of the service client (in this case `AmazonS3Client`) with some configuration values (`AmazonS3Config`). Then, with the instance of the service client, we invoke the asynchronous version of the method `CopyObjectAsync()`. The preceding code snippet is the equivalent of calling the following from the AWS command line:

```
aws s3api copy-object --copy-source <source-bucket> --key <key> --bucket <dest>
```

This pattern is followed for the majority of AWS services, as all AWS service clients inherit from the base class `Amazon.Runtime.AmazonServiceClient` (*https://oreil.ly/5b17a*). This gives all AWS service client objects access to common functionality such as credentials management, logging, metrics, retries, and timeouts, some of which we will cover later in this chapter.

Authentication in the AWS .NET SDK

In order to make calls to AWS APIs, you need to pass credentials to the AWS .NET SDK. There are several methods to do this, and different methods will be applicable in different scenarios. For example, if you are running your code locally for development purposes, you may want to authenticate with the access key and secret stored in one of your AWS profiles. When you deploy your code to AWS, however, you can use the IAM user configured for the specific EC2 instance, App Runner, or AWS Lambda function that is executing your code.

When you use a service client, the AWS SDK for .NET will look for credentials in the following places, in order:

1. Credentials passed to the constructor of a service client object, for example new AmazonS3Client(awsAccessKeyId, awsSecretAccessKey).

2. A named credentials profile on the local machine, as covered previously in "Configuring Visual Studio for AWS Toolkit" on page 208, with the profile name coming from *appsettings.{env}.json*.

3. A named credentials profile on the local machine, with the profile name stored in an environment variable called AWS_PROFILE.

4. A named credentials profile with the name [default], if it exists.

5. Access key, secret, and session tokens stored in the environment variables AWS_ACCESS_KEY_ID, AWS_SECRET_ACCESS_KEY, and AWS_SESSION_TOKEN, respectively.

6. Access key and secret only, in the environment variables AWS_ACCESS_KEY_ID and AWS_SECRET_ACCESS_KEY.

7. IAM role native to the EC2 task, EC2 instance, or other execution environment your .NET code is running on.

The easiest and most flexible way to configure AWS credentials for the SDK, and the way that allows you to best manage multiple credentials for different environments, is to use the *appsettings.{env}.json* files, and load them in using AWSSDK.Extensions.NET Core.Setup, which we will look at next.

Dependency Injection with the AWS SDK

Dependency injection is an extremely common pattern in .NET applications that allows you to configure all your dependencies in one place and inject them into your .NET controllers or other services, achieving inversion of control (IoC). If you are not familiar with dependency injection and IoC, a brief overview can be found on YouTube (*https://oreil.ly/rk9Ql*).

Versions of .NET from .NET Core onward support dependency injection as part of the framework, using the classes found in Microsoft.Extensions.DependencyInjec tion. Services (dependencies) are registered with the container in the *Program.cs* or *Startup.cs* files of your project. Here, an implementation of MyDependency is being registered against the interface IMyDependency in our .NET 6 *Program.cs* file:

```
var builder = WebApplication.CreateBuilder(args);
builder.Services.AddControllers();

// Add a dependency to the DI container
builder.Services.AddScoped<IMyDependency, MyDependency>();
```

When we use the AWS SDK for .NET, we can add AWS service clients into the .NET dependency injection container using similar syntax, with the help of the NuGet package AWSSDK.Extensions.NETCore.Setup. This package allows us to do two important things: register AWS service clients as dependencies, and use an *appsettings.json* file to store our AWS configuration, as previously mentioned.

To load the configuration settings, add the AWSSDK.Extensions.NETCore.Setup NuGet package to your .NET Core / 6+ project and then add these two lines into your service registration code:

```
var awsOptions = builder.Configuration.GetAWSOptions();

builder.Services.AddDefaultAWSOptions(awsOptions);
```

Alternatively, if you are using a `Startup` class, then the code will look like this:

```
public class Startup
{
    public Startup(IConfiguration configuration)
    {
        Configuration = configuration;
    }

    public IConfiguration Configuration { get; }

    public void ConfigureServices(IServiceCollection services)
    {
        services.AddControllers();

        var awsOptions = Configuration.GetAWSOptions();

        services.AddDefaultAWSOptions(awsOptions); ❶
    }

    public void Configure(IApplicationBuilder app, IWebHostEnvironment env)
    {
        // ...
    }
}
```

❶ Add the configuration settings in for use in all resolved service clients.

You can use your *appsettings.<env>.json* settings file(s) reference the name of your AWS credentials profile, among other settings. This allows you to have different AWS credentials for each environment, connecting to AWS under a different IAM user with roles and permissions bespoke to that environment. An example of *appsettings.Development.json* using a local profile called "my-profile-name" would look like this:

```
{
  "AWS": {
```

```
      "Region": "us-east-1",
      "Profile": "my-profile-name"
    },
    "MyKey": "My appsettings.json Value"
  }
```

The settings under the AWS node map to the class Amazon.AWSConfigs and a full list of available properties can be found in the documentation for Amazon.AWSConfigs (*https://oreil.ly/38DIi*).

Once you have default AWS options added to your dependency injection container, you can go ahead and start to register AWS service clients as dependencies for use in your application. Service clients from the AWS SDK will have a concrete class and an interface you can register it against. This allows you to easily mock the interface for unit testing or to otherwise modify the behavior of your application without modifying any of the calling logic. Here is an example using the AmazonLambdaClient service client from AWSSDK.Lambda. This client allows us to invoke a function on AWS Lambda from our C# code:

```
var awsOptions = builder.Configuration.GetAWSOptions();

builder.Services.AddDefaultAWSOptions(awsOptions);

services.AddAWSService<IAmazonLambda>(); ❶
```

❶ Register the AWS Lambda service client using the interface. At runtime this will be injected as an instance of AmazonLambdaClient.

With this service registered, you can inject it into a .NET controller through the constructor:

```
[Route("api/[controller]")]
public class ExampleController : ControllerBase
{
    private readonly IAmazonLambda _lambdaClient;

    public ExampleController(IAmazonLambda lambdaClient)
    {
        _lambdaClient = lambdaClient;
    }

    public async Task DoSomething()
    {
        await _lambdaClient.InvokeAsync(new Amazon.Lambda.Model.InvokeRequest
        {
            FunctionName = "MyLambdaFunction",
            InvocationType = InvocationType.Event
        });
    }
}
```

Notice how we are only referencing the abstraction `IAmazonLambda` in our code and calling `IAmazonLambda.InvokeAsync(...)` to invoke the AWS Lambda function. This allows us to unit test our `DoSomething()` method above by mocking out `IAmazon Lambda`, either by implementing a mock version of this interface or using a tool such as Moq (*https://nugetmusthaves.com/Package/Moq*) to automate the implementation.

The credentials to make this call to AWS Lambda and invoke our function will be retrieved via the use of credentials referenced by the profile in *appsettings.{env}.json* file, allowing us to configure separate credentials for each environment and/or local development user.

Retries and Timeouts

Since the methods in the AWS SDK make HTTP calls over the network to AWS APIs, there is always the chance that something can go wrong and a call can fail. The base `AmazonServiceClient` class that all the SDK service clients inherit from includes functionality to manage retries. Retry behavior can be configured by setting two properties on the service client configuration:

RetryMode
Set to one of three values from the `Amazon.Runtime.RequestRetryMode` enum. These are `Legacy`, `Standard`, or `Adaptive`.

MaxErrorRetry
The number of times to retry a failing call from the SDK service clients before throwing an exception in your code.

You can set these values individually when creating a new instance of any AWS service client, for example:

To follow on from the previous example of dependency injection, however, you may want to set them globally for all service clients used in your application. You can do this by either setting the environment variables `AWS_RETRY_MODE` and `AWS_MAX_ATTEMPTS`, or by adding configuration keys into your AWS config file like this:

```
[default]
retry_mode = Adaptive
[profile profile-name]
region = eu-west-2
```

The AWS config file is located alongside your credentials file under *~/.aws/credentials* (Linux or macOS) or *%USERPRO-FILE%\.aws\credentials* (Windows).

These values will be loaded into the AWSOptions.DefaultClientConfig property of your AWS options object:

```
var awsOptions = builder.Configuration.GetAWSOptions();

// Default retry mode and max error setting for all service clients
var retryMode = awsOptions.DefaultClientConfig.RetryMode;
var maxErrorRetry = awsOptions.DefaultClientConfig.MaxErrorRetry;

builder.Services.AddDefaultAWSOptions(awsOptions);

services.AddAWSService<IAmazonLambda>();
```

From here we can use or modify the values in our code to fine-tune how retries are performed in the AWS SDK.

Paginators

As well as retries and timeouts, the SDK service clients also include pagination functionality for services that may return large arrays of data. For services that support it, pagination is a really nice feature that replaces the continuation token approach with a new object-based approach that returns an async enumerable.

First, let's look at how we can paginate large results set *without* paginators, by using the request.ContinuationToken property. We are calling s3Client.ListObjectsV2Async(...) inside a do...while loop while there is a continuation token in the response:

```
public static async IAsyncEnumerable<string>
        GetAllPaginatedKeys(this IAmazonS3 s3Client, string bucketName)
{
    string? continuationToken = null;
    do
    {
        var response = await s3Client.ListObjectsV2Async(
            new ListObjectsV2Request
            {
                BucketName = bucketName,
                ContinuationToken = continuationToken
            });

        foreach (var responseObject in response.S3Objects)
        {
            yield return responseObject.Key;
        }
        continuationToken = response.NextContinuationToken;
    }
    while (continuationToken != null);
}
```

This is fine; however, despite the advantages we get from returning an IAsyncEnumerable<T>, this is still quite a lot of code to do something as simple as chaining the results from multiple pages. Since version 3.5 of the AWS SDK for .NET, we can now have access to the Paginators property on this IAmazonS3 interface.[1] Here is the same method but using paginators. Notice how the call to Paginators.ListObjectsV2 is *synchronous* whereas the call to listObjectsV2Paginator.S3Objects is asynchronous. The first call encapsulates our request object but does not actually call off to the API until we iterate over the S3Objects property on the paginator:

```
public static async IAsyncEnumerable<string>
    GetAllPaginatedKeys(this IAmazonS3 s3Client, string bucketName)
{
    var listObjectsV2Paginator = s3Client.Paginators.ListObjectsV2(
        new ListObjectsV2Request
        {
            BucketName = bucketName
        });

    await foreach (var s3object in listObjectsV2Paginator.S3Objects)
    {
        yield return s3object.Key;
    }
}
```

The paginator in this example returns IPaginatedEnumerable<S3Object>, which inherits IAsyncEnumerable<S3Object>, allowing us to await foreach over it.

This concludes our look at the AWS SDK for .NET and how you can get the most out of the common features that AWS has included in its service client classes. Next we are going to round out this chapter—and this book—with a look at some of the ways AWS can bring AI into your C# codebase, through their various Artificial Intelligence as a service (AIaaS) products.

Using AWS AI Services

A natural next step in using AWS is to dive into high-level AI services. One of the enormous advantages of using the AWS platform is the high-level AI and ML services available. These services allow the developer to build solutions quickly in services ranging from computer vision to natural language processing. Here is a complete list of AI services on AWS (*https://oreil.ly/oxoiD*). In this chapter, we are going to explore two of these AI services: Amazon Comprehend and Amazon Rekognition. These services offer analysis for text and images, respectively, using pretrained machine

---

1 The example here is just using the Simple Storage Service (S3) client; however, this same Paginators property is available on many different service clients for AWS services that have methods potentially returning a large number of items.

learning models. Between Comprehend and Rekognition we can cover many of the most common usages for AI that a typical .NET application may require.

AWS Comprehend

Let's get started exploring these AI services by using Amazon Comprehend. Amazon Comprehend is a service that uses natural language processing (NLP) to find critical insights about the content of documents. This capability could be essential for a company looking to detect customer sentiment in reports. You can work with one or multiple documents at the same time. The services available include the following items:

Entities
> Amazon Comprehend returns document entities, including nouns like people, places, and locations.

Key phrases
> Amazon Comprehend extracts vital phrases from a critical document to explain what is in the document.

PII
> This function detects the presence of personally identifiable information (PII) (*https://oreil.ly/GjsXC*).

Language
> This function can successfully classify up to 100 languages as the primary language in the document.

Sentiment
> This function detects a document's emotional sentiment, including positive, neutral, negative, or mixed.

Syntax
> This function extracts the parts of speech in a document, finding everything from adjectives to nouns.

One of the best ways to start any AI service on AWS is with the command line using AWS CloudShell. Let's start with a snippet of code that you can paste into a CloudShell Bash terminal. The command uses the following style of aws followed by the name of the service comprehend, then the feature of the service detect-sentiment:

```
aws comprehend detect-sentiment \
    --language-code "en" \
    --text "I love C#."
```

The output shown in Figure 8-8 returns a JSON payload that includes the Sentiment Score, i.e., the emotion of the text.

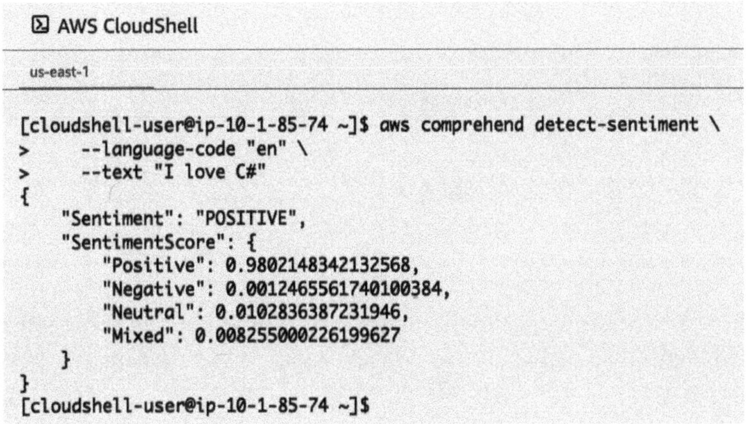

```
⊠ AWS CloudShell

us-east-1

[cloudshell-user@ip-10-1-85-74 ~]$ aws comprehend detect-sentiment \
>     --language-code "en" \
>     --text "I love C#"
{
    "Sentiment": "POSITIVE",
    "SentimentScore": {
        "Positive": 0.9802148342132568,
        "Negative": 0.0012465561740100384,
        "Neutral": 0.0102836387231946,
        "Mixed": 0.008255000226199627
    }
}
[cloudshell-user@ip-10-1-85-74 ~]$
```

Figure 8-8. Async listing buckets

Another way to explore this API is by dynamically piping text from a website into our CLI. This step works through the use of lynx. Let's run this to help us determine the sentiment around Albert Einstein on Wikipedia:

1. First, install lynx:

   ```
   sudo yum install lynx
   ```

2. Next, dump the page for Albert Einstein and pipe it into less to explore it:

   ```
   lynx -dump https://en.wikipedia.org/wiki/Albert_Einstein | less
   ```

3. By using wc -l, we get a count of the lines:

   ```
   lynx -dump https://en.wikipedia.org/wiki/Albert_Einstein | wc -l
   ```

4. To get the number of bytes, we can use wc --bytes:

   ```
   lynx -dump https://en.wikipedia.org/wiki/Albert_Einstein | wc \
   --bytes
   ```

   The result shows:

   ```
   432232
   ```

If you run aws comprehend detect-sentiment help, it can only process 5000 bytes. Because of this, we need to truncate the output. The truncation is done via head and then assigned to a Bash TEXT variable:

```
TEXT=`lynx -dump https://en.wikipedia.org/wiki/Albert_Einstein | head -c 5000`
```

Next, the command's output using the $TEXT shows that Wikipedia content around Albert Einstein is generally NEUTRAL with a significant POSITIVE percentage of 34%:

```
aws comprehend detect-sentiment --language-code "en" --text "$TEXT"
{
    "Sentiment": "NEUTRAL",
    "SentimentScore": {
        "Positive": 0.3402811586856842,
        "Negative": 0.0033634265419095755,
        "Neutral": 0.6556956768035889,
        "Mixed": 0.0006596834864467382
    }
}
```

The Bash command line also makes building one solution and pivoting into another common. In the following example, we switch to detecting entities from the same blob of Wikipedia text. Notice that we use --output text to use the power of Bash to filter the output:

```
aws comprehend detect-entities \
    --language-code "en" \
    --text "$TEXT" \
    --output text | head
```

The output of the command shows the following entities:

```
ENTITIES    20     29     0.632317066192627     Wikipedia          ORGANIZATION
ENTITIES    126    141    0.9918091297149658    Albert Einstein    PERSON
ENTITIES    151    160    0.7205400466918945    Wikipedia          ORGANIZATION
ENTITIES    230    236    0.9783479571342468    German             OTHER
ENTITIES    256    264    0.9940117001533508    Einstein           PERSON
ENTITIES    305    313    0.9899683594703674    Einstein           PERSON
ENTITIES    341    356    0.9821130633354187    Albert Einstein    PERSON
ENTITIES    379    394    0.990595817565918     Albert Einstein    PERSON
ENTITIES    401    409    0.814979076385498     Einstein           PERSON
ENTITIES    410    414    0.9937220215797424    1921               DATE
```

We could go even further and count the unique entities found using Bash. The following Bash pipeline converts entity column to lowercase then formats to easily count unusual occurrences. It isn't perfect, but it gets us a close enough proof of concept to know how to prototype APIs with Bash before moving on to C#:

```
aws comprehend detect-entities \
    --language-code "en" \
    --text "$TEXT" \
    --output text \
    | cut -f 5 \
    | tr -cd "[:alpha:][:space:]" \
    | tr ' [:upper:]' '\n[:lower:]' \
    | tr -s '\n' \
    | sort \
    | uniq -c \
```

```
| sort -nr -k 1 \
| head
```

The output of the Bash pipeline shows us that several entities are worth exploring more, at least from the initial part of the text extracted:

```
12 einstein
 9 of
 6 university
 4 german
 4 empire
 4 Albert
 3 kingdom
 2 Zurich
 2 wrttemberg
 2 Wikipedia
```

 You can also watch a walk-through of using Bash to extract entities from scratch on O'Reilly (*https://oreil.ly/NzKhQ*) or YouTube (*https://oreil.ly/DwlYG*).

With those explorations out of the way, let's move to code up a solution in C#.

Again, select a Visual Studio Console App and install Comprehend via NuGet as shown in Figure 8-9.

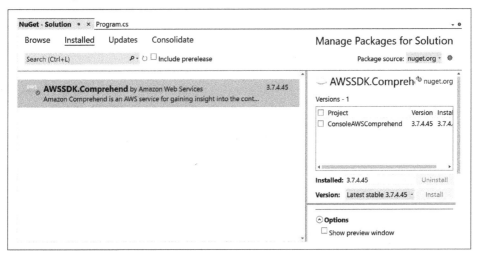

Figure 8-9. NuGet Comprehend install

Here is the sentiment detection done using the `DetectSentimentAsync()` method of the service class found in the AWSSDK.Comprehend package:

```
using Amazon;
using Amazon.Comprehend;
using Amazon.Comprehend.Model;

// Display title
Console.WriteLine("AWS AI API Sentiment Detector" + Environment.NewLine);

// Ask for phrase
Console.WriteLine("Type in phrase for analysis" + Environment.NewLine);
var phrase = Console.ReadLine();

// Detect Sentiment
var comprehendClient = new AmazonComprehendClient(RegionEndpoint.EUWest1);
Console.WriteLine("Calling DetectSentiment");

var detectSentimentResponse = await
comprehendClient.DetectSentimentAsync(
new DetectSentimentRequest()
{
    Text = phrase,
    LanguageCode = "en"
});
Console.WriteLine(detectSentimentResponse.Sentiment);
Console.WriteLine("Done");
```

Running the Console Application and entering some text, as illustrated in Figure 8-10, shows our statement is a MIXED sentiment.

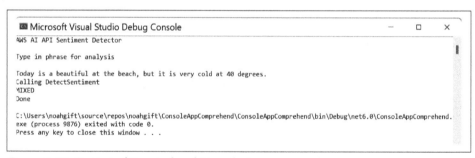

Figure 8-10. Output of Comprehend Console App

 You can also watch a walk-through of using C# with AWS Comprehend on O'Reilly (*https://oreil.ly/bNhVs*) or YouTube (*https://youtu.be/zhiNMmg8FxA*).

This example has used DetectSentimentAsync() to detect the *sentiment* (overall mood) of the text; however, we can just as easily perform entity detection on our text by calling client.DetectEntities() and inspecting the list of entities AWS detected in the text. Another service that offers entity detection, but this time in an image, is AWS Rekognition.

AWS Rekognition

Rekognition is AWS's computer vision service for both images and video. It provides a number of pretrained machine learning models to fit a range of different image recognition needs, all in an easy-to-use API available through the .NET SDK and priced using a pay-as-you-go model. You can try the service out with your own image by searching for "Rekognition" in the AWS Management Console and clicking the Try Demo button. From here you can upload an image from your machine (or choose a sample image provided by AWS) and select from one of the pretrained models. Figure 8-11 shows the results of the *label detection* algorithm, as you can see AWS Rekognition has identified this image as 98.1% likely to contain a cat.[2]

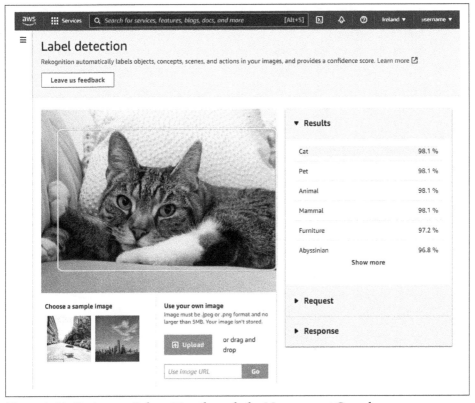

Figure 8-11. Testing out Rekognition through the Management Console

---

2 We almost got to the end of this book without including a picture of James's cat.

Calling AWS Rekognition from your C# code is as simple as installing the AWSSDK.Rekognition package from NuGet and utilizing the `Amazon.Rekogni tion.AmazonRekognitionClient` service class to call the API. You can inject or instantiate this service class in any of the ways we have seen earlier in this chapter; in this example, we have registered it with `services.AddAWSService<IAmazonRekog nition>();`:

```
using Amazon.Rekognition;
using Amazon.Rekognition.Model;
using Microsoft.AspNetCore.Mvc;

namespace AwsRekognitionExample.Controllers;

[Route("api/[controller]")]
public class ImageController
{
    private readonly IAmazonRekognition _rekognition;

    public ImageController(IAmazonRekognition rekognition)
    {
        _rekognition = rekognition;
    }

    [HttpGet]
    public async Task<string> GetFirstLabel()
    {
        var response = await _rekognition.DetectLabelsAsync(
            new DetectLabelsRequest
            {
                Image = new Image()
                {
                    S3Object = new S3Object()
                    {
                        Name = "cat.jpg",
                        Bucket = "photos-bucket",
                    },
                },
                MaxLabels = 10,
                MinConfidence = 75F,
            });

        return response.Labels.FirstOrDefault()?.Name ?? "None";
    }
}
```

In this example, we are calling `IAmazonRekognitionDetectLabelsAsync(...)` and passing a reference to the image in an S3 bucket. The Rekognition API works by loading the image data from an S3 bucket over accepting image data in the HTTP call to invoke the function. Saving large data files like images to S3 first, and then calling services such as AWS Rekognition is a good pattern to follow in a cloud native

AWS application as it allows you to architect an event-driven system. If you need to upload the image first, you could utilize an S3 trigger much like we did in "C# Résumé Uploader example: event-driven" on page 114.

Critical Thinking Discussion Questions

- What are a few real-world consequences of using timeouts in communicating the AWS SDK in production code?
- What are a few real-world consequences of using retries in communicating the AWS SDK in production code?
- What new workflows are enabled by using async communication using the AWS SDK?
- What architecture patterns are most cost-effective to avoid duplicate API calls in production systems?
- What unique advantages does .NET coupled with AWS give you?

Exercises

- Set up the AWS Toolkit for Visual Studio if you haven't already and use it to create a new S3 bucket, create a folder inside the bucket, and finally upload an image or file from your desktop.
- Expand on the AWS Rekognition example and convert it to a web service deployed on AWS App Runner.
- Expand on the AWS Comprehend example and convert it to a web service deployed on AWS App Runner.
- Create a portfolio project highlighting a complete master of .NET on AWS showing end-to-end development skills, including IaC and frontend.

Conclusion

We have used the term cloud native several times in this book, and you have no doubt encountered it many times in the wild, but let's think about what it really means and why it matters. Cloud native code runs either exclusively in, or at least is optimized for, the cloud. By writing our code with the intention of running it exclusively on AWS, we can adopt a much deeper level of integration with AWS services such as message queues, databases, logging, and reporting. If our C# code is born in the cloud (the dictionary definition of the word *native*), we can write it to best take advantage of the services around it. Sure, there are trade-offs. Local development is more difficult if you have architected your application to use exclusively AWS Lambda functions. Complexity can increase exponentially if you increasingly integrate AWS

X-Ray tracing for performance monitoring into every execution path. There are trade-offs; however, the benefits you gain in performance, flexibility, and often cost, will often vastly outweigh these drawbacks.

Remember, whether you prefer to develop in Visual Studio, VS Code, or Cloud9, there is a C# AWS workflow to suit you. The AWS Toolkit for Visual Studio has been around in one form or another since Visual Studio 2008 and is regularly updated to keep pace with additions to both AWS and Visual Studio itself. The latest version of the toolkit is even rolling out a new Publish to AWS experience that aims to make publishing your code to the cloud even simpler, allowing you to rapidly test your code in the environment it will be native to: the cloud. For us, we love Cloud9 for its seamless integration into AWS services and ability to access it from anywhere you have a web browser. Web-based IDEs may not be for everyone, but if you regularly change development machines or use portable or loaner devices for development, having your code accessible from anywhere in the cloud can be a game changer.

Amazon Web Services is the most broadly adopted cloud platform in the world and has been supporting .NET in the cloud since 2008. With over 200 services offering everything from a simple Windows virtual machine you can spin up for any task imaginable, to machine learning services like those we have visited in this chapter, AWS supports .NET on 485 instance types, 255 different AMIs for Windows workloads, and 40 different Linux AMIs with .NET or SQL Server preconfigured. This all means deploying to and integrating with AWS from your C# codebase has never been easier.

In this book we have covered many of the ways you can leverage AWS in your application, but there are many more we have not had time to cover. There are open source .NET tools, Windows samples for AWS CodeBuild, an MQTT client for leveraging Internet of Things (IoT) services, and over 20 AWS services for machine learning alone. Among these, AWS SageMaker is a service that allows you to train and deploy your own ML models, a topic we could fill an entire book with by itself.

What we have covered, however, should give you an entry point into Amazon's cloud services and help you plan the next stage of development for your .NET codebase(s). Whether that be a migration, containerization, or rewrite from the ground up, we hope the topics on these pages have given you enough food for thought.

Benchmarking AWS

One way to get a more profound knowledge of AWS is to benchmark the performance of different machines. Part of the value of AWS is the ability to use many various services and other abstractions to solve problems in the most efficient manner possible. You can view many code examples in this example GitHub Repository on benchmarking (*https://github.com/noahgift/benchmarking-aws*). Notice that there are substantial differences in sysbench benchmarks from 1 core to a 36 core to a 96 core machine as shown in Figure A-1.

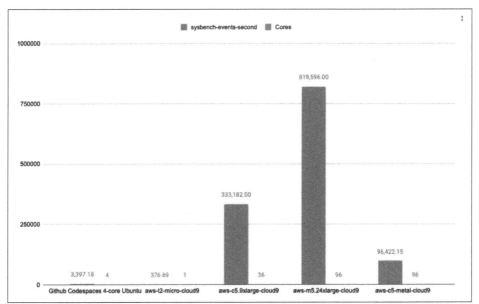

Figure A-1. Benchmarking AWS instances

As your organization determines the correct Amazon Linux 2 machine to run .NET Core on Linux, it would be a great idea to do some initial benchmarking. To run these benchmarks in a repeatable manner on Amazon Linux 2, you can refer to this Makefile (*https://oreil.ly/IF5rR*). Notice how sysbench only needs two lines to install and run the ./benchmark.sh script.

The actual benchmark script is as follows:

```
#!/usr/bin/env bash
CPU=`python -c "import multiprocessing as mp;print(f'{mp.cpu_count()}')"`
echo "Running with CPU Count and Threads: " $CPU
sysbench cpu --threads=$CPU run
```

The makefile command can be run as make benchmark-sysbench-amazon:

```
benchmark-sysbench-amazon:
        #install sysbench
        curl -s https://packagecloud.io/install/repositories/akopytov/\
        sysbench/script.rpm.sh | sudo bash
        sudo yum -y install sysbench
        #run CPU benchmark
        ./benchmark.sh
```

The benchmark script uses a "one-liner" to determine how many cores are available and then passes this into a CPU benchmark:

```
#!/usr/bin/env bash

CPU=`python -c "import multiprocessing as mp;print(f'{mp.cpu_count()}')"`
echo "Running with CPU Count and Threads: " $CPU
sysbench cpu --threads=$CPU run
```

A free tool like Cinebench (*https://oreil.ly/ROql2*) works to benchmark a Windows OS. It is always good to perform multiple measures, including an OS-level benchmark and application load test, on the actual environment in which an application gets deployed.

Getting Started with .NET

Start with the interactive documentation for Hello World in the browser (*https://oreil.ly/nExkF*).

Hello World in GitHub Codespaces for C#

Next up, try out GitHub Codespaces and the Visual Studio Code tutorial (*https://oreil.ly/G6CcZ*).

First, create a new Console App from the CLI and name it HelloWorld:

```
dotnet new console -n HelloWorld
```

This step creates a console project. Next, change the code in *Program.cs* to the following example:

```
using System;

namespace HelloWorld
{
    class Program
    {
        static void Main(string[] args)
        {
            Console.WriteLine("Hello World C# on AWS!");
        }
    }
}
```

Next, cd into the directory (**cd HelloWorld**) and run the code **dotnet run**. The output of the command will be the following:

```
Hello World C# on AWS!
```

Hello World in GitHub Codespaces for F#

Create a new F# Console App:

```
dotnet new console -lang "F#" -n FSharpHelloWorld
```

Change the code to the following:

```
open System

// Define a function to construct a message to print
let from whom =
    sprintf "from %s" whom

[<EntryPoint>]
let main argv =
    let message = from "F# on AWS" // Call the function
    printfn "Hello world %s" message
    0 // return an integer exit code
```

Next, cd into the directory (**cd FSharpHelloWorld**) and run it with **dotnet run**. The output will be the following: Hello world from F# on AWS.

 You can watch a walk-through of this process on the O'Reilly platform (*https://oreil.ly/Zqv9z*) or YouTube (*https://youtu.be/7kkDXf3I4sQ*).

Index

metric math, 188
metrics
    CloudWatch, 183-185
    CloudWatch arithmetic functions, 188
MGN (Application Migration Service), 67-71
Microsoft .NET Upgrade Assistant, 76-79
migrating legacy .NET framework application
    to AWS, 59
    choosing a migration path, 59-66
    choosing a migration strategy, 63
    rearchitecting, 61
    rebuilding, 62
    rehosting basics, 60
    rehosting on AWS, 66
    replatforming basics, 61
    replatforming via containerization, 71-74
    repurchasing, 61
    retaining a legacy codebase, 62
    Strategy Recommendations Service, 63-66
monitoring, 157
    (see also logging, monitoring, and instru-
        mentation)
    CloudWatch anomaly detection, 189
    CloudWatch dashboards, 185-190
    DevOps best practices and, 157
multifactor authentication, 7

N
natural language processing (NLP), AWS Com-
    prehend and, 222-227
.NET
    basics, 1-24
    C# Résumé uploader example, 88-91
    choosing serverless components for .NET
        on AWS, 88-116
    containerization of (see containerization
        of .NET)
    getting started with, 233-234
    migrating legacy framework application to
        AWS (see migrating legacy .NET frame-
        work application to AWS)
    website, 10
.NET 6
    containerized .NET 6 API, 132
    containerized .NET 6 on Lambda, 132
.NET applications
    modernizing to serverless (see serverless
        applications)
.NET Core

moving to, 75-83
NFS (Network File System) storage, 33-35
NoSQL, DynamoDB, 49

O
OpenTelemetry, 195

P
paginators, 220
PDCA (Plan-Do-Check-Act) cycle, 152
Platform as a Service, 5
Porting Assistant, 80-83
PowerShell, 13
    (see also AWSPowerShell.NETCore)
    CloudShell and, 14-17
    installation, 13
pricing options, 41
principle of least privilege (PLP), 7, 45
pure functions, 87

R
RDS (Relational Database Service), 54
rearchitecting
    AWS Porting Assistant, 80-83
    basics, 61
    Microsoft .NET Upgrade Assistant, 76-79
    moving to .NET (Core), 75-83
rebuilding, 62
rehosting, 66
    Application Migration Service, 67-71
    basics, 60
    Elastic Beanstalk, 70-71
Rekognition, 227-229
Relational Database Service (RDS), 54
replatforming
    basics, 61
    containerization, 71-74
repurchasing, 61
Resource Health view, 195
retaining a legacy codebase, 62
retries, SDK and, 219
Rider, AWS Toolkit for, 214

S
S3 (Amazon Simple Storage Service), 28-35
    benefits of, 29
    developing with, 29-31
    Lifecycle configuration, 30

About the Authors

Noah Gift is the founder of Pragmatic AI Labs. He lectures at many top universities, including Duke Data Science and AI programs. He teaches and designs graduate machine learning, MLOps, AI, and data science courses, and consults on machine learning and cloud architecture for students and faculty. He is also an AWS ML Hero and Python Software Foundation Fellow. As a former CTO, individual contributor, and consultant, he has over 20 years' experience shipping revenue-generating products in many industries, including film, games, and SaaS. He is also the author of hundreds of technical publications, courses, and books.

James Charlesworth is an engineer, manager, public speaker, and the founder of *traintocode.com*. With a background in industrial control systems, James has taken that pragmatic, engineering approach to build both high performing software and high-performing teams. Through *traintocode.com*, James's mission is to bring skills into the software development industry from all walks of life and all backgrounds, by treating software development as a creative skill and not simply a bucket of knowledge.

Colophon

The animal on the cover of *Developing on AWS with C#* is a banded cotinga (*Cotinga maculata*). They are endemic to Brazil, primarily living in the southeastern subsection of tropical, humid lowland Atlantic forests.

Males are bright and eye-catching, predominantly covered in cobalt-blue feathers. Black dots spread across their wings, turning into solid black tips, matching those on their tails. A radiant shade of purple covers their bellies and throats, bisected by a band of blue feathers, like a collar around their necks. These striking colors are advantageous for winning over females in elaborate courtship rituals.

Females are much more subtle. Their back and wings are covered in brown and white mottled plumage, occasionally streaked with golden yellow. Similar feathers cover their underside, shifting towards an off white.

Similar to other cotinga, their diet relies heavily on fruits, with the occasional consumption of seeds and insects. They are shy birds that prefer to live high up in the forest canopy.

Unfortunately, banded cotinga are a critically endangered species. Their habitat is small and fragmented due to deforestation, and people illegally capture them for trade and collect their feathers. Their population is continuously decreasing, with its current estimate being between 250 to 999 mature birds. Many of the animals on O'Reilly covers are endangered; all of them are important to the world.

The cover illustration is by Karen Montgomery, based on an antique line engraving from Lydekker's *Royal Natural History*. The cover fonts are Gilroy Semibold and Guardian Sans. The text font is Adobe Minion Pro, the heading font is Adobe Myriad Condensed, and the code font is Dalton Maag's Ubuntu Mono.